On the Prairie of Palo Alto

On the Prairie

of Palo Alto

Historical Archaeology of the U.S.–Mexican War Battlefield

CHARLES M. HAECKER AND JEFFREY G. MAUCK

Texas A&M University Press, College Station

The paper used in this book meets the minimum requirements of the American
National Standard for Permanence of Paper for Printed Library Materials, Z39.48-1984.
Binding materials have been chosen for their durability.

Library of Congress Cataloging-in-Publication Data
Haecker, Charles M.
    On the prairie of Palo Alto : historical archaeology of the U. S.–Mexican War
Battlefield / by Charles M. Haecker and Jeffrey G. Mauck.
        p.   cm. — (Texas A&M University military history series ; 55)
    Includes bibliographical references and index.
    ISBN 0-89096-758-X
    1. Palo Alto Battlefield National Historic Site (Tex.)   2. Archaeology and
history—Texas—Palo Alto Battlefield National Historic Site.   3. Mexican War,
1846–1848—Battlefields—Texas.   4. Texas—History, Local.   5. Texas—
Antiquities.   I. Mauck, Jeffrey G. (Jeffrey Gordon), 1959–   .   II. Title.
III. Series.
E406.P3H35   1997
973.62—dc21   97-12335
                                                                                  CIP

Contents

Illustrations

Preface

The antecedent and nucleus of this book is the National Park Service report *A Thunder of Cannon, Archaeology of the Mexican–American War Battlefield of Palo Alto*. It was one of several planning documents used toward creating Palo Alto Battlefield National Historic Site. Sometimes such limited distribution reports evoke a much wider response than expected, and fortunately this is what happened with *A Thunder of Cannon*. Quite a number of professional and avocational historians and historical archaeologists submitted written responses, usually positive in tone and almost always constructive in nature. After several months of receiving these responses, it seemed appropriate that a significantly expanded and improved book be produced.

The other purpose of *On the Prairie of Palo Alto* is to pull from undeserved obscurity the first battle of a half-forgotten war. In so doing, we have synthesized data obtained from historical documents and archaeological evidence. A history of events that led up to the battle is included, as well as detailed descriptions of both countries' abilities to wage war during the first half of the nineteenth century. Without this background information we believe General Zachary Taylor's campaign during the spring of 1846 would be incomprehensible and the reasons for the outcome of the battle of Palo Alto difficult to understand. In the annals of American military history, Palo Alto does not exactly possess the same level of name recognition or catch the imagination of, say, Gettysburg and Little Bighorn. So be it. Nonetheless, Palo Alto possesses all the needed qualities of a great battle story, and toward this end we offer the following chapters.

We would like to express our appreciation to the primary organizations and individuals mentioned below and apologize if we have inadvertently overlooked anyone. Within the National Park Service we thank historian Neil

Mangum and archaeologist James Bradford, both of whom offered insightful comments and encouragement; scientific illustrator Jerry Livingston, who produced the meticulous artifact photographs; and artist Carmen Silva, who produced the detailed line drawings of nineteenth-century weaponry.

A number of other historians and archaeologists contributed their comments: Museum Director Steven Allie, Frontier Army Museum at Fort Leavenworth, Kansas; Professor Silvia M. Arrom, Brandeis University; Dr. James E. Ayres; Professor Joseph E. Chance, University of Texas–Pan American; Dr. William C. Gist, Jr., of the Aztec Club of 1847; Dr. Berle R. Clay, State Archaeologist for Kentucky; Mark Megehee, director of the Fort Sill Museum, Fort Sill, Oklahoma; Charles M. Niquette and Dr. Henry McKelway, both of Cultural Research Analysts, Inc., Lexington, Kentucky; Professor David M. Pletcher, Indiana University; Tennessee archaeologist Dr. Fred Prouty; Dr. Douglas D. Scott, National Park Service, Midwest Archaeological Center, Lincoln, Nebraska; and historian Kevin R. Young.

Other experts volunteered their knowledge in the identification of problematic artifacts: Dr. Richard Ahlborn, supervisor-curator with the Smithsonian Institution; Bill Brown, National Park Service, Harpers Ferry Design Center; James Moore, Office of Archaeological Studies, Santa Fe, New Mexico; historian Samuel Nesmith; and Dr. Jack S. Williams, Center for Spanish Colonial Archaeology, Mesa, Arizona.

The excellent pen-and-ink illustrations of Mexican and American soldiers at Palo Alto are the work of artist-historian Gary Zaboly. We are indebted to the Aztec Club of 1847, which provided invaluable support by commissioning two of Gary's battle scenes for their specific use in *On the Prairie of Palo Alto*. It should be noted that the Aztec Club of 1847 was founded by American veterans of that war, and whose present members are their direct descendants. By encouraging research on that conflict this organization bestows honor both to the memory of its founders and to itself.

Many people of the Brownsville area made significant contributions during both the fieldwork and report phases of the Palo Alto Archaeology Project. We would like to single out for recognition park superintendent Tom Carroll and park historian Dr. Aaron Mahr, both of Palo Alto Battlefield NHS; Bruce Aiken, executive director, Historic Brownsville Museum; Tom Fort, assistant director, Hidalgo County Historical Museum; and Walter E. Plitt, III, chairman, Palo Alto Battlefield Committee. Not enough praise can be given to the good-natured members of the survey crew who, as a group, worked hundreds of hours under a merciless Texas sun. Archaeologists T. G. Futch and Melissa Payne ably assisted the project director during the 1992 and 1993 field seasons, respectively. Volunteers included Cecil Allison (now deceased), Bob Anderson, Rod Bates, Gary Chauvin, Robert Garcia, David Gray, David Martinez, Paul Mitchell, James and Grace Pointinger,

Stosh Prukop, and Robert Zamarripa. The principal author thanks each of you for your friendship and tolerance of his bad puns.

To the historian, memoirs expressly written for publication are suspect, and battle recollections or participants in their old age are notoriously unreliable. For this reason we have made every effort where practical to utilize private diaries and letters of the battle participants. It is in such documents that truth will most likely be found, since they are usually free of rationalizations and justifications. Fortunately, quite a number of American research institutions have in their possession the very documents needed to present an original account of the battle of Palo Alto. A comprehensive listing of all of these institutions is presented in the bibliography. We are most appreciative of the help we received from James Holmberg and James T. Kirkwood, archivists of the Filson Club in Louisville, Kentucky; the Beineke Library, Yale University; the Hargrett Rare Book and Manuscript Library, University of Georgia; Special Collections, the United States Military Academy at West Point; the Library of Congress; the National Park Service Spanish Colonial Research Center in Albuquerque; and we especially thank Katherine Goodwin, chief archivist, Library Special Collections, University of Texas–Arlington, for her extra effort on our behalf.

National partiality is among the most difficult of biases to overcome for anyone conducting research on a historic event such as a battle, and differing language and customs can only exacerbate divisiveness. We are, therefore, most appreciative of the excellent research conducted on our behalf by Professor Patricia Fournier and her assistant Maribel Piña-Calva, both of Escuela Nacional de Antropologia, Mexico, D.F. We believe their thorough compilation of pertinent Mexican documents has provided an essential counterbalance to the otherwise overwhelming American historical data collected by the authors.

Finally, we reserve a special thanks to Louanna Haecker. Louanna spent many hours reading and re-reading the various manuscript drafts before they crossed the editor's desk, translating the professional jargon of a historian and an archaeologist into more readable prose.

Our results would have been inadequate without the interest, expertise, and very active support obtained from the cooperative efforts of these, and many other, people and organizations. Any errors, omissions, or misinterpretations in this book are, of course, the faults of the authors.

On the Prairie of Palo Alto

Introduction

This is a frequent problem in military history: One always knows the results of a battle;
the difficulty is in reconstructing the course of events during it.

—Barbara W. Tuchman,
Practicing History: Selected Essays

War is a faithful companion of humanity. Yet, despite this truism, military history is considered a somewhat unsavory field of research by many in the academic community. Perhaps the scars left on the national consciousness by the Vietnam War have supported the belief that the study of warfare is tantamount to its glorification. If humanity's darker side is ignored, according to this reasoning, it will somehow go away. We strongly disagree. Through this study of the battle of Palo Alto, the first battle of the U.S.-Mexican War, we hope to make a significant contribution toward a better understanding not only of this particular conflict but also of warfare in general. To do so we have used an interdisciplinary approach, combining the perspectives of the historian with those of the historical archaeologist. This approach reveals certain subtle events of the battle not noted by previous studies and places Palo Alto within the larger context of nineteenth-century human behavior and national development.

On May 8, 1846, a U.S. army of 2,228 men, commanded by General Zachary Taylor, defeated a Mexican force of at least 3,700 men under General Mariano Arista on the prairie of Palo Alto, a few miles north of modern Brownsville, Texas (map 1). On the following day, Taylor attacked and virtually destroyed the demoralized but still much larger Mexican army at the battle of Resaca de la Palma, located within what are now the northern suburbs of Brownsville. The two Mexican setbacks were a sign of things to come. In September, 1846, Taylor's reinforced but still outnumbered army captured the key city of Monterrey, which gave the United States firm control of the entire Lower Rio Grande Valley. In February, 1847, Taylor's 4,700-man army checked the advance of General Antonio López de Santa Anna's 15,000-man force at Buena Vista, called the battle of Angostura by the Mexicans. This was the last major campaign of the war in northern Mexico, although guerrilla-style warfare continued here until the end of the war. General Taylor fought no more battles but returned home a national hero.

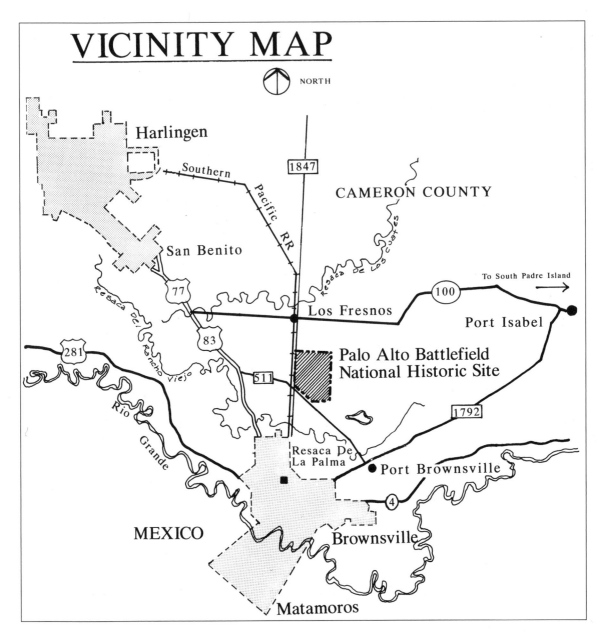

VICINITY MAP

NORTH

Harlingen

Southern

Pacific RR

1847

CAMERON COUNTY

San Benito

77

Resaca de Los Cuates

To South Padre Island →

100

Los Fresnos

Port Isabel

83

Resaca del Rancho Viejo

Palo Alto Battlefield
National Historic Site

281

511

1792

Rio Grande

Resaca De
La Palma

Port Brownsville

4

MEXICO

Brownsville

Matamoros

*map 1. Vicinity map
showing the location of
Palo Alto Battlefield
National Historic Site,
near Brownsville, Texas.
Courtesy National
Park Service*

In 1848 the once-obscure officer was elected president, spending the last sixteen months of his life in the White House.

Despite its crippling losses in the north, a proud Mexico refused to negotiate a peace that would demand territorial concessions. President James K. Polk, therefore, ordered General Winfield Scott to capture the strategic port of Veracruz, then advance on Mexico City. Scott took Veracruz in March, 1847. During the ensuing march toward the Mexican capital, the Americans, though always outnumbered, won a series of hotly contested battles, captured Mexico City in August, and occupied it during the resulting peace negotiations. In the Treaty of Guadalupe Hidalgo of 1848, Mexico agreed to

On the Prairie of Palo Alto

accept the annexation of Texas by the United States, as well as to cede the vast territory that included all or parts of the present states of New Mexico, Arizona, California, Nevada, Colorado, and Utah.

For the United States, this incredible victory soon brought about a bitter division. As early as August, 1846, questions about the ultimate purpose of the war were forced to the forefront of political debate when Congressman David Wilmot of Pennsylvania introduced his famous "proviso"— actually an amendment to an Army appropriations bill—that demanded any territory taken from Mexico be closed to the institution of slavery. The proviso passed in the northern-dominated House, but the Senate finally defeated it. Southerners bitterly resented this intrusion into what they considered to be a local issue, and sectional tensions rose to unprecedented levels.

The crisis abated for a time after the war, but in 1850 the sectional conflict heated up when California applied for statehood. Under the so-called Compromise of 1850, California was admitted as a free state. The South, in return, received several concessions. But the political crisis continued throughout the 1850s, and it usually centered on the question of whether western territories would be settled as slave or free. Abraham Lincoln had opposed the U.S.-Mexican War. During the 1850s he was a "free soiler," dedicated to halting the expansion of slavery into the western territories. When Lincoln was elected president in 1860, the southern states began to secede. Over 630,000 would die during the ensuing Civil War—sixty-three times more than the number of Americans who lost their lives during the earlier war with Mexico.

In May of 1846, General Taylor's army included fifty-one future Civil War generals. Ulysses S. Grant and John C. Pemberton were brother-officers at Palo Alto; seventeen years later, at Vicksburg, they were adversaries. So, too, did James Longstreet and George Gordon Meade share the victory of Palo Alto. Their paths would cross again, but on opposing sides at Gettysburg. While the battle raged on the prairie of Palo Alto, a few miles away a smaller force defended Fort Texas. Among its defenders were George Thomas, Braxton Bragg, Lafayette McLaws, and John F. Reynolds. The friendships made among officers in the peacetime army continued to strengthen over the next year and a half of hard fighting in Mexico. In October, 1847, during the occupation of Mexico City, some of the American officers established the Aztec Club as a means of cementing their close ties and mutual respect for one another. Their club survived the war as a fraternal organization; however, it was sorely tested during the subsequent years of civil war, when many of its members became bitter enemies.[1]

The U.S.-Mexican War was undoubtedly a seminal event in the history of both nations. Unfortunately, historical accounts of this war were often colored by excessive nationalism. Until recently most American historians tended to justify the war as an unavoidable event in the expansion of a great nation. Since about 1970, however, a new, more objective, and less polemical scholarship has emerged. For example, studies by K. Jack Bauer, David M. Pletcher, Josefina Zoraida Vázquez, Lorenzo Meyer, and Richard Griswold del Castillo have treated objectively the military campaigns, diplomatic background, and consequences of this conflict, thereby contributing new dimensions toward its understanding. The historiography of the U.S.-Mexican War has matured, and the time is right to explore new approaches that will explain its impact on both the United States and Mexico.

Historians depend primarily on the written record for their interpretation of past events. They understand the system of accessing primary historical documents, and they consequently have a working familiarity with the various document repositories. Rarely, however, does their profession require them to actually visit the physical location of a historic event. For some historians, undoubtedly the close analysis of musket balls would lead to nothing more than dirty hands. Historical archaeologists likewise use primary and secondary documents, but the information gleaned from these sources is conjoined with data obtained from the material culture: artifacts, structures, and the like. Their ultimate goal is identification of patternings of human behavior that cannot be classified from the written word alone.

It is assumed that the historical archaeologist is both a historian and an archaeologist, having mastered the skills and knowledge that are demanded in both disciplines. A good number of historical archaeologists, in fact, do just that. We suspect, however, that there is a tendency for historical archaeologists to overemphasize the archaeology half of this duality at the expense of fully investigating the written record. This is unfortunate, since a detailed social context is required for a better interpretation of the material culture. To avoid this pitfall, we believe historians and historical archaeologists should work in tandem because they share a common goal of better understanding the human past. This is the approach we have chosen in our study of the battle of Palo Alto.

To obtain a true interdisciplinary methodology, it was necessary for us to become familiar with the historiography of battlefields in general. Historian John Keegan has noted that from the time of Homer and his semi-mythical narrative of the Trojan War to the early twentieth century, historians of warfare have usually focused on contributions of the commanding generals. Unfortunately, they also tended to depict common soldiers as faceless automatons. Regiments, battalions, and divisions seemingly moved about the battlefield as manageable, homogeneous blocks in obedient response to their commanders' orders. The grand view of battle was still the focus of attention in such accounts, with nonheroic and faceless soldiers deemed irrelevant and, by implication, unworthy of study.[2]

During the Second World War, however, army historian S. L. A. Marshall and his team of researchers undertook the first systematic study of human behavior in combat. In what was probably an unintended result, their work had a profound impact on military historiography. One important finding was that a soldier in combat closely bonds with only a few of his comrades for mutual survival. The soldier's motivation during combat is ultimately tied to the dynamics of this small group, not to the larger units of which he is a member. It is now believed that a key determinant in the outcome of a battle is the soldier's strong desire to fight or flee with these few men.[3] Analysis of battle events, therefore, demands recognition of the interrelationship between commanders and the sometimes autonomous dynamics of small combat units.

The U.S.-Mexican War generated a respectable number of firsthand accounts. However, given that most of the rank-and-file regulars who fought at Palo Alto were illiterate, the history of its events is largely told by the usually better-educated commissioned officers. Regardless of their sources, personal battle accounts convey details that were perhaps overly simplified or else considered inappropriate for inclusion in the commanding officer's post-battle report. But such accounts, invaluable as they are, also have their flaws. A soldier's power of perception is sharply narrowed and often confused by the literal and figurative "fog of battle," exacerbated by his exhaustion, privation, pain, and other traumatic combat factors. Physical obstacles can also limit a soldier's field of vision. For example, the extreme flatness of the terrain and the high grass at Palo Alto undoubtedly restricted observation to only those who were either mounted or standing on one of the few slight bumps on the landscape (overstated as "hills" by some of the battle participants). It is not surprising, then, that such accounts are often contradictory. In fact, many traditional descriptions of famous military operations have been exposed as frauds by some military historians simply by their inspection of the battlefield terrain.[4]

The most abundant evidence of the soldiers' participation in battle is the physical residues of combat, which, if interpreted properly, can reflect their experience. What is needed, then, is a method by which one can integrate the written record of the battle with the physical evidence of the battlefield. Artifacts have a story to tell as well and, as inanimate objects, have the added bonus of being incapable of prevarication. The discipline of archaeology, with its fundamental tenet that human behavior is patterned, can provide this needed complementary evidence—and battlefields are simply the locales of the most violent expression of human behavior.[5] A professional army, having a rigid command structure, demands from its soldiers strict adherence to a code of behavior that includes the learning of specialized training. In combat, the well-trained are expected to perform duties as ordered without concern for personal welfare.[6] One example of selfless behavior in combat is that of the Mexican regiments at Palo Alto, who followed orders and stood at attention while undergoing several hours of a horrendous artillery attack. Such sanguinary conduct is most definitely patterned behavior.

One of the most compelling and influential studies regarding patterned behavior on a battlefield is the one presented by Douglas Scott, Richard A. Fox, Jr., et al., which addresses General George A. Custer's debacle at the Little Bighorn.[7] Over the last 120 years this tragedy has generated volumes of written material ranging in literary quality from cogent speculation to the worst of Victorian-era bathos. As a counterpoint to all this verbiage, archaeological research has identified what really happened at Custer's Last Stand. A grass fire in 1983 cleared the vegetation that covered the Little Bighorn battlefield, allowing National Park Service archaeologists to conduct a thorough examination. Although their research is continuing, a number of important discoveries have been made.

Artifact patterning indicates Custer and his men did not put up a determined, defensive posture against overwhelming odds, as many Custer devotees would have one believe. Instead, there occurred "a sudden, unexpected, and irreversible collapse in the tactical capabilities of Custer's force." It is a military truism that when the stability of a military force disintegrates, a commander loses the power to maneuver the various units and maintain overall control. What was once a disciplined force is now transformed into a frightened mob whose members are united only by the common desire to escape and survive. During this period, the final phase of battle, the victorious force can conduct "mop-up" operations. The archaeological research at Little Bighorn has yielded the reasonable premise that tactical stability will be reflected by a more or less ordered array of artifacts and features; a haphazard, unstructured array indicates tactical instability.[8] As will be revealed in the following chapters, the Palo Alto battlefield holds incontrovertible evidence that both tactical stability and instability took place here as well.

Analysis of the nature of armaments used during a battle is a basic objective of any battlefield investigation. For instance, cartridges, cartridge cases, and rifle bullets make up the majority of artifacts recovered from Little Bighorn. Modern firearm identification analyses, such as those used in crime labs, provided the key for the archaeologists' identification of ammunition calibers, firing pin and extractor signatures on cartridge cases, and rifling marks on bullets. Based on these clues, it was possible to identify specific combat areas for both troopers and Indians and to assign these areas along a time line of battle events.

Cartridge signature analysis is an appropriate and highly productive avenue of research when investigating battles of the Civil War era and later. However, in contrast with the combatants at Little Bighorn, those who fought at Palo Alto almost exactly thirty years earlier possessed a fundamentally different armaments system. Both American and Mexican armies at Palo Alto were supplied primarily with smoothbore weaponry, rifles playing a relatively minor role during the battle. Firearm ammunition came in the form of round lead balls and black powder usually wrapped together into a cartridge made of paper. Metal cartridges did not make their debut on battlefields until about fifteen years later.

The era of smoothbore weaponry, which was coming to a close at the time of the U.S.-Mexican War, required a complex set of tactics. These tactics, the product of hundreds of years of development, quickly became obsolete with the wholesale adoption of rifles as combat weapons a few years later. We recognize at Palo Alto a type of artifact patterning more reflective of eighteenth-century European warfare than the American Civil War fought a few years later. Furthermore, it is a pattern quite different from those identified at battle sites of American Indian wars fought after 1865. To translate artifact patterning found at Palo Alto into behavioral dynamics of the smoothbore period, it is essential that we compare and assess the respective arms, equipage, and logistics of the two armies as well as deduce the overall competency of the leaders and morale of the led.

Research Purpose and Objectives

Congress, in its desire to recognize the significance of the battle of Palo Alto and the U.S.-Mexican War as a whole, authorized in 1978 the establishment of a park two miles north of the city limits of Brownsville, Texas. Establishment of a new park by the National Park Service (NPS) requires that an archaeological investigation be conducted in conjunction with in-depth and ongoing documentary research. Regarding Palo Alto, the resultant information would provide NPS with a sound plan for identifying and interpreting the physical locations of various battle events known to have taken place. Consequently, an archaeological reconnaissance survey was completed the following year, but the limited scope and results of this survey were deemed inconclusive for NPS planning needs. A more thorough investigation was not possible, however, until Congress passed the Palo Alto Battlefield National Historic Site Act in June, 1992.

Preparations for the 1992 field season, and the subsequent 1993 season, included the development of a research design. The overriding goal of our research was acquisition of enough archaeological and documentary data to determine the major battle-line positions of the two opposing armies. Investigative interests included:

(1) A comprehensive search for and the study of a variety of pertinent historical documents and eyewitness battle accounts. Synthesis of these data would be used as a basis of comparison with expected archaeological data.

(2) Correlation of specific topographic features described at the time of the battle with those features found on the battlefield today.

(3) Assessment of postbattle history as it relates to topographic and artifact patterning modifications.

(4) A detailed analysis of artifact types and the patterning they form on the battlefield. Such analysis would also provide a database for researchers investigating other battlefields of the smoothbore period.

The degradation process of artifact patterning began at Palo Alto almost as soon as the battle drew to a close. Artifact removal from the battlefield accelerated as a result of relic hunters using metal detectors, and we feared before beginning our fieldwork that little of research value would remain. We were pleasantly surprised to find this fear was unjustified. In fact, we now believe significant archaeological information still remains to be discovered, which may fill in some of the blanks of history if it is retrieved under scientifically controlled conditions. All archaeologically productive sites are part of our common cultural heritage. Some are significant primarily on a community level, reflecting early developmental stages of that community; others are of importance to a region, mirroring trends that helped form its social, political, and economic fabric. Only a handful of archaeological sites can be viewed as part of our shared national heritage. Certainly, the event that took place at Palo Alto on May 8, 1846, meets all of the above levels of significance.

Two Notes of Consideration

First, in this study we follow Webster's New Unabridged Dictionary, second edition, regarding the usage of the word *army* in its capitalized and noncapitalized forms. When capitalized, "the Army" or "Regular Army" refers to a country's entire land forces of permanent, professionally trained troops. During the U.S.-Mexican War, a period of national emergency for both Mexico and the United States, the Regular Army of each country also included various units of semi- and nonprofessional citizen-soldiers. In noncapitalized form, *army* refers to a specific military unit, usually consisting of two or more subunits, together with auxiliary troops. This is a field army. For example, the Mexican army at Palo Alto consisted of four infantry regiments, supported by cavalry and engineer battalions, artillery batteries, nonprofessional irregulars, a field hospital, and baggage train. A field army, therefore, is a subset of the Regular Army.

Second, the English system of measurement is used because this system was predominant in the nineteenth-century United States. The nineteenth-century Mexican linear unit of measurement, the *vara*, was variable in length but comparable to about thirty-three inches. For this study, the *vara* has been converted to English measurement, thereby allowing for comparisons and avoiding possible confusion.

Historical Overview

You might as well attempt to turn the current of the Mississippi as to turn
the [Democratic Party] from the annexation of Texas to the United States. . . .
Obtain it we must—peaceably if we can, but forcibly if we must.
—former President Andrew Jackson, 1844

Diplomacy of Manifest Destiny, 1803 to 1846

The 1840s have often been referred to as the Age of Manifest Destiny in
United States history, for it was during this decade that the expansionist
movement reached its apogee and much of the western United States was
added to the national domain. That expansion came largely at the expense
of Mexico, and the issue that brought the two nations to war was the status
of Texas.

The United States first laid claim to Texas in 1803 when President
Thomas Jefferson tried to persuade Spain that this region was part of the
Louisiana Purchase and that the Rio Grande should serve as the border
between the two nations. This, of course, was stretching the truth, for Spanish
settlers had established San Antonio, the region's principal community,
nearly a century before. The two countries could not agree on the status of
Texas until President James Monroe's secretary of state, John Quincy Adams,
negotiated the Transcontinental Treaty with Spain in 1819. This agreement
set the border at the Sabine River and clearly established that Texas was
Spanish territory. Adams made this concession only after Spain agreed to
cede Florida to the United States. Mexico declared its independence from
Spain in 1821, and two years later Adams became president. He tried to
persuade Mexico to sell Texas to the United States, but to no avail. At the
same time, however, Mexico opened the area to settlement by American
citizens, and thousands emigrated there over the remainder of the decade.
Adams's presidential successor, Andrew Jackson, continued the American
effort to annex the region, but he, too, was rebuffed.[1]

In 1836 the Texans, which included both the Anglo-American settlers
and their Hispanic allies, revolted against the Mexican government. After
General Sam Houston and his Texan army defeated the Mexican army at
the Battle of San Jacinto in 1836, the rebels captured President Antonio

López de Santa Anna and forced him to sign the so-called Treaty of Velasco, which granted Texas independence and recognized its border with Mexico at the Rio Grande. Treaties signed at gunpoint have little validity in international law, however, and a new Mexican government quickly repudiated the agreement. For the next decade, Texas was an independent republic. Vicious border skirmishes periodically flared up between Texas and Mexico, which still claimed Texas as a wayward state in rebellion. Even if Mexico had been willing to recognize Texas' independence, it is unlikely that the two sides could have agreed on a border. Texans demanded the Rio Grande, while in coming years Mexico would consistently—and correctly—assert that the historic border between the rebellious state and Tamaulipas had always been the Nueces River, over a hundred miles to the north.

After independence was secured on the battlefield, many Texans hoped to join their infant republic to the United States. But President Jackson

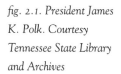
fig. 2.1. President James K. Polk. Courtesy Tennessee State Library and Archives

On the Prairie of Palo Alto

(1829–37), who tried to buy Texas during his first term, now proved cool to an annexation agreement, which might inject the slavery issue into American politics or precipitate a war with Mexico. Jackson's successor, Martin Van Buren (1837–41), followed the same course. The Texas issue did not come to the forefront of American politics again until President John Tyler (1841–45) sent a treaty of annexation to the Senate in 1844. Complications over slavery caused its failure. During the presidential election campaign of 1844, Democrat nominee James K. Polk of Tennessee pledged to annex Texas and Oregon (the latter region was also claimed by Great Britain). His narrow victory over Whig nominee Henry Clay of Kentucky, who was less expansionist-minded, demonstrated to Congress the people's will (fig. 2.1). Even before the new president was inaugurated, Congress voted to annex Texas through a joint resolution in February, 1845. For Mexico, which had never accepted Texas's independence, this was an act of war. If no diplomatic settlement could be reached, the matter would ultimately be settled by arms.[2]

National Development and Military Power: United States and Mexico

THE AMERICAN ARMY

The U.S. Army of the 1840s was, in many respects, the product of a reform movement that began shortly after the War of 1812, a war that had revealed glaring weaknesses regarding the nation's defense establishment. The army adopted a series of reforms during the decades following independence, but few of these reforms resulted in permanent improvements. The Constitution of 1787 had created a federal government with sufficient taxing power to establish credit and pay its troops. During the 1790s, the Washington and Adams administrations created a small but credible Army and Navy. But much of what had been accomplished under the Federalists was lost when the Jefferson administration, responding to public anger over taxation, dramatically reduced military expenditures.

When Congress declared war in 1812, the nation was ill-prepared to fight. In the first major action, General William Hull surrendered Detroit to a British force half the size of his garrison. Other humiliations followed, including the burning of Washington in August, 1814. By then, however, the conflict had turned into something of a stalemate. British and American negotiators signed the Treaty of Ghent on Christmas Eve, 1814, ending the war and returning to the status quo antebellum—essentially the way things were before the war. American demands for respect of "neutral rights" and guarantees against future impressment were not met. Many Americans, however, chose to forget the setbacks after General Andrew Jackson inflicted a stunning defeat upon a British expeditionary force at New Orleans in January, 1815, two weeks after the peace treaty had been signed. It was easy then to claim a glorious victory instead of accept the reality of an ignominious draw.[3]

After the war, a group of young generals—Jacob Brown, Edmund P. Gaines, Alexander Macomb, and Winfield Scott—realized how close the nation came to defeat and, in subsequent years, spearheaded a reform movement to prepare American land forces for the next war. Their vision was a better-organized, -educated, and more professional officer corps to direct future mobilization. To wage an effective war, the nation needed centralized strategic planning. When the country entered the next war, it would need a well-trained Regular Army to take the fight to the enemy. They remembered well how a hastily mobilized force of mostly militia and poorly trained volunteers failed to wrest Canada from its small British garrison in 1812. Their ideas were not wholly altruistic, for these were ambitious men who saw the military as their career. Nevertheless, the young generals accomplished much, but only because they occasionally found allies in the executive branch.

Crucial to the successes of the reform movement were Secretaries of War John C. Calhoun (1817–25) and Joel Poinsett (1837–41). A series of reforms over the next two decades substantially improved the American Army. Beginning in 1817, Superintendent Sylvanus Thayer standardized the curriculum of the United States Military Academy at West Point. In 1818, the Army began a long-term process that standardized ordnance and other equipment. Secretary of War Calhoun began a program of coastal fortification, created a general staff, and centralized supply bureaus in Washington. Beginning in 1821 the Army initiated a policy of commissioning only graduates of the military academy, with the exception of a few posts in the pay and medical departments. The percentage of West Pointers in the Army gradually rose from less than 15 percent in 1817 to almost 64 percent in 1830. Unfortunately, the Jacksonian egalitarian "reforms" of the 1830s undermined this policy, specifically when the executive branch began commissioning unqualified individuals directly into the armed services. Despite this setback, just before the Civil War at least three-quarters of all officers were West Point graduates.[4]

It was not until the 1830s, however, that the artillery arm of the land forces began to feel the full effects of the reform movement. American military and political leaders became cognizant of the potential of this arm largely because of Napoleon's effective use of it. Consequently, the U.S. Army in 1808 gained congressional approval to create an artillery regiment. An important development was the creation of light artillery units, which eventually played a key role in winning the war with Mexico. Captain George Peter's experimental light artillery company staged a memorable drill for Congress in July, 1808. His horse artillery battery rode from Baltimore to Washington at an impressive six miles an hour. Before the gathered dignitaries the men galloped three miles, dismounted, unlimbered, fired a national salute, returned to the starting point, and fired a second salute, all in twenty-two minutes. Powerful congressional leaders were impressed, and the future of American light artillery looked bright. But after Jefferson left office in 1809, William Eustis, President Madison's secretary of war and a former contract army surgeon, decided that the regiment's horses were a waste of money and disbanded the unit.[5]

In 1821 Congress again authorized the creation of a light artillery, this time in the form of one company in each of the four artillery regiments. But for the next seventeen years nothing was done, and American artillery fell into decline. Artillerymen ended up serving mainly as foot soldiers in coastal and frontier forts. Indians, not Europeans, were the potential adversary; the services of artillery were not highly valued. It took the personal initiative of Secretary of War Joel Poinsett to help revive the artillery arm. In 1838 Poinsett decided to mount four light batteries as the 1821 law allowed. The first company was organized under the command of Captain (Brevet Major) Samuel Ringgold of the 3rd Artillery. He received six new field guns and horses and set to work. The next summer, Poinsett created a "camp of instruction" at Trenton, New Jersey, and put the artillery on display to the public. Ringgold was the star of the show. A journalist for the *New York American* recounted that as spectators took their places, "Ringgold and his flying artillery sweeps by at speed, the ear is startled with the earthquake rumble of his death-dispensing cannons." Then: "The reviewing being accomplished, the troops performed a variety of evolutions—the light artillery rushed across the field, swung their pieces to the front—unlimbered—the men dismounted—the horses ranged to the rear, almost of themselves—and the cannon were discharged, limbered, loaded, and off again, almost in a time as short as that occupied in reading this paragraph."[6]

THE MEXICAN ARMY

The character of the Mexican Army was shaped during the struggle for independence. In 1811, Father Miguel Hidalgo led a rebellion against Spanish authority, which attracted considerable support from the lower classes and Indian peoples. But most of the propertied classes, clergy, and Creole Army officers distrusted this movement from below and remained loyal to Spain. In a few years, however, the rebellion was isolated to a handful of outlying areas, primarily in the south, and posed no threat to Spanish authority. The key turn of events came in 1820 when the Spanish Cortes passed legislation that threatened the privileged legal status of the military and clergy in the Spanish empire. Now the royalist military establishment in Mexico City changed course and, joined by many of the clergy and other social elites, turned against the viceregal authority.

In February, 1821, a group of royalist officers, led by Augustín de Iturbide, declared the Plan of Iguala, which called for the establishment of a constitutional monarchy. Shortly thereafter, the revolutionary officers joined their former insurgent enemies. In September, Iturbide entered Mexico City in triumph. Once in power, he rewarded his supporters with wholesale promotions that included elevating numerous enlisted men to officer rank. Many of these new officers, however, were totally unqualified. Furthermore, the promotions produced more officers than available billets. At the end of 1821, for every two soldiers in Mexico City there was one noncommissioned or commissioned officer. Three hundred to five hundred of these needless appointees were housed and paid at taxpayers' expense. In 1822, the revenue of the government was only one-half that of the viceregal government before 1810, yet the army was three times as large. Iturbide declared himself emperor in July, 1822, but could not afford to continue paying the army and was thus overthrown in February, 1823. A cycle began wherein the generals tended to support those in power, but only as long as promotions and pay were forthcoming. One historian has noted that

> a main feature of the age of Santa Anna . . . was chronic political upheaval and the Mexicans' apparent incapacity to establish a stable and enduring system of self-government. As both cause and effect of this turmoil, no president save the first managed to retain office for his full elected or appointed term, and governments changed with bewildering frequency. An incalculable number of revolts, or pronunciamentos, took place and military action by ambitious army officers became the normal method of expressing dissent or pursuing political change.[7]

A further stimulus to instability was the tacit agreement among the officers that leaders of the losing side would not suffer severe punishment. In many cases, they simply had to go into exile for a short time and could return to their former place and rank. Enemies in one coup became allies in the next. In these "games of chess," as one observer called them, there was usually little fighting and casualties were limited. From independence in 1821 to the outbreak of war with the United States in 1846, Mexico saw thirty-one presidential administrations and thirty-nine changes in the ministry of war. It should be noted, however, that some individuals held the same office more than once. Santa Anna, for example, was either president or interim president eleven times in his career (fig. 2.2).

These repeated coups weakened the nation in a number of ways. During times of instability and civil war the property of foreigners was often seized or destroyed, leading to a plethora of claims by foreign governments. Mexico was unable to pay these claims, and the resultant tension ended any real chance the new nation had of obtaining allies abroad. The coups and civil wars fostered costly military maneuvers and action. In their aftermath, officers who had backed the winning side had to be satisfied with promotions

fig. 2.2. Antonio López de Santa Anna. He was a major leader of Mexico but in exile at the time of the battle of Palo Alto. *Courtesy Special Collections Division, University of Texas at Arlington Libraries, Arlington, Texas*

or pay. The cycle served to drive an already indebted nation only deeper in debt. The threat, or opportunity, of coups tended to keep military forces near the capital and unable to defend the frontier from Indian raiding, which in turn created separatism in the northern states. Furthermore, it is impossible for any military, so caught up in the political arena, to possibly meet its larger obligation as protector of the nation. Instead, the Mexican Army became one of the major causes of the new nation's ills.[8]

One of the greatest weaknesses of the Mexican Army was its recruitment process. With little or no money to attract enlistees, it relied on brutal methods to fill the ranks. Jean Louis Berlandier, who later served with the Mexican army at Palo Alto as an aide-de-camp, described the process in the early 1830s. It had changed little before the war with the United States.

> *There exist few countries on earth where the formation of disciplined troops is accomplished as arbitrarily and dishonorably as in Mexico. . . . When the government has need for troops, the governors of the states or departments, who are charged with sending contingents to the commandants general, have the alcaldes seize, pell-mell and without warning, vagabonds and often poor but honest men. Those who have thus been seized, and whom no master or protector reclaims, are destined by force to military service, where they are*

mingled with convicts and prisoners of every condition, whom the courts of justice have condemned to a career of warfare. . . . When these levies do not suffice to complete the number of men demanded, the alcaldes drag from the bosom of their families citizens upon whom they wish to avenge themselves. . . . Lastly as a crowning misfortune, very few of these new soldiers can become officers, no matter what their merits, because of the custom of drawing officers from the ranks of cadets or privileged soldiers. . . . It is impossible to deny, however, that such a system incites to desertion and is more worthy of a feudal country than of a government which vaunts itself as within to proclaim liberty.[9]

War or Peace: The Final Crisis

Under the administration of President James K. Polk (1845–49), the United States sought to persuade Mexico to sell lands for American expansion south to the Rio Grande and west to the Pacific Ocean. Persuasion included steady diplomatic, economic, and military pressure. The strategy of "graduated pressure" was conceived in an atmosphere ignorant of the realities of Mexican domestic politics. Since the loss of Texas north of the Nueces River, no Mexican government dared discuss the voluntary surrender of additional land to the United States for fear of being overthrown. In fact, a substantial number of Mexican citizens favored war with the United States to recapture Texas. Polk's aggressive tactics in diplomacy convinced various Mexican leaders that their northern neighbor was attempting to annex their country. Such suspicions regarding the motives of the United States effectively stifled Mexican efforts to steer the dispute toward a peaceful resolution. Polk made matters worse by adding a military threat to the diplomatic process. On May 29, 1845, Polk ordered Brevet Brigadier General Zachary Taylor to move fifteen hundred regular troops from Fort Jesup, Louisiana, to a point near the Rio Grande (fig. 2.3).

Zachary Taylor was born on November 24, 1784, in Orange County, Virginia. He received a commission as a second lieutenant in the U.S. Army in 1808 and first saw action at the outbreak of the War of 1812. As commander of isolated Fort Harrison in present-day Indiana, he rallied a demoralized garrison and consequently drove back an Indian attack but was largely inactive for the rest of the war. Taylor ended the war as major but in the postwar reduction of forces was retained as a captain. Insulted, he quit the military and returned to Louisville. In 1816 his second cousin, President Madison, gave him a commission as major in the 3rd Infantry. In 1819, he was appointed lieutenant colonel of the 4th Infantry in New Orleans.

Taylor's first and only chance to command men in battle before the U.S.-Mexican War was at the battle of Okeechobee in December, 1837, during the Second Seminole War. Taylor's force of 1,032 men encountered some

400 Seminoles who had taken a position on a low rise in the middle of a swamp. Taylor's tactics that day were simple and straightforward. He ordered his men to dismount and place their baggage at the edge of the swamp; he then had the Missouri volunteers form a line and advance against the enemy. The 4th and 6th Infantries formed a second line, apparently to take over the fight if the volunteers faltered. The 1st Infantry formed the reserve. The men stumbled through the swamp and soon began suffering heavy casualties. The Missourians eventually broke and ran toward the rear, and, according to Taylor's report, they could not "again be brought into action as a body . . . although efforts were repeatedly made by my staff to induce them to do so." The 4th and 6th picked up the fight and after three hours drove the Indians off from their position onto the shore of Lake Okeechobee, where they dispersed. Taylor's force had suffered 26 killed and 112 wounded—probably far more than the Indian casualties—but they held the field. The Indians, of course, fought with an entirely differ-

fig. 2.3. General Zachary Taylor. Courtesy Filson Club Historical Society

ent philosophy; having inflicted heavy casualties, they were probably as equally sure that they had carried the day. Nevertheless, the public and the Van Buren administration, eager for success against the Seminoles, considered the bloody affair a victory. Taylor was promoted to brevet brigadier general.[10]

On receiving his orders from Polk, Taylor chose Corpus Christi, Texas, for his base, located at the mouth of the Nueces River. By the end of July, he and his troops were encamped there. During the succeeding months, the camp increased in size to approximately forty-three hundred men, slightly over half of the entire regular U.S. land forces. Taylor's force contained the elements of four infantry and one dragoon regiments plus a regiment-sized battalion of "red-legged infantry," or artillerymen serving as infantry. The infantry and dragoon units arrived fresh from service on the Indian frontier, while the artillerymen came from coastal defenses.

Organization of infantry regiments was in ten companies of forty-two

---

fig. 2.4. The drilling of recruits at Corpus Christi (from Frost, History of the Mexican War*). Courtesy Special Collections Division, University of Texas at Arlington Libraries, Arlington, Texas*

men each. Each regiment contained one company formed as an elite grenadier unit, its members hand-picked for leading attacks. A second company was trained and equipped as light infantry that functioned as skirmishers and sharpshooters. Light infantry companies were often combined to form a special battalion. American infantry excelled at individual and company drills, but the normal practice of stationing troops in small detachments of two to five companies offered little opportunity for battalion drill. Taylor instituted a battalion training program at Corpus Christi in the autumn of 1845, but its effectiveness was questionable. There was also a strenuous training program for new recruits (fig. 2.4); however, the effort slackened as the harsh fall and winter weather attacked the troops in their poorly protected encampment. Despite a growing sick list and the presence of increasing numbers of grog shops, prostitutes, and gambling dens, the army maintained its underlying discipline.

The horse regiments were dragoons instead of true cavalry since they were mounted men armed and trained to fight primarily on foot. Dragoon regiments consisted of ten companies of fifty-four men each, normally deployed for frontier police duties stressing rapid movement by heavily armed men. Dragoons were too few in number to play a major role in the coming battles of the U.S.-Mexican War. The artillery regiments were trained to serve both as gunners for the coastal defense batteries and as temporary

On the Prairie of Palo Alto

infantry for supporting local militia. Their versatility allowed the artillery companies to function as the army's strategic reserve. One company in each of the four artillery regiments was armed as a light or field battery of four cannon, usually consisting of two six-pounder guns and two twelve-pounder howitzers.[11]

In 1845 the U.S. Army contained no truly specialized troops. Fatigue parties drawn from line units and supervised by engineer officers did engineering work. These officers were normally among the most promising graduates of the United States Military Academy at West Point, which was still the nation's largest single source of trained engineers during the first half of the nineteenth century. In May, 1846, Congress authorized the formation of the Company of Sappers, Miners, and Pontoniers, which would not see action until spring, 1847. Logistic support of the army in the field was the responsibility of the quartermaster, commissary, forage, and ordnance departments. Each relied on hired civilians to staff its wagons and depots under the control of officers belonging to the departments. Similarly, the medical department consisted of medical officers but no enlisted men. Nurses and others who helped staff the hospitals were either civilians or soldiers detailed to that duty. The regimental band also assisted in the removal of the dead and wounded.[12]

In November, 1845, President Polk received intelligence from the American consul in Mexico City that Mexico would receive a diplomatic emissary "to settle the present dispute in a peaceful, reasonable, and honorable manner." Accordingly, he named Senator John Slidell of Louisiana as the new American minister to Mexico. Polk instructed Slidell to gain leverage for a boundary settlement by emphasizing unpaid claims of American citizens against the Mexican government, estimated to exceed $5 million. Polk, hoping a nearly bankrupt Mexico would settle for money, offered a sliding scale of payments for various Mexican territorial cessions. The president demanded the Rio Grande as the boundary for Texas, which he insisted Santa Anna had acknowledged in 1836. For this minimum settlement, Polk would have the United States government accept the claims of its citizens against Mexico. The United States would also add an additional $5 million if Mexico would cede New Mexico. Additionally, Polk offered greater amounts for more land, including a top price of $25 million and assumption of claims for the cession of upper California (now the state of California), New Mexico, and the Rio Grande boundary for Texas.[13]

In early December, Slidell arrived in Mexico City to negotiate. His mission, however, soon foundered in diplomatic technicalities. Mexican president José Joaquín de Herrera secretly agreed to negotiate with a United States *comisionado*, or commissioner, but Polk apparently received a poor translation of Mexico's terms and mistakenly appointed Slidell as "minister plenipotentiary," a high-ranking diplomat. For Mexico to accept and bargain with such a minister would have implied restoration of full diplomatic relations, which in turn would have allowed Herrera's political opponents to charge that he accepted the annexation of Texas. Mexico could not afford to grant such concessions before the negotiations even began. Therefore, on December 16, the secretary of foreign relations, Manuel de la Peña y Peña, informed Slidell that his credentials would have to be changed to those of commissioner before talks could begin.[14]

Despite this snub of Slidell, Herrera was overthrown in January, 1846, by certain factions accusing him of weakness in dealing with the United States. Major General Mariano Paredes y Arrillaga, commander of the Army of the North, assumed the presidency. Paredes adopted an uncompromising attitude over the issue of the Mexico–United States dispute by vowing to uphold Mexican sovereignty all the way to the Sabine River. Word of Slidell's failure reached Washington in January, 1846. Polk's reaction was to increase pressure on Mexico by ordering Taylor to move his troops to the Rio Grande. Taylor departed Corpus Christi on March 8. Heavy artillery, supplies, and the sick traveled by water under naval escort to the village of Frontón de Santa Isabela on Point Isabel, on the coast just north of the mouth of the Rio Grande. The troops marching overland traversed a desolate, semiarid land. On March 20, as the leading elements of the American army approached the Arroyo Colorado, a small stream about thirty miles north of Matamoros, they encountered a Mexican force on the south side. This detachment threatened to contest the Americans' crossing. General Taylor brought up his trailing brigades and prepared to make an assault. His light companies and dragoons, covered by artillery, dashed across the stream. But the Mexicans disappeared into the brush.

On March 24 the Americans reached the junction of the roads from Point Isabel and Matamoros, located within the area known as Palo Alto, and bivouacked opposite Palo Alto Pond. Their encampment was later named Worth's Camp, after second-in-command Colonel William Worth. Taylor had left Worth in charge of the infantry while he proceeded to the coast with the dragoons. The Mexicans set fire to the village of Frontón de Santa Isabela at Point Isabel just before the dragoons and Taylor arrived. Waiting offshore were the baggage transport ships, which had arrived at about the same time the village was set to the torch. Taylor garrisoned the base with two artillery companies under Major John Munroe and ordered work started on a fort that would protect the supplies.[15]

On March 27 Taylor and the dragoons rejoined the main body of soldiers at Palo Alto, some ten miles from the Rio Grande. Upon their arrival at the river, the Americans began construction of a star-shaped, earthen-walled fortress that they named Fort Texas. The Mexican commander at Matamoros, General Francisco Mejía, made no attempt to dislodge Taylor. Instead, he improved the artillery positions and earthworks of Fort Guerrero, located adjacent to Matamoros and across from Fort Texas. During this initial period of relatively peaceful confrontation, the Mexicans made strenuous efforts to induce American soldiers to desert to their cause. At one time, the Mexicans believed the entire U.S. 7th Infantry, a largely Irish and German unit, would desert en masse. The actual number of deserters crossing into Mexico, however, was well under a hundred men. On April 4, José María Tornel y Mendevil, Mexico's minister of war and marine, ordered Major General Mariano Arista, a veteran officer, to command the Army of the North (fig. 2.5). Arista also received secret orders to attack Taylor's force on the Rio Grande.[16]

Mariano Arista was born in San Luis Potosí, Mexico, on July 16, 1802. At eleven he became a cadet in the Spanish Royalist Army and rose to the rank of lieutenant until he abandoned it for the insurgent forces in 1821. During the 1820s, Arista slowly rose in rank but at the same time demonstrated a tendency to change allegiance in order to further his career. He was sometimes an ally and at other times a rival of Santa Anna, who promoted him to general of a division in 1832.

fig. 2.5. General Mariano Arista. Courtesy University of Texas at Austin

In 1833 Arista was exiled to the United States, but he returned to Mexico in 1835 and reentered the service with little damage to his career. During the 1838 French invasion of Veracruz, Arista was captured while serving under Santa Anna but was released two months later. In 1839 he commanded a brigade to suppress a revolt in Tampico and was appointed commandant of Tamaulipas. From that point forward, Arista's career was mostly centered in the north. In 1839 the general was named commander in chief of the Army Corps of the North, and he played a significant role in the Federalist wars. Arista resigned in 1841 over an accusation that he participated in a separatist movement and revolution. As was typical of his checkered career, however, he was soon back in command in the north.

Arista was in command of the Mexican forces on the Texas border in 1844–45 and was surely more familiar with the potential theater of war than Taylor. But the Mexican general had little confidence that he could defeat the invaders. Before Polk's election, Arista had argued for a war with Texas in the hope that the errant state would be conquered before annexation could be completed. By January, 1845, when he learned that annexation of

Texas to the United States was inevitable, Arista wrote the minister of war demanding more troops to augment his small force in the north. Although Arista had received four thousand recruits since 1841, most had long ago deserted. In February, Arista informed Mexico City that his army was immobilized by lack of the basic necessities. An American force might appear on the banks of the Rio Grande any day, and all he had to defend his nation was "an insignificant force, poorly clothed and without equipment." In July, 1845, Arista privately ridiculed American military maneuvers aimed at preventing an invasion of Texas. They had little to fear from his army, "which was in a state of dreadful misery." He was removed from command for a brief time after General Mariano Paredes came to power for failing to support the coup but returned to take control of Mexican forces at Matamoros on the eve of battle.[17]

During April, 1846, American troops in Fort Texas experienced both hard work and boredom in the semitropical heat, their monotonous existence broken only by occasional skirmishes with local guerrillas. On April 10, Colonel Trueman Cross, chief quartermaster, and Lieutenant Theodoric Porter were killed not far from Fort Texas. Mounted patrols were sent to apprehend or kill the guerrillas. One of these patrols was ambushed and a lieutenant killed. On April 11, Major General Pedro de Ampudia arrived in Matamoros to supervise Mexican military operations. Shortly afterward, Brigadier General Anastasio Torrejón followed with 2,200 troops. Ampudia immediately ordered Taylor to withdraw from his position on the river. The American general both refused this demand and ordered a naval blockade of the mouth of the Rio Grande, thereby cutting Ampudia's maritime supply route. Ampudia took no overt action since he knew General Arista was about to replace him.[18]

On April 23, President Paredes issued a manifesto that declared "a defensive war," in which the Mexican armed forces would defend "every point of our territory which may be attacked." This reference was to Taylor's presence south of the Nueces. Because there was little chance that the Americans would withdraw, it was only a matter of time before Mexico attacked. The following day, General Arista arrived in Matamoros to resume command of the Mexican army on the border, replacing Ampudia, who was widely detested in the region.[19] Arista immediately held a council of war with his generals to detail an offensive strategy. He reviewed his assembled forces. General Francisco Mejía commanded the 1st and 10th Line Infantries, the 2nd Light Infantry, the 7th Cavalry, an elite battalion of *zapadores* or sappers, one squadron of auxiliary troops from different northern villas, various presidial companies, and a battalion of the local national guard. General Ampudia commanded the Regiment of Light Infantry of Mexico; General Torrejón commanded the 4th Infantry, the 8th Cavalry, and eighty cannoneers with six artillery pieces; and General Antonio Canales was commander of a mounted auxiliary regiment of irregulars. Arista's army totaled 5,200 men and twenty-six pieces of artillery.

Arista also informed General Taylor that hostilities between the two countries had commenced and launched his attack the next day. His plan called for Torrejón, with about sixteen hundred sappers, cavalry, and light infantry, to cross the river at the village of La Palangaña west of Matamoros and strike east to sever the American supply line to Point Isabel. Arista, with the main portion of the army, would cross at a point east of Matamoros and join Torrejón's force, threatening to cut off Fort Texas. Upon learning of Torrejón's crossing, Taylor sent out dragoon patrols to determine the location of these Mexican forces. On April 25, Torrejón ambushed a patrol led by Captain Seth Thornton at Rancho de Carricitos, twenty miles upriver from Fort Texas (map 2). In the ensuing fight, American casualties included eleven killed, six wounded, and forty-six captured, the latter including Thornton.

News of the debacle reached General Taylor on the twenty-sixth. He sent a dispatch to President Polk, stating that "hostilities may now be considered as commenced." The dispatch arrived in Washington on May 9. Polk had already considered a declaration of war: the fighting on the Rio Grande played perfectly into his plans. On May 11 he sent a message to Congress asking for a declaration of war. It made no mention of the Mexican claim to the Nueces or that the American army was in disputed ter-

map 2. Map showing the vicinity of Palo Alto at the time of the battle. Courtesy National Park Service

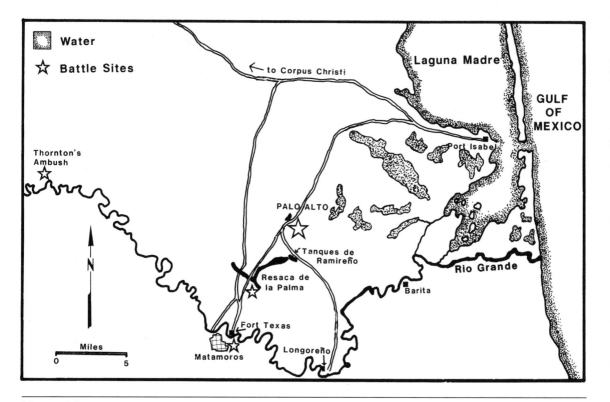

fig. 2.6. A Texas Ranger at Palo Alto (from Frost, History of the Mexican War). Courtesy Special Collections Division, University of Texas at Arlington Libraries, Arlington, Texas

ritory but boldly declared that the movement to the Rio Grande had been undertaken to defend Texas from an invasion. The United States, Polk declared, had "tried every effort at reconciliation" and that, in response, "Mexico has invaded our territory and shed American blood on American soil." On May 13, Congress declared war on Mexico. By that time, Arista's army on the Rio Grande had been annihilated in two days of fighting.[20]

After destroying Thornton's command, Torrejón turned his cavalry toward the Point Isabel–Matamoros Road. Another small victory came his way on April 28. A Mexican patrol surprised a portion of Captain Samuel Walker's Texas Rangers at their encampment near Palo Alto (fig. 2.6). The Mexicans had accomplished the first phase of Arista's strategy, that of cutting the Americans' supply route between Fort Texas and Point Isabel. Word of Torrejón's feat quickly filtered back to the coast, causing a near panic at

On the Prairie of Palo Alto

Point Isabel. Major John Munroe, in command of the forces there, pulled together five hundred artillerymen, Texas volunteers, and sailors to defend the unfinished fort. Luckily for the Americans, Torrejón did not advance on Point Isabel, nor did he remain at Palo Alto and wait for Arista's reinforcements as initially planned. Mexican strategy changed because of a rumor that American snipers were poised to assassinate Arista while he and his forces crossed the Rio Grande. A suddenly worried Arista ordered Torrejón to abandon his position astride the road at Palo Alto and march to the Rio Grande to protect the troop crossing at Rancho de Longoreño, thirteen miles downriver from Matamoros. The Point Isabel–Matamoros Road was open again, if only for a few days.[21]

Captain Walker, whose men just two days earlier had been so ignominiously surprised by Torrejón's men, arrived at Fort Texas to deliver Major Munroe's appeal for immediate assistance. Now that Arista had the upper hand, General Taylor belatedly realized the importance of securing both installations. He put every man "not detained by other indispensable duty" to work completing the walls of Fort Texas. Once the fort was ready to withstand a siege, Taylor could march to the aid of Munroe and reopen the supply line. Taylor's quickened efforts came none too soon, for Arista was moving to regain the road. General Pedro de Ampudia led the first brigade of Mexican infantry across the river at Rancho de Longoreño on April 30. Arista followed the next day with the second brigade. General Francisco Mejía remained behind with 1,400 men to garrison Matamoros, ready to attack Fort Texas.[22]

Taylor learned of the crossing on the afternoon of May 1, too late to attack the Mexican bridgehead. Logically assuming that Arista's objective was Point Isabel, Taylor lost no time in starting for his supply base. Within two hours a relief force of about twenty-three hundred men, led by Taylor, left Fort Texas. The Mexicans watching from across the river rejoiced, for they assumed the departure signaled an American retreat. They were wrong. Major Jacob Brown remained at the still-incomplete fort with the 7th Infantry, Captain Allan Lowd's four eighteen-pounders, and a field battery under Lieutenant Braxton Bragg, a future Confederate general—a total of some five hundred men. Brown's orders were to hold Fort Texas until Taylor and his force returned from the coast with supplies sufficient to withstand a lengthy siege. On May 1, Taylor's force marched until midnight and bivouacked on the plain at Palo Alto. They rose early on the second and resumed the march, arriving at Point Isabel around noon. The soldiers immediately began improving its defenses and organizing a train of some 270 supply wagons for the return trip to Matamoros.[23]

Arista completed ferrying his men across the Rio Grande and divided his command on May 2. Ampudia led the 4th Infantry, the Puebla Battalion, some sappers, and about two hundred light cavalry up the river to lay siege to Fort Texas. Arista's force of 3,500 hurried to the crossroads at Palo Alto, arriving on May 3. Although the Mexican army was one day too late to stop the Americans from reaching Point Isabel, it could still block their return to Fort Texas. The Mexicans soon discovered, however, that the water supply at Palo Alto was inadequate for their needs. It was also possible that Taylor could bypass their position by marching south of Palo Alto. Accordingly, Arista pulled out to Tanques de Ramireño, about three miles to the south on the Matamoros road, arriving on May 5. This location had an abundance of good water and was an excellent position from which to monitor all roads and trails that led to the Fort Texas–Matamoros area.[24]

The Mexican batteries opened fire on Fort Texas at five in the morning on May 3. The rumble of artillery reverberated across the prairies of the Rio Grande delta, and its muffled sound reached the American forces at Point Isabel. A now-anxious Taylor sent several Texas Rangers to make their way into the besieged fort, with orders for Major Brown to hold out at all costs. The Rangers returned the next day and informed Taylor that Brown's force was in no immediate danger. By May 7, Fort Polk, as the post at Point Isabel was now known, was secure and the supply wagons ready for the march to Fort Texas.

On the banks of the Rio Grande, the Mexican bombardment of Fort Texas consisted of an almost continuous artillery barrage from positions in Matamoros. Major Brown rationed his counterfire because of limited gunpowder; nevertheless, it was apparently sufficient to discourage a major assault. Damage to the earthen walls of Fort Texas was minimal, while its defenders remained relatively protected inside bunkers. Casualties were low, but Sergeant Horace A. Weigert of the 7th Infantry was killed on the first day of the siege, and Major Brown was mortally wounded on the morning of the sixth. That afternoon the Mexicans formally requested that the garrison surrender, but the acting commander, Captain E. S. Hawkins, refused. Major Brown died the afternoon of May 9, shortly before Taylor relieved the fort.[25]

By May 6 reinforcements had arrived to secure Fort Polk, and Taylor's force to secure Fort Texas was almost ready. On the morning of the seventh, he advised his subordinates to be ready to march that afternoon. One of Taylor's aides, Lieutenant George Gordon Meade, the future victor at Gettysburg, wrote his wife that the army was in excellent spirits and ready to fight. Meade worried, however, that Taylor had overburdened his army with some 270 supply wagons and two eighteen-pounder siege guns drawn by oxen. All of this would severely limit his maneuverability. The army moved out that day. Because of the late start and slow pace, the American force of 2,228 bivouacked after a march of only seven miles. They continued the trek before sunrise on May 8, with the general riding in "a jersey wagon of ponderous materials and questionable shape."[26]

Mexican scouts observed the signs of Taylor's column early on the morning of the eighth, then rushed south to inform Arista. The Mexican commander, still not convinced, sent out another patrol to reconnoiter. Although they were ambushed by a scouting party of Texas Rangers just east of Palo Alto, most of the patrol made it back to Tanques de Ramireño to confirm that Taylor was indeed advancing. Arista gave the order to break camp and march to meet the enemy. He knew he needed more men, however, and dispatched orders to Ampudia, who was besieging Fort Texas, to rejoin him at Palo Alto. Ampudia moved out by noon, with General José López Uraga's 4th Line Infantry, a company of sappers, a pack train of two hundred horses, two artillery pieces, and Canales's mounted irregulars. Fearing Arista would do battle before his arrival, Ampudia set a fast-paced march to the rendezvous. While Ampudia marched, Arista positioned his battalions just south of Palo Alto Pond and astride the road. At around 1 P.M. the American army cautiously entered the northern end of the prairie of Palo Alto. By this time, Taylor and his men could clearly see the long Mexican battle line waiting for them to the south.[27]

The Battle of Palo Alto

The prairie of Palo Alto, or "Tall Timber," took its name from the relatively tall stands of mesquite that began there and, interspersed with patches of open ground, stretched southward toward the Rio Grande. Then, as now, the roughly two-mile-wide open plain was covered by stiff, chest-high, and sharp-pointed grass that deals misery to anyone moving through it on foot. As would be demonstrated once the fighting began, this species of grass also has the peculiar ability of burning easily while still green. In addition to a semipermanent pond, the Palo Alto prairie included shallow depressions and old river meanders, termed *bolsones* and *resacas*, respectively, by the Mexicans. Because of heavy rains, these features on the day of battle either held standing water or were marshy. A belt of mesquite- and scrub-covered low rises and resaca levees demarcated the northern, southern, and eastern limits of the grassy plain. Bushes and tall mesquite both bordering and obscuring a resaca and its low, broad levee defined the western limits of the imminent battlefield.

Two roads connected Matamoros with Point Isabel: El Camino de Santa Isabel and El Camino de los Indios. The former was six miles shorter and the preferable route in dry weather. When it rained, however, this road was avoided because of the black clay mud that made it almost impassable. Owing to recent rains, Taylor's army had to take El Camino de los Indios, the "wet weather road." To pass through Palo Alto on this road, the Americans first had to skirt along a marshy area, El Tule Grande, the present-day Tule lake bed. The road then followed along the low levee that marked the western

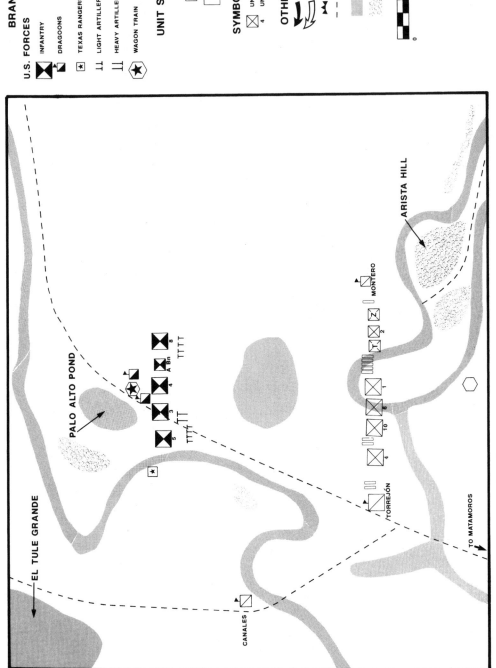

BRANCH SYMBOLS

U.S. FORCES

INFANTRY	
DRAGOONS	
TEXAS RANGERS	
LIGHT ARTILLERY	
HEAVY ARTILLERY	
WAGON TRAIN	

MEXICAN FORCES

INFANTRY	
CAVALRY	
TAMPICO CORPS	
ZAPADORES (SAPPERS)	
LIGHT ARTILLERY	
WAGON TRAIN	

UNIT SIZE SYMBOLS

COMPANY

BATTALION

REGIMENT

SYMBOL DEFINITION

UNIT SIZE AND BRANCH

4   UNIT NUMBER

OTHER SYMBOLS

U.S. TROOP MOVEMENTS

MEXICAN TROOP MOVEMENTS

TROOPS UNDER ATTACK

WAGON ROAD

STANDING WATER/MARSH

HIGH GROUND

0   3000 FT

N

EL TULE GRANDE

PALO ALTO POND

CANALES

TORREJÓN

TO MATAMOROS

MONTERO

ARISTA HILL

A Bn

map 3. Initial battle lines, approximately 1 P.M. Courtesy National Park Service limits of the prairie. By noon of May 8, however, the left flank of Arista's army had blocked this segment of the road.[28]

The American army may have had its first view of the massed Mexican army at about the time they reached the southeastern end of El Tule Grande. Taylor halted his column about two miles north of the Mexican battle line to allow the wagon train to catch up. Then his army, in column formation, advanced again until they were about three-quarters of a mile from the enemy and adjacent to a body of standing water on their right. This was Palo Alto Pond and perhaps the nearby resaca as well. Here they halted to water the horses and fill their canteens, half of each regiment at a time. Once refreshed, the troops formed in predetermined battle order to the right and left of the road (map 3). Meanwhile, Taylor ordered the train to move up and take a defensive position near the pond under the guard of a squadron of dragoons. Taylor's battle plan was to mass troops on his right and hit the Mexican left with a bayonet charge. Whether this plan was based on a perceived weakness in the Mexican line, on the lay of the ground, or simply on the fact that the road ran in that direction is unknown. Like his battle strategy at Okeechobee years before, it consisted of a simple assault on the enemy position, accepting that casualties had to come and driving the enemy from its position. It was not pretty, but from Taylor's viewpoint, it was how battles were fought.[29]

In keeping with this plan, General Taylor placed Brigadier General David Twiggs's right wing astride the road. Within this wing, Lieutenant Colonel James McIntosh's 5th Infantry took the extreme right, followed by Brevet Major Samuel Ringgold's field battery; Captain Walker's mounted Texas Rangers, numbering twenty-five men, performed right-flank picket duty west of the road and in the mesquite thicket; two eighteen-pounders under Lieutenant William Churchill, supported by Captain Lewis Morris's 3rd Infantry, held the road; and the 4th Infantry, under Major George Allen, was Twiggs's easternmost unit. Taylor held in reserve Captain Charles May's dragoon squadron. Brevet Lieutenant Colonel William Belknap's left wing deployed, from west to east, the "Foot" Artillery Battalion of Lieutenant Colonel Thomas Childs, Captain James Duncan's battery, and the 8th Infantry led by Captain William Montgomery. Captain Croghan Ker's dragoon squadron had the dual responsibility of guarding the train parked near the pond and supporting the American left wing.

Once positioned, American troops had about an hour to stare at Mexican bayonets and lance heads glinting in the sunlight and enemy pennons and flags rippling in the gulf breeze. Brightly uniformed Mexican troops formed a line stretching over one mile long, double the length of the American line. General Arista could be seen riding his horse along the line, exhorting his soldiers to throw back the invader. The soldiers responded with tossed banners and shouts of "*¡Viva la República!*" which mingled with martial strains from the regimental bands. Almost half a century later Cadmus Wilcox could still remember that "in response to this sight, the [American] regimental colors were then stripped of their coverings, and amidst deafening cheers unfurled in defiance, and thrown to the breeze."[30]

Taylor apparently conceived his order of battle without any intelligence regarding the placement of the Mexican artillery. He belatedly sent Captain Charles May and his dragoon squad to reconnoiter the Mexican line and, if possible, to draw artillery fire. But the Mexican artillery were hidden by the tall grass and ranks of infantry, so this attempt by the dragoons failed. At that point, two volunteers stepped forward to make another effort: Lloyd Tilghman and Jacob Blake. Tilghman, a West Pointer who had left the Regular Army less than a year after graduation to become an engineer, had joined Taylor's army as a volunteer civilian aide-de-camp to General Twiggs. He assisted Lieutenant Jacob Blake of the Topographical Engineers. They galloped forward across the prairie and down the entire length of the Mexican line within its musket range. No effort was made by the Mexicans to drive off this unwanted inspection. At one point the two men dismounted, noted in detail the position of one of the Mexican batteries, remounted, and returned to report. According to Taylor's postbattle report, their reconnaissance "resulted in the discovery of at least two batteries of artillery in the intervals of their cavalry and infantry."[31]

The resaca anchored Arista's left flank, which straddled the Matamoros road at a point where the road skirted the mesquite forest. Located somewhere within this forest was General Antonio Canales, a lawyer of rather questionable character from the Rio Grande town of Camargo, with some four hundred mounted *rancheros*. For some unknown reason, Canales's force never fought during the coming battle. General Torrejón's cavalry brigade held the road. His men were arranged with the *presidiales* on the extreme left, followed, as one moved to the right, by the 8th Cavalry, 7th Cavalry, and the Light Cavalry. To the right of the Mexican cavalry stretched a long line of infantry interspersed with artillery batteries.

General Pedro de Ampudia's column arrived just before the fighting broke out. His 4th Infantry, commanded by General José Uraga, took its place on the left. To its right was General Romulo Díaz de la Vega's brigade, which consisted of the 10th and 6th Infantries centered by two eight-pounders; then the 1st Infantry, with five four-pounders stationed on its right flank. Completing the infantry line were the Tampico Coastal Guards, the 2nd Light Infantry, and a battalion of *zapadores,* or sapper-engineers, on whose extreme right stood a lone four-pounder. The remaining light cavalry, under Colonel Cayetano Montero, waited between the infantry and two low rises, or *motitas,* that also anchored the Mexican right flank, and around whose bases ran the road to Tanques de Ramireño. A protective screen of sharpshooters, or *cazadores*, was thinly spaced in front of the Mexican line (fig. 2.7). Interestingly, in his journal, Jean Louis Berlandier stated that Arista's army also included an unknown number of nomadic Indians. The Mexican baggage train, hospital, and camp followers were located several hundred yards to the rear of the Mexican center.[32]

The number of Mexican troops at Palo Alto is uncertain. One contemporary Mexican account set the number at 3,000; this source also said both armies were roughly of the same size. Arista later testified at a Board of Inquiry that he had 3,461 enlisted men and 365 officers on his battle line. Unclear, however, is if this number also included those troops not actually on the battle line: for example, Canales's irregulars. In contrast, contemporary American sources consistently estimated the Mexican troop count at more than double or even triple that of Taylor's army of 2,228 men.[33]

Arista arranged his men as a trap for an infantry attack either across the plain or down the road, the latter being exactly what Taylor planned to do. In either case, Mexican cavalry could envelop the attackers. The weakness of the formation was the length of the double Mexican line: it absorbed all available men, with no reserves to contain a breakthrough or counterattack. Also, because Mexican artillery was difficult to shift on the battlefield, Arista could not significantly rearrange his formation once it was set.

Taylor ordered his infantry to advance in columns. Around 2:30 P.M. Mexican artillery opened the contest, the first full-scale battle of the U.S.-Mexican War. A solid shot arched over the advancing Americans and into an artillery caisson behind them, instantly killing its driver. Seeing this hit, the Mexican soldiers shouted, *"¡Viva México!"* The American force halted while Ringgold's and Duncan's two batteries of six- and twelve-pounders quickly wheeled forward to respond. At the same time, the 8th Infantry moved slightly back and to the left, then formed a square to secure the left flank. The other infantry units all moved from column to line formation.

The two batteries moved forward about a hundred yards in front of the American line and within seven hundred yards of the Mexican left flank. They opened fire with rapid, accurate, and destructive precision. At the same time the oxen-drawn eighteen-pounders, which were confined to firm ground because of their ponderous weight, slowly swung into position on the road and under the personal supervision of General Taylor. The Americans concentrated their fire on Torrejón's cavalry on the Mexican left flank.

The Mexican 4th Infantry Regiment arrived just as the battle started and began taking its place to the left of the 10th Regiment, which was already in line formation. To the Americans one-half mile away, the sudden arrival of this column suggested the massing of troops for a bayonet attack. In response, all of the American batteries poured fire onto the hapless 4th Infantry Regiment. American cannoneers watched as a single shot appeared

fig. 2.7. Overleaf: a cazador in action at Palo Alto. The rifleman in the foreground is from the Mexican Sixth Line Regiment, as indicated by the number six on the infantry bugle insignia. This was worn both on his barracks cap band and on his cartridge-box cover flap. Following illustrations by A. Nieto, A. S. Brown, and J. Hefter El soldado mexicano: organizacion, vestuario, equipo. The Mexican Soldier: Organization, Dress, Equipment, Mexico City, 1958, the rifleman's uniform is distinguished by white lapels, a matching white band on his barracks cap, and white turnbacks on his tailcoat and is faced with a colored plastron having plain brass buttons. White spatterdashes protect his shoes from the rain and mud. Black leather cross belts are centered by a brass plate. Attached to the plate is a chain that secures a wire vent-pricker and pan brush, tools used to service his rifle. His canteen is an American-made tin model, and he is armed with a British-made Baker rifle. The Baker buckle with a snake design is attached to his waist belt. At the rifleman's feet are fragments of paper cartridges and a waist belt with the brass buckle of the Mexican Fourth Line Regiment. Burning cordgrass in the background, the result of wadding from U.S. cannon fire, partly obscures a detachment of Mexican lancers on the horizon. Another cazador, wearing a leather shako, is nearby. Illustration by Gary Zaboly

---

to take out a whole platoon and as large gaps opened in the Mexican lines. With *vivas* the gaps would quickly close, only to be reopened by another round of fire (fig. 2.8). According to several accounts, many American rounds also fell to the rear and landed in and around the Mexican field hospital, "which was obliged to change position."[34]

At some point during the first hour or so of the artillery exchange, Taylor realized that a costly bayonet charge was not needed. The general's experience with artillery was nearly nonexistent, but anyone could see that the American rounds were quickly decimating the Mexican forces. In contrast, the effectiveness of Mexican shot was usually lost as it rolled and tumbled through the tall grass toward the American battle line. One observer, then-Brevet Lieutenant Ulysses S. Grant (fig. 2.9), noted that for most of the battle American infantry "stood at order arms as spectators, watching the effect of our shots upon the enemy, and watching his shots so as to step out of their way." In some American units, notably the Artillery Battalion and the 8th Infantry, officers had their men sit on the ground to avoid the bouncing balls. For the most part, the Mexican artillerymen focused their fire on the American batteries because they were closer and were the sole cause of their mounting casualties.[35]

Of all the American units, it was Samuel Ringgold's "flying artillery" that proved most effective. His batteries darted about the field, loading, firing, and redeploying before counterbattery fire could catch up with them. With their rapid fire, the gunners demonstrated their ability to pick specific targets instead of simply taking blank aim at masses of men. For example, a

fig. 2.8. Overleaf: Mexican Fourth Line Regiment, under artillery attack. The illustration depicts Mexican infantrymen in "arms at high" position, after de Orga, Prontuario en que se han reunido las oblicaciones del soldado, cabo y sargento. A private's uniform in this regiment is believed to have consisted of dark-blue pants and a waistcoat fronted by a red plastron with plain brass buttons. The white leather cross belts are centered by a brass plate showing the cutout number four. Attached to the plate by a chain are the musket vent-pricker and powder pan brush. Infantrymen carry either a keg-shaped, one-quart canteen as described by A. Nieto, A. S. Brown, and J. Hefter El soldado mexicano: organizacion, vestuario, equipo. The Mexican Soldier: Organization, Dress, Equipment, Mexico City, 1958, or a round wooden canteen obtained through U.S. imports before the war. The privates are armed with British India Pattern Brown Bess muskets. The wounded man on the ground is a first sergeant, as noted by the fringed epaulets on his shoulders. His damaged sword is an infantryman's briquet. In the lower left foreground is a fragment of a saddlecloth or shabraque, with a brass number one signifying the First Line Regiment. Illustration by Gary Zaboly

---

Mexican regimental band began to play the martial tune *Los Zapadores de Jalisco*, "The Engineers of Jalisco," to rally the troops. An American gunner carefully aimed his fieldpiece and destroyed the entire band with one explosive shell. One of the most telling accounts of the flying artillery at Palo Alto was by C. M. Reeves of the 4th Infantry.

> The gunners went into it more like butchers than military men; each man stripped off his coat, rolled up his sleeves, and tied his suspenders around his waist; they all wore red flannel shirts, and, therefore, were in uniform. To see them limbering and unlimbering, firing a few shots, then dashing through the smoke, and then to fire again with lightning-like rapidity, partly hid from view by dense clouds of dust and smoke, with their dark-red shirts and naked arms, yelling at every shot they made, reminded me of a band of demons rather than of men.[36]

Mexican counterbattery fire was so ineffective that Taylor ordered Lieutenant William H. Churchill to move his lumbering eighteen-pounders, each pulled by a team of eight oxen, farther down the road to be closer to the Mexican lines. The huge bovines made excellent targets, yet most survived the battle unscathed. A few, however, "were converted into beef by the shot of the enemy during the action."[37]

The decimation of his army forced Arista to abandon his plan for a double envelopment of the American flanks with infantry and cavalry. One historian speculated that the tactic might have worked early in the battle when the Mexican soldiers were eager to fight and the American batteries would not have done much more harm at closer range. Apparently, Arista

---

fig. 2.9. A ca. 1845 daguerreotype of Brevet Lieutenants Ulysses S. Grant (left) and Alexander Hays, taken at Camp Salubrity, Louisiana. Courtesy U.S. Military Academy at West Point

believed it impractical for his men to wallow forward through the tall grass under such withering fire. Something had to be done, however, since his troops grew impatient. After about an hour of this punishment Arista ordered Torrejón, with some one thousand lancers (fig. 2.10) and two four-pounders, to turn the American right flank (map 4). Reluctantly, Torrejón obeyed. With trumpets sounding, his men advanced through the grass, across a resaca, and into the chaparral. The lancers' horses soon bogged down in another, deeper resaca that suddenly appeared in the low brush. Torrejón's slow progress through the morass was observed and reported to Taylor, who took a moment from writing a message to laconically reply, "Keep a bright lookout for them." Colonel David Twiggs, in charge of the threatened right flank, sent his right flank regiment, the 5th Infantry, about five hundred yards to its right and front and into the chaparral, where it formed a square. The walls of bristling bayonets presented by this type of formation ensured that the American right flank would not be rolled up by Mexican cavalry.[38]

Meanwhile, Torrejón's cavalry regrouped on firmer ground and then charged the U.S. 5th en masse. The Mexicans in front included the unseasoned *presidiales,* many of whom discharged their short-barreled *escopetas* at too great a range. The west face of the 5th's square held their fire until the lancers approached within fifty yards and then delivered a volley. After two such charges and a loss of at least ten men, the Mexicans retreated approximately three hundred yards. American casualties in this attack were limited to a few wounded.

At about this time, the U.S. 3rd moved into a defensive square to the right and south of the wagon train. Torrejón sent word to Arista that the terrain and dense vegetation made a charge impractical. Arista ordered

fig. 2.10. A Mexican lancer at Palo Alto (from Frost, History of the Mexican War). Courtesy Special Collections Division, University of Texas at Arlington Libraries, Arlington, Texas

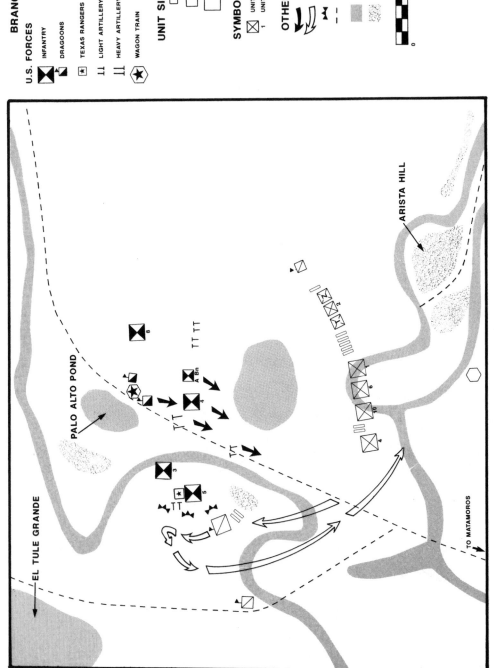

map 4. *Battle lines, approximately 2–4* P.M. *Courtesy National Park Service*

BRANCH SYMBOLS

U.S. FORCES
INFANTRY
DRAGOONS
TEXAS RANGERS
LIGHT ARTILLERY
HEAVY ARTILLERY
WAGON TRAIN

MEXICAN FORCES
INFANTRY
CAVALRY
TAMPICO CORPS
ZAPADORES (SAPPERS)
LIGHT ARTILLERY
WAGON TRAIN

UNIT SIZE SYMBOLS
COMPANY
BATTALION
REGIMENT

SYMBOL DEFINITION
UNIT SIZE AND BRANCH
UNIT NUMBER

OTHER SYMBOLS
U.S. TROOP MOVEMENTS
MEXICAN TROOP MOVEMENTS
TROOPS UNDER ATTACK
WAGON ROAD
STANDING WATER/MARSH
HIGH GROUND

0   3000 FT

EL TULE GRANDE

PALO ALTO POND

ARISTA HILL

TO MATAMOROS

Torrejón to try again. This time Torrejón's men maneuvered farther north, then turned east, both to avoid the murderous fire from the 5th and to get at the wagon train. Instead, the Mexicans received a devastating volley from another face of the 5th's square. Furthermore, the presence of the 3rd Infantry dissuaded Torrejón from pressing the attack further. The Mexicans retreated after suffering considerable losses.

About this time Torrejón's two four-pounders finally crossed the swampy resaca and, under the protection of retreating lancers, prepared to fire on the U.S. 5th, located four hundred yards away. But a section of Ringgold's battery, under the command of Lieutenants Randolph Ridgley and Samuel French, arrived "at full speed" to defend the threatened infantry square. Walker's Rangers, assigned to protect the 5th, leveled their rifles at the approaching enemy cavalry and delivered their fire with "their usual coolness and deadly aim." At the same time American cannon opened fire with canister and spherical case shot "so promptly and with such effect that the enemy's artillery were completely routed and retreated . . . under the protection of their cavalry without discharging a gun." The Mexicans lost dozens of men with the remainder driven back to their lines.[39]

It was now around 4:00 P.M. The wind blowing in from the gulf increased, and a smoldering cannon wad discharged by Duncan's battery ignited the tall cordgrass (fig. 2.11). Smoke and flames quickly spread and obscured both armies, causing the cannon fire to slacken. Some Mexican wounded, lying in no man's land, tragically burned to death. George A. McCall described the event in a letter home.

> Soon the red flames began to dance and pitch into the air high above our heads. Directly the wildfire beyond the control of man darted forward—cleft through the light blue clouds that had sprung from the cannon's mouth & overspread the plain, hissing and crashing like a mighty Damon [sic] of the prairies, roused from his slumbers by the voice of battle. Onward he rushed between the contending hosts, belching volumes of murky smoke into their very faces & lifting his red army on high, as if he reveled in the midst of human carnage.[40]

Taylor rode along the line during the lull, casually chatting with officers and waiting for the contest to begin anew. American soldiers collected their dead and wounded, repaired cannon carriages and caissons, and replenished their ammunition. The intense heat of the day was only worsened by the flames on the prairie, so the men were allowed to fall out to get water. Taylor also issued orders for a realignment. He had the eighteen-pounders moved down the road to a spot close to the original position of the Mexican left flank. The U.S. 4th was to the left of these cannon. The 5th moved forward and anchored the extreme right flank to prevent a repetition of Torrejón's earlier flanking attempt. The effect was to pivot the entire American line counterclockwise.[41]

*fig. 2.11. Captain
Duncan's battery during
the final phase of the battle
of Palo Alto. Courtesy
Special Collections
Division, University
of Texas at Arlington
Libraries, Arlington,
Texas*

Arista also realigned his forces, pivoting them counterclockwise, so that his right flank advanced about four hundred yards. His 4th Infantry and lancers fell back to the south and east. Apparently this mutual counterclockwise movement gradually continued through the remainder of the afternoon. Major T. Staniford, 5th Infantry, noted in his report that, at some time during the latter half of the battle, "we were ordered to take position on the right of the new line, which had been formed by throwing forward our right—the enemy having changed his front nearly perpendicular to his first line."[42] The Mexican realignment left the wagon road open for an American advance of the eighteen-pounder battery. As before the lull, several shallow pools of water lay between the two forces. These pools discouraged a frontal assault by either side. Any effective infantry and cavalry attacks had to be conducted on the flanks. The spatial distance between the battle lines remained nearly unchanged from what it was before the prairie fire.

The smoke had lifted sufficiently by around 5:00 P.M. for the artillery duel to resume (map 5). Arista's batteries directed their fire toward Churchill's eighteen-pounders that had wreaked so much havoc in the Mexican line. In response, the big American guns blasted gaps in the Mexican ranks. General Taylor now seized the initiative and ordered May's squadron, supported by the 4th Infantry and Ringgold's battery, to turn the Mexican left. May's

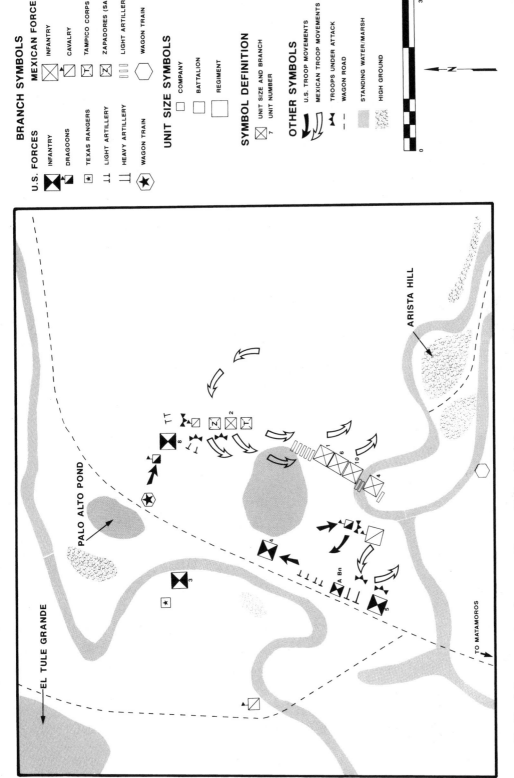

BRANCH SYMBOLS

U.S. FORCES

INFANTRY

DRAGOONS

TEXAS RANGERS

LIGHT ARTILLERY

HEAVY ARTILLERY

WAGON TRAIN

MEXICAN FORCES

INFANTRY

CAVALRY

TAMPICO CORPS

ZAPADORES (SAPPERS)

LIGHT ARTILLERY

WAGON TRAIN

UNIT SIZE SYMBOLS

COMPANY

BATTALION

REGIMENT

SYMBOL DEFINITION

UNIT SIZE AND BRANCH

7 UNIT NUMBER

OTHER SYMBOLS

U.S. TROOP MOVEMENTS

MEXICAN TROOP MOVEMENTS

TROOPS UNDER ATTACK

WAGON ROAD

STANDING WATER/MARSH

HIGH GROUND

0   3000 FT

N

EL TULE GRANDE

PALO ALTO POND

ARISTA HILL

TO MATAMOROS

map 5. Final battle lines, approximately 5–7 P.M. Courtesy National Park Service

fig. 2.12. U.S. Artillery Battalion in square formation, under attack by Mexican lancers. Battalion wagons, band, color guard, officers, and casualties are positioned inside the square. Surgeons, assisted by the bandsmen, are tending the wounded. The eighteen-pounder battery is in the foreground on the wagon road, with both cannon firing canister at the oncoming lancers. Several mounted dragoons are protecting the cannon crews, the latter supplied from caissons (lower left) pulled by oxen. Dead and wounded oxen have been dragged off the road. Illustration by Gary Zaboly, courtesy the Aztec Club of 1847

men advanced against intense cannonading and small-arms fire only to meet Torrejón's massed cavalry. May shied away from pressing his attack with his sixty-eight dragoons and fell back after two men were wounded and four horses lost. The fight was not totally one-sided. During this phase of the battle, the U.S. 4th, positioned next to the eighteen-pounders, received "a most galling fire" from the Mexican batteries and suffered a number of casualties. Second Lieutenant Ulysses S. Grant watched in horror as just a few feet in front of him a solid shot took off an enlisted man's head and then

On the Prairie of Palo Alto

tore away Captain John Page's lower jaw. The 4th was forced to pull back with May's dragoons and rejoined the right wing.[43]

Childs's Artillery Battalion then moved up to take the place of the 4th, between the eighteen-pounders and the 5th Infantry. The infantrymen found some protection from the Mexican round shot and canister after their commanders ordered them to sit down in the tall grass. While Arista's cannon kept the American right pinned down, his cavalry attempted another flanking maneuver. Torrejón again organized his cavalry for a massive charge against the Americans crouching in the grass. But Churchill's eighteen-pounders quickly broke up the massed cavalry with canister. Repulsed but not destroyed, the Mexican horsemen then turned on Childs's battalion, now standing in square formation (fig. 2.12). The battalion fired a single, close-range volley that drove Torrejón's men back to the main Mexican battle-line position.[44]

Because of the effectiveness of Ringgold's and Churchill's guns, the Mexican artillery concentrated on them. So effective was their counter battery fire that it drove Ringgold's unit back. During the withdrawal, Major Ringgold was hit by a Mexican four-pounder shot, which tore the flesh from the front of one thigh, passed through his horse, then ripped through his other thigh (fig. 2.13). Although carried from the field alive, he died two days later, aware that his "flying batteries" had carried the day. The Mexican artillery continued firing for well over an hour until they exhausted their ammunition.

Captain Duncan's battery on the American left poured a continuous fire into the inactive troops on the Mexican right. A Mexican account of the fighting stated that "the troops . . . tired of being slaughtered for no use, demanded with a shout to be led on to the enemy with the bayonet, for they wished to fight hand to hand, and to die like brave men." Arista granted them their wish. He ordered Montero's light cavalry, supported by the 2nd Light Infantry, *zapadores*, and the Tampico Coastal Guards, to turn Taylor's left flank.[45]

Duncan's view of this development was partially obscured by the lingering smoke of the grassfire. His men were hitching up their cannon to go to Ringgold's assistance on the American right when Duncan spotted the Mexican cavalry leaving the chaparral. He realized that, if left unchecked, the enemy could reach the wagon train. He positioned one section of his battery directly in front of the Mexican column (fig. 2.14), with the other placed where it could fire canister at point-blank range into the Mexican flank. In his report written four days after the battle, Duncan recalled the action.

A strong body of the enemy's infantry, supported by two squadrons of cavalry,
debouched, from the extreme right point of the chaparral, and moved steadily

fig. 2.13. The wounding of Major Ringgold. Courtesy Special Collections Division, University of Texas at Arlington Libraries, Arlington, Texas

forward to the attack:—one section of the battery opened upon them, with round shot, shells, and spherical case. So well directed, that the whole advance, horse and foot, fell back in disorder to the bushes. The other section played in the meantime upon the masses of cavalry, that had halted at the sight of the guns. . . . Although these shots were well delivered, and each one made an opening through an entire squadron, this part of the enemy's line stood unshaken.[46]

The artillerymen were soon joined by Captain Croghan Ker's squadron and the 8th Infantry, but it was the fire from the "flying battery" that halted the Mexican attack. The Mexican soldiers tried to return the fire but were frustrated by the setting sun shining directly in their eyes. When the Mexicans finally fell back, Duncan again moved to the attack and advanced his batteries to within three hundred yards of the Mexican right flank. From there he opened an enfilade fire that rolled back the Mexican line. General Luis Noriega's cavalry increased the panic among the Mexican infantry by riding through them. Arista and some of his officers halted the flight, but to prevent a rout he ordered a second attack by the broken infantry units supported by Colonel Cayetano Montero's Light Cavalry Regiment. The Mexican troops were too disheartened to push home the attack and were easily turned aside by a sweep of Duncan's cannon fire along the lengths of their columns. They fled across the front of the Mexican line, taking all the troops with them as far as the 6th Infantry.[47]

On the Prairie of Palo Alto

fig. 2.14. A Company C "flying artillery" fieldpiece in action. This scene portrays the moment when one section of Captain Duncan's battery fired directly into the front of the final Mexican flanking attack. The gunners are servicing a model 1841 six-pounder gun, which is about to be loaded with a canister round. Objects on the lower right are a Mexican four-pounder copper cannonball, a smashed U.S. canteen, and an American forage cap. A four-pounder copper cannonball, a U.S. canteen spout, and an American spur buckle were found near where Duncan's battery was likely stationed toward the end of the battle. Illustration by Gary Zaboly, courtesy the Aztec Club of 1847

It was now around 7:00 P.M. Because his artillery had expended its available ammunition, Arista ordered his army to withdraw onto the mesquite-covered ground behind his right wing to bivouac for the night. With the chaos in the Mexican lines, this was the time for the American infantry to charge with the bayonet and turn the retreat into a rout. But darkness was fast approaching, and exposing the train of wagons to the possibility of capture or a cavalry raid was unwise. So as the Mexicans fell back, Taylor's forces bivouacked. "The surgeon's saw was going the livelong night" as searching parties brought in the wounded. Ulysses S. Grant wrote home that "we then encamped on our own ground, and the enemy on theirs. We supposed that the loss of the enemy had not been much greater than our own, and expected of course that the fight would be renewed in the morning." From their camp the Americans could see torchlights as Mexican soldiers searched the battlefield for fallen comrades. The Mexicans were unable to bury many of their dead because they lacked pickaxes and shovels. Their wounded were brought to the field hospital for rudimentary care, but the surgeon to whom the medicine chests had been entrusted disappeared with them during the battle. The luckier ones were piled into wagons and sent back to Matamoros. Mexican morale had been dealt a devastating blow.[48]

American casualties at the battle of Palo Alto included five killed, forty-three wounded, and two missing. An additional two officers and eight enlisted men later died of their wounds. Mexican losses were substantially higher. Arista admitted to 252 killed, while Lieutenant George Gordon Meade, after interviewing captured Mexican officers, placed the number closer to 400. In his official account of the battle, Arista stated that his army lost only 102 men.[49]

Sometimes word of battle travels slow. While the two armies battled at Palo Alto, the defenders of Fort Polk listened to the sound of guns echoing across the coastal plain without a clue as to which side was winning. It appeared to them that the American army, "if not retreating, was not advancing," and many wanted to abandon the works and march to Taylor's aid. As dark fell, still no word arrived from the field until about midnight, when a camp follower arrived at the fort and told Major Munroe that Taylor had suffered a devastating defeat. Several of the naval officers wanted to send out a force and requested permission from Commodore David Connor aboard his ship. Connor refused the request since his men were poorly trained in the use of shoulder arms and could be easily cut up by Mexican cavalry. Soon, however, word filtered back that the Americans held the field.[50]

The battle at Palo Alto did not proceed as Taylor had anticipated since he had abandoned his initial plan of a bayonet charge. According to military historian K. Jack Bauer, Taylor's apparent flexibility probably reflected his inexperience as much as anything. Palo Alto was his first large engagement and the first time he had seen the "flying artillery" in action. Their performance could not have failed to impress him. Also, the battle was the only time Taylor saw cavalry perform in combat. Their flexibility and speed, theorizes Bauer, "clearly worried a general whose force was hobbled by a large and vulnerable wagon train." This threat to the train and his flanks is the probable explanation for Taylor's decision not to attack.[51] In a tactical sense, Taylor's men had won the battle since they held the field at little cost to themselves while inflicting heavy casualties on the Mexicans. But strategically the battle was a draw. Neither side had accomplished its objective: Taylor had not reopened the road to Fort Texas, and Arista had not destroyed the American force.

Palo Alto: The Human Cost of Battle

Too often military historians in recounting battles have focused on the day of the fighting and perhaps its strategic and political consequences without considering the long-term human costs involved. Those wounded on nineteenth-century battlegrounds often suffered for months and even years since this was an age when medical science could offer them little relief. We know all too little of the consequences for the many Mexican soldiers maimed by the hail of metal from the American artillery.

A glimpse of their predicament is offered by American surgeon Madison Mills, who visited some of the wounded in Matamoros. He was horrified that many of the amputations had been badly performed; in such cases, as the wound healed the bone would protrude from it in a most ghastly manner. Mills attributed this to the lack of training of the Mexican surgeons. Perhaps a better explanation is that many of these procedures were performed in battlefield conditions on the night of May 8, after the long bombardment at Palo Alto. A single case illustrates the horror of the aftermath of Palo Alto, that of Captain John Page of the 4th U.S. Infantry. Ulysses S. Grant was standing next to Page when a cannonball tore away the latter officer's jaw. Page's wounds must have caused horrible suffering but were not immediately fatal. Taken back to Point Isabel, Page lingered in the hospital while authorities notified his new bride of her husband's condition. She caught a ship from New Orleans but on arriving at Point Isabel found that her husband had already been sent back to New Orleans. They were finally united there, and she nursed him on a long journey up the Mississippi on a steamboat. Page eventually died on the ship, off Cairo, Illinois, on July 12.[52]

It was Ringgold's batteries, of course, that played the crucial role at Palo Alto. As fate would have it, Ringgold was one of the few Americans who lost their lives during the battle. Navy surgeon J. M. Foltz tended the dying Ringgold after the battle. Foltz described the scene:

> The numerous friends of Major Ringgold will doubtless be anxious to know the particulars attending his melancholy end. . . . The engagement of the 8th was entirely in the hands of the artillery, and Major R took a most active and important part. . . . About 6 o'clock he was struck by a six pound shot. He was mounted, and the shot struck him at right angles, hitting him in the right thigh, passing through the holsters and upper part of the shoulders of his horse, and then striking the left thigh. . . . On the evening of the 9th he reached this camp. . . . He was immediately placed in comfortable quarters, and his wounds dressed. An immense mass of muscles and integuments were carried away from both thighs—the arteries were not divided, neither were the bones broken. I remained with him all night. He had but little pain, and at intervals had some sleep. On dressing his wounds in the morning, they presented a most

unfavorable aspect. . . . During the night he gave many incidents of the battle and spoke with much pride of the execution of his shot. He directed his shot not only to groups and masses of the enemy, but to particular men in their line; he saw them fall, their places occupied by others, who were in turn shot down. . . . He continued to grow worse until one o'clock last night, when he expired. He survived his wounds 60 hours.[53]

Postbattle History

MAY 9, 1846, TO MAY 8, 1893

Arista's army withdrew the morning after the battle. Taylor's army followed the retreating Mexican force several hours later but only after defensive measures were taken for the American wagon train. Lieutenant Jeremiah Scarritt, Taylor's staff engineer, reported, "On the morning of the 9th [General Taylor] directed me to secure the train in the best manner possible. . . . By 12 o'clock, I had the train so that it could resist any attack of cavalry—come in what direction it might and it would have required very steady cavalry to have marched upon it." The earthworks were posi-

fig. 2.15. Lieutenant Scarritt's sketch of his earthen fortification that protected the U.S. wagon train after the battle. Note the placement of two eighteen-pounders and two twelve-pounders behind earthen redoubts and abutting Palo Alto Pond. Wagons are depicted as rectangles. Courtesy National Archives

On the Prairie of Palo Alto

tioned in the immediate vicinity of the pond where, the day before, American troops, horses, and livestock pulling the wagon train had found water. Two eighteen-pounder cannon, two twelve-pounder howitzers, and a detachment of artillerymen were left with the teamsters to defend the wagon train (fig. 2.15).[54]

With his wagon train now secured, General Taylor began his cautious advance following the Mexican army. The American soldiers marched through the battlefield and the area where the Mexican soldiers had decamped just a few hours before. The grisly remains of the battle left a strong impression on Captain William S. Henry:

> I took advantage of a halt [of the army] to go over the field of battle. It was truly a shocking sight: our artillery had literally "mowed them down;" there were heaps of dead lying hither and yon, with the most ghastly wounds I ever saw; some had died with a smile on their countenance, others, in the agony of death, with a fierce convulsive struggle had caught at the rank grass, and died with their hands clinched firmly in it, looking defiant at the enemy. It was a shocking picture.[55]

During this temporary halt Major Belknap placed several of his men on burial detail, interring eleven badly mangled Mexican bodies.[56] An official battlefield inspection report, as well as the musings of several of the idle curious, noted the effectiveness of canister and spherical case shot on massed troops. For example:

> I visited the place . . . where the two 18 pounders were for a time directed, convincing evidence of the skill with which our Artillery was used were still perceptible upon that part of the field, for although [the Mexicans] were permitted to bury their dead, and afterward returned in numbers and spent considerable time in that employment, I counted some thirty bodies stretched out as they fell in that immediate vicinity.[57]

Army surgeon Madison Mills wrote:

> During this halt, which was fully four hours, I took occasion to go over the whole field of battle and saw sights that made my heart sick. . . . Groups of men on horseback, others on foot (camp followers) were riding or running over the field in all directions, looking at the enemy's dead and wounded and picking up trophies of the ever memorable battle of Palo Alto. . . . They left dead on the field at least 200 and from appearances must have buried a large number. I saw two large graves newly covered with brush and dirt; in the immediate vicinity of which I found instruments and dressings which told me that some of my own species [surgeons] had been there. What havoc and what horrid wounds our artillery made. I saw heads and limbs severed from their bodies and trunks strewed about in awful confusion. Many a body I saw that

had been cut in twain by our 18 pdrs and such ghastly spectacles I hope never to behold again. I picked up a lance and a few other trophies from the field which I hope to retain and take home with me. . . . The 1st Brigade buried a number of the enemy's dead but there were about 150 left on the field unburied.[58]

The American dead were temporarily buried on the battlefield. The locations of their graves, like the Mexicans', are presently unknown. One postbattle casualty was soon added to the relatively small number of American graves. Lieutenant Jacob Blake, a topographical engineer, was accidently killed after the battle when he unbuckled his holsters and dropped them on the ground; one of the pistols discharged, killing him almost instantly. That night, after the battle of Resaca de la Palma, his body was taken to the Palo Alto battlefield and buried by torchlight. Major Ringgold's remains were later removed for reburial at his home in Maryland. Torrential rains flooded the battlefield a few days later, and this situation continued for weeks owing to unusually severe seasonal rains. The more shallowly buried bodies reportedly floated away; others were exposed to the vultures and wolves. Thereafter, the battlefield became an object of curiosity for off-duty soldiers who were stationed in the area. Collecting souvenirs of the battle was probably their major pastime. Several companies of volunteers joined them later that summer.[59] No doubt there were civilians who, while traveling through Palo Alto, stopped to look for mementos as well.

Seven months after the battle, a Tennessee volunteer wrote: "Nothing was to be seen on the ground, save the graves, many of which had been disturbed by the wolves and the scattered skeletons of very many who had not found a burial. Those laid as they fell: here in rows, from the sweeping effects of the artillery; there singly, from musketry or bayonet."[60]

Except for its occasional use as a pasture for Fort Brown's livestock, the battlefield entered a phase of civilian exploitation. On July 14, 1847, the Army of Occupation newspaper, the *American Flag* (published in Matamoros), carried this advertisement:

Palo Alto House. This house is now open for the reception of guests on the battleground of Palo Alto. Comfortable conveyance furnished from the opposite side of the river, at a reasonable price. Preparation is being made for horse-racing to come off on Sunday next and we advise those who wish to see "lots of fun", not to fail going.[61]

The "house" or inn was just off the Point Isabel–Matamoros wagon road. Its probable location has been identified by archaeologist Jake Ivey of the National Park Service, who noted structural traces and an associated trash dump dating to circa 1845–55. These traces may be the inn or one of several houses built within a few years after the battle. An inspection of this site during the summer of 1992 resulted in locating one copper and one iron canister shot. The battlefield is over one-half mile to the south, so it is possible these artifacts were dropped by guests of the inn and were not a direct result of battlefield combat. Since its discovery in January, 1992, relic collectors have removed artifacts from the inn location.[62]

The battlefield was becoming a local tourist attraction. Officers stationed at nearby Fort Brown—formerly Fort Texas—sometimes gave informal tours of Palo Alto to visitors. Major attractions included the location of the Mexican mass graves and the battle lines (the latter still visible where the cordgrass was trampled down) along with the occasional scatters of horse and human bone. American troops were stationed at Palo Alto shortly after the conclusion of the U.S.-Mexican War, and no doubt they added to the postbattle impact on the battlefield.

A reminder that Palo Alto was still very much on the frontier occurred in May, 1849, when a band of Comanches attacked a wagon train as it passed in front of the Palo Alto Inn. The following year ten robbers broke into a house at Palo Alto, killed the resident, and took everything portable. In 1853, the Point Isabel–Matamoros Road was relocated farther to the west. Shortly thereafter, the little community of Palo Alto was abandoned. During the 1992 survey, archaeologists recovered postbattle artifacts dating to the turn of the century, found in relative abundance on or near the presumed route of the abandoned wagon trail. These findings support historical accounts that local ranchers still used the trail, although abandoned as the main route between Point Isabel and Matamoros.[63]

The battlefield, although now almost literally off the beaten track, was not forgotten. In 1853 President Antonio López de Santa Anna issued a decree calling for commemoration of all Mexican soldiers who had fallen in the war against the United States, including those who had perished at Palo Alto and Resaca de la Palma. In addition, Santa Anna requested that the Mexican war dead who lay in the United States be exhumed and returned to Mexico for a dignified reburial. United States officials presumably took no action since there is no documentation of any attempts by private parties to locate and remove Mexican remains.

For the next several decades the battlefield remained essentially as it had appeared in 1846, an expanse of cordgrass bisected by a wagon road, bounded by mesquite thickets and resacas and used as a pasture. In 1893, local resident Felipe Martínez, a self-described former scout in Arista's army, gave a battlefield tour. Martínez remembered the resaca levee as a "ridge" where Taylor halted his army and allowed his men to fill their canteens from the nearby pond. Presumably, the wagon road ran along the top of the levee. An 1893 newspaper article noted that "this ridge is now known as *fortincitos*, meaning little forts. After the battle the army returned to this ridge and erected these forts, three in number." On May 8, 1893, a private group of citizens from Brownsville dedicated a monument on the Palo Alto battlefield. The monument, consisting of a marble tablet "like a quartermaster's tombstone," was placed approximately one hundred yards south of the barely discernible wagon fortification at the pond. In recent times, a Brownsville, Texas, historian placed one of the three fortifications at the pond and facing northwest. The other two, he believed, were to the east and alongside the wagon road.[64]

If correct, such placement suggests that the two easternmost fortifications paralleled the wagon road, thereby providing some protection for those wagons that had arrived during the battle. Land-leveling activities in and around the now dry pond apparently obliterated any vestiges of this defensive position that might have existed after 1893. An inspection of the pond area during the 1992 field season also revealed the presence of numerous small, shallow depressions. Presumably these depressions resulted from relic hunters' searches for Scarritt's position.

POST-1893 TO THE PRESENT

During the early 1900s, the army used Palo Alto and the surrounding unoccupied lands as a firing range. Untold numbers of 75-mm artillery rounds exploded over the battlefield, scattering lead ball shrapnel in the process. In later years, these lead balls caused some confusion with the battlefield archaeological record. In 1914 General James Parker, commander of the Brownsville Military District, initiated interest in the placement of monuments at historic sites in the Brownsville area, including the Palo Alto battlefield. In a memo to the adjutant's office, General Parker described the Palo Alto battlefield thus: "On an old partly unused route, [the battlefield's] position is unknown to the inhabitants of that vicinity, except a few old persons. . . . [The battlefield] is an open plain covered in places with salt marsh grass. . . . The terrain is flat with a few clumps of mesquite trees which mark the position of some of the old roads." General Parker also noted in this memo that the 1893 monument was damaged and its inscription partially obliterated "so that even the name of the battle is partly gone."[65]

Shortly thereafter, General Parker directed the installation of an upright eighteen-pounder cannon barrel of Civil War vintage a few hundred feet south of the 1893 monument. In 1917, a Board of Officers of the 1st Provisional Infantry Division convened in Brownsville to determine battlefield locations in the area. The board toured the Palo Alto battlefield under the guidance of Judge Frank C. Pierce, a historian of the Lower Rio Grande Valley. Pierce's knowledge of the battle was based in part on his interviews of a battle participant named Wabeski or Werbiski, who claimed he had been an enlisted man in May's dragoons. Neither name spelling, however, appears on the muster rolls of any of the units that fought at Palo Alto.[66]

The board incorporated Pierce's information with what they learned from written accounts to reconstruct the approximate positions of the United States and Mexican battle lines. The board of officers determined that the 1893 monument was correctly placed where the American army initially deployed; that is, immediately south of the old wagon road and the pond. The U.S. army's next position, at the initiation of cannon fire by the Mexicans, was approximately six hundred to eight hundred yards farther to the south and east. The American army's final right-flank position was estimated to be about thirteen hundred yards farther to the southeast, making a partial left wheel. The board recommended that General Parker's monument be moved to a place marking the main action of the battle, or the American army's right flank, approximately where the 5th Infantry and Ringgold's battery repulsed the Mexican cavalry attack. The board's recommendation, however, was never enacted.

In 1938, the Palo Alto battlefield was recorded in the National Survey of Historic Sites and Buildings. The site at the time encompassed about fifty acres, located east of the junction of Farm Roads 1847 and 511. These roads were the western and southern boundaries of the battlefield, respectively. In 1960, the battlefield was designated as a national historic landmark by the National Park Service under the authority of the 1935 Historic Sites Act. It was around this time that General Parker's cannon barrel monument was moved to its present location, the northeast corner of the intersection of Farm Roads 1847 and 511. A state of Texas granite marker dated 1936 can be found there.[67]

Although recognized as a historic landmark since 1893, the battlefield has undergone various localized land alterations since the early twentieth century. In addition to the exploding 75-mm rounds, it has endured excavations for ponds and a major drainage ditch, damming of a resaca, removal of mesquite thickets, strip plowing for the planting of experimental grazing grasses, placement of a buried natural gas pipeline, land leveling within and around Palo Alto Pond, and deep plowing for crops. Relic collecting has also had an immeasurable effect on the battlefield since the day after the battle. There is an apocryphal account of the owner of a portion of the battlefield who, during the 1930s, removed "hundreds" of cannonballs from his plowed field and dumped them into a resaca. Another battlefield landowner reported two cannonball concentrations in one of his plowed fields, but relic collectors took them all during the 1960s. In at least one instance, a collector resorted to using a backhoe to locate the fabled payroll chest that General Arista somehow managed to misplace on the battlefield. The use of increasingly sophisticated metal detectors by collectors has also resulted in a significant loss of artifacts normally protected by vegetation cover and soil deposition.[68]

In 1974, Texas A&M University Anthropological Laboratory personnel, under the direction of Harry J. Shafer, conducted preliminary field studies along several proposed routes for the Brownsville-Matamoros railroad relocation project. The resultant report noted that two of the routes would cross the battlefield site, necessitating compliance with the provisions of section 106 of the 1966 Historic Preservation Act. Shafer's survey did not locate any battle-related artifacts. His report recommended that a proton magnetometer survey be performed to locate and recover metal artifacts and detect subsurface soil anomalies such as burials and earthworks.[69]

In 1976 the Brownsville Navigation District contracted with the Texas A&M Anthropological Laboratory to conduct intensive investigations on the Palo Alto battlefield. The contract included a documentary research program and a reconnaissance survey of the presumed battlefield area. The subsequent report noted a number of discrepancies in the historic reports and maps of the battle, concluding that "a major portion of the battle occurred just north and northwest of Loma Alta," an extensive low hill situated approximately one-half mile to the southeast of the actual battlefield. Much of this conclusion was based on the assumption that the lead balls found in the supposed battlefield area were deposited by combatants at the battle of Palo Alto. It was later determined that these balls were really the above-mentioned lead ball shrapnel derived from 75-mm artillery rounds. Also, none of the other artifacts collected during the 1976 survey could be definitely attributed to the 1846 battle.[70]

Following the authorization of the Palo Alto Battlefield National Historical Site (NHS) by Congress in 1978, the National Park Service (NPS) initiated a research project seeking to delineate the parameters of the battle. Reevaluation of the battlefield location problem was prompted largely because of information supplied in 1979 by A. A. Champion of Brownsville, a longtime student and investigator of the battle. Champion strongly recommended that any further research should concentrate on the area commemorated as the battle site in 1893 and 1914 instead of the Loma Alta area. For over fifty years Champion visited the site and, by using an aerial photo with information obtained from written eyewitness accounts of the battle, had identified historically significant topographic features. Champion's recommendation was independently supported by two previously unknown sources that surfaced at this time: two maps drawn by battle eyewitness Jean Louis Berlandier, which provided views of the locations of the opposing forces as well as some of the area's topographic features; and Lieutenant Scarritt's written descriptions, including a sketch of the wagon fortifications.

In March, 1979, a team of archaeologists from Texas A&M, under the direction of Clell L. Bond, conducted a reconnaissance-level survey of the Loma Alta area and the region identified by Champion as the actual battlefield location. A few battle-related artifacts were found, but nothing definitive was determined. The NPS decided that Bond should conduct an intensive archaeological survey, making use of a proton magnetometer, metal detectors, aerial photography analysis, and limited test excavation. Accordingly, Texas A&M developed a research design accepted by the NPS. Fieldwork followed during June and July, 1979. This survey failed to produce large quantities of statistically testable information because the archaeologists recovered only twenty artifacts that were directly attributable to the battle. These artifacts were too few to address the specifics of the survey research design. The survey, however, did meet the overall project purpose: to determine the extent and complexity of the battlefield.

Bond concluded that the use of a proton magnetometer was inappropriate because of the numerous and recent man-made soil anomalies and the relatively small magnetic variation caused by isolated artifacts. Bond also determined that metal detectors, although potentially capable of locating quantities of artifacts, would be greatly hindered by the existing vegetation. The report recommended the following: conduct further documentary research, including examination of the Mexican archives; document Mexican arms and accoutrements, especially Mexican cannon ordnance possibly used in the battle; interview and analyze information from individuals who collected artifacts from the battlefield; further delineate the location of the Mexican and American battle lines by conducting a more thorough field investigation; and require future surveyors of the battlefield to use metal detectors along a series of north-south transects, incorporating those areas where significant numbers of artifacts have been found. Bond discovered at Palo Alto that the cordgrass, growing in dense clumps often three feet across and four feet in height, usually obscured the ground surface. Even when mowed with a tractor-driven rotary mower, the remaining stiff stubble prevented the search coil of a metal detector from touching the ground surface, thus precluding a reliable subsurface survey. Bond recommended a 100 percent removal of the sample area vegetation in future site investigation.[71]

No further professional archaeological investigations of Palo Alto occurred during the next thirteen years. However, in 1991, the NPS contracted with Walter Plitt III, chairman of the Palo Alto Battlefield National Park Committee, to provide provenience information for those artifacts recently located on the battlefield by collectors. The resulting document yielded important artifact patterning data, which were incorporated in part into this report. In addition, the National Park Service continued funding the historical research of this battle and assisted the efforts of local interested parties who helped make this park a reality.[72] All of the above actions ultimately led to the Palo Alto Battlefield National Historic Site Act of 1991 and the preparation of a general management plan. This plan included funding for an additional, more intensive archaeological survey of the Palo Alto battlefield. The survey occurred during July and August of 1992, with a follow-up survey done in March and April, 1993.

Weapons, Accoutrements, and the Soldier

The U.S.-Mexican War was fought just before the widespread impact of the industrial revolution on Euro-American armaments manufacture, along with its concomitant effects on tactical and strategic thought. A new generation of military theorists was on a threshold of change, advocating alternatives to the orthodox methods of waging war from the Napoleonic era. Yet, given all this technological and theoretical ferment, most of the weaponry, equipage, and tactics displayed at Palo Alto would not have been out of place on a battlefield from the late eighteenth century. Infantrymen were still armed with the smoothbore musket and bayonet, which perpetuated the use of classic line-and-column tactics, the saber-and-lance cavalry charge, and smoothbore artillery as both an offensive and defensive arm.

But the series of firearms inventions that would influence radical changes in such tactics had already begun in 1814 with the invention of the percussion cap. In 1832, a British officer invented the cylindroconoidal bullet: when fired, its hollow base expanded to engage the rifling of the barrel, giving the bullet a horizontal spin unobtainable with the smoothbore musket. In 1843, the French captain Claude Etienne Minié perfected this principle and invented the "Minié ball." The Minié ball could be dropped down the muzzle of a rifle almost as easily as if it were round. Previously too slow to load, the rifle now became a practical weapon on the battlefield with its additional range, velocity, and accuracy.

Bureaucratic and political resistance to major innovations hindered the transition to rifled percussion muskets in both Europe and North America. The armed forces of various European powers, as well as the United States, all experienced this lag during the mid-nineteenth century. In 1851 the British adopted the rifled musket after much delay, followed by the Enfield rifle in 1854. The Tige rifle was approved for general use by the French army in 1857. The Prussian army began to introduce its breechloading "needle gun" in 1840, but only by 1865 was its entire infantry armed with it. The United States began its conversion to the rifled musket during the 1840s but rejected both the repeating rifle and the breechloader for use by infantry in the Regular Army because of mechanical problems. Even then, there were still those champions of the smoothbore musket who believed only skirmishers should be armed with rifles.[1]

The United States possessed the world's most advanced shoulder arms when it went to war in 1846. What British admirers termed "the American system of manufacture" was developed between 1820 and 1850 by the United States' Springfield arsenal and private gun makers of the Connecticut River Valley. The basis of this system was automatic and semiautomatic milling machines that produced interchangeable parts, permitting assembly of firearms without the delicate filing and parts adjustments required by hand manufacture. This technology made it possible to produce large orders of high-quality firearms in a short period of time, and it was a valuable asset for a country on the brink of war. Although Great Britain was the most technologically advanced nation in the world, its firearms industry lagged behind that of the United States.

In contrast, Mexico during the 1840s was an impoverished, politically unstable, preindustrial country almost totally dependent on other nations for the tools of war. Before its independence, Mexico had an arsenal that produced firearms comparable in quality to any manufactured in preindustrial Europe. Mexico's war for independence, however, left the arsenal machinery in a state of disrepair, and its trained personnel dispersed. Santa Anna's military forces entered the 1846–48 war equipped with an assortment of firearms, many of which dated to the eighteenth century. In addition, Mexico had acquired from various European nations a large number of obsolete flintlocks discarded in favor of technologically superior percussion firearms. Great Britain, in particular, had arsenals full of surplus equipment from the Napoleonic wars. This situation, combined with its crippling war debt, spurred the British to sell off many thousands of flintlocks to less technologically advanced nations like Mexico.

For differing reasons, then, both the United States and Mexico armed their infantry predominantly with flintlock muskets. The flintlock ignition system operated on the principle that sparks result when a sharp piece of flint strikes steel. On a flintlock musket, the jaws of the cock gripped the flint, the latter partly padded with a leather or lead patch to secure the grip. With the pull of the trigger the flint, which was held firmly in place by a lock, struck a hardened steel frizzen. The frizzen then pivoted forward, allowing the sparks to fall into a small pan of gunpowder. When the powder burned, it transmitted a spark through a small hole in the gun barrel and into the main powder charge, which then exploded. The discharged projectile was a large lead ball that killed, or tore a gaping, ghastly wound, if it hit an enemy.

On the Prairie of Palo Alto

Loading and firing a flintlock musket was slow. Holding the weapon horizontally, the soldier pulled the cock back to half-cock position and tipped the frizzen forward to expose the pan. He then drew out a cartridge from his cartridge box. The paper cartridge contained a measured amount of gunpowder and a round lead ball that was slightly smaller than the inside diameter of the barrel and usually weighing about one ounce. The cartridge often contained an additional two or three smaller lead balls, or buckshot; this would be a "buck-and-ball" cartridge. The shooter then tore the end of the cartridge open with his teeth, poured a small amount of powder into the pan, and closed the frizzen over it. The remainder of the powder was then poured down the barrel, followed by the lead balls and finally the cartridge paper used as wadding, all of which was then seated firmly onto the powder with the ramrod. The flintlock could then be cocked for firing. The entire process required as many as seventeen motions, but a trained soldier armed with a flintlock musket could get off two to three rounds a minute if he did not become rattled in the din of battle.

A percussion musket was simpler to load. The soldier poured all of the cartridge powder into the barrel and rammed home the lead balls. Then he pulled the cock, or hammer, to half-cock position. He placed a small copper or brass cup-shaped percussion cap on the cone, or nipple, and loading was complete. To fire, one simply cocked the hammer and pulled the trigger. The hammer fell onto the nipple, exploding a small charge of fulminate of mercury in the percussion cap, which sent a spark through the nipple and into the main charge.

The advantages of rifles had long been familiar to European gunsmiths, who discovered as early as the end of the fifteenth century that a rifled barrel, by imparting spin to the bullet, could assure a smooth flight through the air. But rifles cost more to make and were slow to fire, since it was necessary to force the cloth-wrapped lead ball down the barrel with a mallet in order for the round to fit tightly against the rifling. This took time and care, commodities not normally available during battle. Both Mexico and the United States used rifle units for skirmishing and to cover the flank of a larger unit, but for the most part rifle fire was viewed as a support to musketry. Rifles were expected to draw the enemy's fire, whereas muskets and bayonets decided the issue.[2]

Mexican Firearms

INDIA PATTERN MUSKET

During the early 1830s the Army of the Republic of Mexico began a program of replacing its worn-out, colonial-era firearms. Mexico was unable to manufacture its own arms because of the dilapidated condition of its national arms factory, and the money needed for repairing the factory's machinery

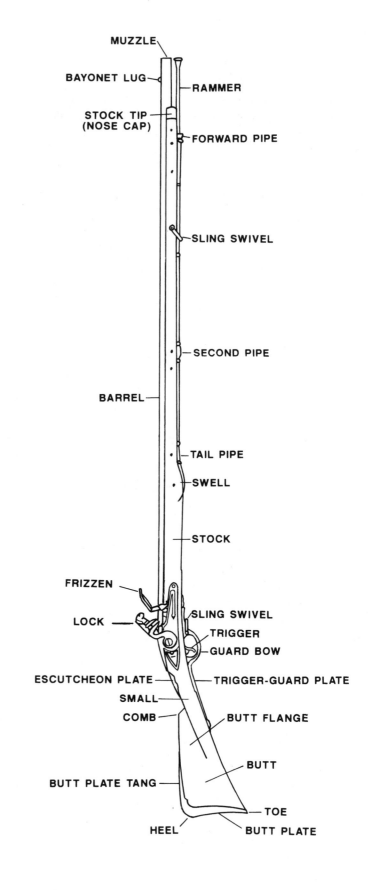

MUZZLE

BAYONET LUG

RAMMER

STOCK TIP
(NOSE CAP)

FORWARD PIPE

SLING SWIVEL

SECOND PIPE

BARREL

TAIL PIPE

SWELL

STOCK

FRIZZEN

SLING SWIVEL

LOCK

TRIGGER

GUARD BOW

ESCUTCHEON PLATE

TRIGGER-GUARD PLATE

SMALL

COMB

BUTT FLANGE

BUTT

BUTT PLATE TANG

TOE

HEEL

BUTT PLATE

INCHES

0

6

12

fig. 3.1. British India Pattern Brown Bess musket. Courtesy National Park Service was nonexistent. Fortunately for Mexico, Great Britain possessed a vast surplus of armaments from the Napoleonic wars. In addition to captured French weapons, Britain had some 440,000 India Pattern "Brown Bess" muskets in its arsenals (fig. 3.1). Mexico probably purchased quantities of these, as well as other surplus weapons through private arms dealers or the East India Company. By December, 1838, Mexico had amassed a total of 18,542 *fusiles ingleses* or English muskets: 2,428 were categorized as new, 12,270 were used, and the remaining 3,844 were defective.[3]

The India Pattern musket was a relatively inexpensive firearm that had been manufactured for the British East India Company, hence the name India Pattern. In 1793 an ill-prepared Great Britain found itself once again at war with France, having only 110,000 muskets for 250,000 men. As a stopgap measure, the East India Company was required to sell all of its muskets to the Board of Ordnance; yet this was still not enough to meet the growing needs of the armed forces. In order to speed up firearms production, in 1797 the board required gunsmiths to stop making the superior Short Land Pattern muskets and, in their place, supply exclusively the India Pattern. The latter musket model was inferior in design to the earlier model Short Land musket. Its metal fittings were simplified or eliminated and the barrel shortened from forty-two to thirty-nine inches, walnut for the stock was inferior grade, and inspectors were less exacting in quality control. The India Pattern weighed nine pounds eleven ounces, the bayonet adding another 1.5 feet and an additional pound.

Yet, even with all its deficiencies, the 1793–94 introduction of the India Pattern musket to British regiments relieved a serious arms shortage. This long-arm model remained the standard weapon of the British infantry throughout the Napoleonic wars, modified only by the introduction of a reinforced cock in 1809. Between 1804 and 1815, some 1,603,711 India Pattern muskets were manufactured. In spite of its substandard workmanship, this musket was an effective weapon up to one hundred yards. Tests conducted on this model in 1841 indicated that it could hit a target twice as high and twice as broad as a man three out of four times at one hundred fifty yards; at any greater range, not one hit was registered. One must keep in mind that, in the context of Napoleonic warfare, it was sufficient that a musket could register a hit anywhere upon a large mass of troops. Indeed, the very inaccuracy of muskets demanded tactics involving the maneuver of compact blocks of troops.

By the 1830s the India Pattern musket had become obsolete; the British Army had replaced it with the New Land Service percussion musket. During this same period, Great Britain unloaded onto the international arms market great quantities of its outdated weaponry. Mexico was just one of many impoverished countries that purchased India Pattern muskets, most of which had been condemned as unserviceable before they were sold.[4]

The Mexican government bought many thousands of bargain-priced India Pattern muskets in order to arm the majority of its regular infantry. In addition, it purchased hundreds of the more expensive Baker rifles for the elite sharpshooter troops. Like the Indian Pattern musket, the flintlock Baker rifle was by this time obsolete, being replaced in the British armed forces by the percussion Brunswick rifle. The British probably chose to sell to Mexico its oldest, least serviceable versions of the Baker rifle during the early 1830s because, until 1839, it was still an official British small arm.

The Baker, first issued to the British Army in 1800, was actually a rifled and more decorative version of a musket. Its initial .75-caliber musket bore was later reduced to a .625-caliber bore; this was the version purchased by Mexico. Its thirty-inch barrel was especially suited for skirmish duties and was equipped with a wide-bladed sword-bayonet for use in close combat. The trigger mechanism was made of brass instead of steel, as was the British musket. Also distinguishing the Baker rifle was a brass trigger guard that curved down away from the stock to form a type of pistol grip more accurate for shooting. Rifle fittings included a brass-lidded patch box in the butt, and later patterns incorporated cleaning tools in the butt box as well. The Baker rifle weighed 9.5 pounds, minus the 2-pound bayonet.

As with all rifles of this period, loose powder and ball were normally used with the Baker. The powder, carried in a flask or horn, was measured and poured into the muzzle. The .615-caliber ball, encased in a patch of cloth or leather, was hammered down using a mallet in conjunction with a ramrod. As the loading process required some time, the trained rifleman was capable of only about one shot per minute. Unlike the musket, the Baker rifle could be loaded and fired in the prone position, enabling marksmen to take advantage of small cover. For situations requiring more rapid fire, the Baker sharpshooter used prepared cartridges intended for the Baker cavalry carbine rifle. The effect of this ability to hit a specific target at long range enabled the riflemen-skirmishers to single out enemy noncommissioned and commissioned officers, thus causing disorder in the ranks of their opponents. Without a patch for the ball, however, there was not a tight enough fit for accurate firing; the Baker rifle then became nothing but a short-barreled, highly inaccurate musket.[5]

Although slower to load than a musket, the Baker rifle was far more accurate. A British marksman armed with the Baker was expected to hit an enemy's cross belts up to two hundred yards and his head and shoulders thereafter. The Mexican army provided the Baker rifle for their elite companies of *cazadores*, or light infantry, and *grenaderos*, or grenadiers, of the line battalions. They also purchased Paget rifled carbines for their cavalry troops. However, because of limited training, the Mexicans could not fully exploit what relatively few rifles they had. By December, 1838, the Mexican army possessed a total of 357 rifles in varying degrees of disrepair, none of which came equipped with a bayonet.[6]

The Paget flintlock carbine was the primary weapon of the British cavalry until at least 1815, the end of the Napoleonic wars. The Paget was still used by the British until the 1830s, when it was replaced by percussion carbines. Distinctive features of the Paget were the short barrel length, the swivel ramrod, and the bolted lock. Some of its brass furniture, such as its upper ramrod pipe, was exactly the same as that on the India Pattern musket. A Paget carbine nosecap was found within the Mexican battle line at Palo Alto, suggesting that this firearm model was one of the Mexican purchases from the British.

ESCOPETA

The *escopeta*, called a "scuppet" by American soldiers, was a sort of blunderbuss used by Mexican cavalrymen who presumably were not issued the Baker carbine. This weapon used the antique-style miquelet lock characteristic of seventeenth- and early eighteenth-century Spanish small arms. Unlike the firing mechanism of later flintlocks, the miquelet lock had a robust hammer able to hold irregularly shaped lumps of flint. Ideal for use by irregular light cavalry, almost anything could be rolled down the flaring-mouthed short barrel. The *escopeta* often had the Catalan-style stock, an archaically shaped butt with a square cut end and a "hook" on the underside. *Escopetas* saw long and hard service on the Mexican frontiers and were often subjected to crude repair work, which correspondingly lessened their overall effectiveness.[7]

PISTOLS, UNITED STATES AND MEXICAN

Until the appearance of reliable repeating pistols during the mid-nineteenth century, the military handgun played a relatively minor role on the battlefield. Single-shot pistols of the period simply had neither the rifle's accuracy nor the musket's close-range shock value. Pistols were viewed as another indication of an officer's rank, and they were also useful when fighting in close quarters or when the long-arms were empty. Since one bullet was often not enough to be effective, single-shot military pistols were usually supplied in pairs. Mexico purchased quantities of British flintlock pistols, presumably obsolete and condemned surplus from the Napoleonic wars. During those wars, Britain manufactured a wide variety of pistols in pistol- and carbine-bore. Barrel lengths varied from the twelve-inch Heavy Dragoon pistol to the nine-inch Light Dragoon. There was also an East India Company variety. The common Land Pattern pistol had a swivel ramrod; another pattern was the nine-inch-barreled, carbine-bore pistol with a swivel ramrod. As in all national armies of the time, the Mexican army issued pistols only to their cavalrymen and officers. Those who could afford it purchased their own brace of pistols, ranging from deluxe percussion versions of regulation patterns to ornate duelers. In December, 1838, the Mexican Armed Land Forces listed a total of 389 pistols: 48 were new and 104 used, with an additional 237 considered unserviceable.[8]

The American Army issued pistols chiefly to mounted men, who carried each pair in holsters slung across the saddle pommel. The regulation American military pistol of the period was a .54-caliber smoothbore with either a 8.5- or 6-inch barrel. Both model 1836 flintlock and model 1842 percussion pistols were in service during the 1840s. However, Ordnance Bureau shipping records indicate that pistol flints were *not* provided to Taylor's command between August, 1845, and July, 1846. This strongly supports our belief that virtually all of the American pistols at Palo Alto were the percussion model. Regardless of model and quality, the general inaccuracy of single-shot pistols made them inferior to shoulder weapons, at least when dealing with a target at long range. A veteran British officer of the Napoleonic wars once remarked, "Pistols . . . are only a superfluous addition of weight and incumbrance [*sic*]. . . . We never saw a pistol made use of except to shoot a glandered horse." Another officer noted the range of a pistol was so limited that its discharge was pointless "until you feel your antagonist's ribs with the muzzle," at which range it was easier to use a sword. Not until the development of reliable repeating handguns did this attitude toward pistols begin to change.[9]

United States Shoulder Weapons

Conversion of existing American military flintlocks to percussion design began in 1842. By 1845 both the Springfield and Harpers Ferry Arsenals were manufacturing percussion muskets. Toward the end of 1846, these two factories had produced over 17,000 percussion muskets; by the end of the U.S.-Mexican War, all the national arsenals together had constructed over 78,000 more. Ordnance Bureau records indicate that over 100,000 percussion caps, in addition to 220,000 musket flints and 30,000 rifle flints, were shipped to Taylor's army between August, 1845, and April, 1846. Yet Ulysses S. Grant stated in his *Memoirs* that, during the U.S.-Mexican War, the regular infantrymen were all armed with flintlock muskets. Regardless of the recognized superiority and availability of percussion weapons, relatively few American troops were armed with them during the entire war. The reason for this policy was that officials of the Ordnance Department did not want the soldiers to fight a war with unfamiliar weapons. These officials believed there was little time to train troops with the new muskets before their deployment to Mexico, especially since virtually none of the drill manuals then in print addressed percussion arms. Also, the executives were concerned that

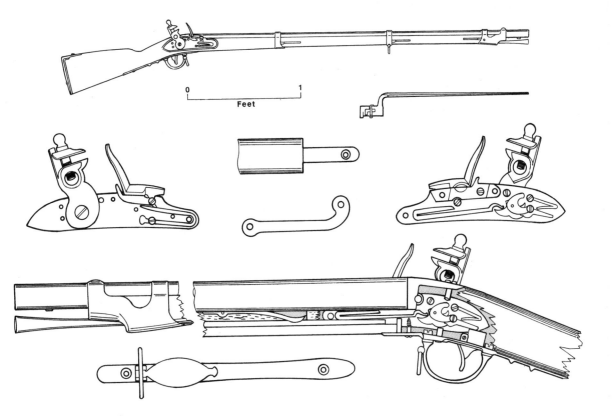

an adequate supply of percussion caps could not be maintained. A soldier who lost his flint could use a local source to replace it, but a soldier without percussion caps had a useless weapon.[10]

It is likely, therefore, that the American infantry at Palo Alto was armed with both models 1816 and 1835 flintlock muskets (fig. 3.2). The percussion caps were probably for pistols, Hall models 1833/1836/1843 carbines, and perhaps some refurbished 1819 Hall rifles. Possibly the model 1841 percussion rifle, the so-called Mississippi rifle, was present as a nonregulation firearm used by the Texas Rangers. It is doubtful, however, that any of the regulars were armed with model 1842 percussion cap muskets for the reasons given above.

fig. 3.2. U.S. model 1835 flintlock musket (adapted from Hicks, Notes on United States Ordnance, *vol. 1: Small Arms, 1776–1946). Courtesy National Park Service*

MODELS 1816 AND 1835 MUSKETS

The model 1816 flintlock musket was manufactured for the American military until the late 1830s. This weapon possessed the qualities of both sturdiness and excellent design, representing an achievement in producing machine-made interchangeable gun parts meeting exacting specifications. Model 1835 was the last flintlock musket built for the American military, incorporating improvements standardized in the model 1822 musket. Production of model 1835 began in 1839 and ended in 1845, even while the American arsenals were converting from flintlock to percussion design. Because of the planned phase-out of the flintlock ignition system, only about thirty thousand model 1835s were available just before the war. This was not enough to meet the needs of the armed forces on a wartime footing and a limited budget. Thus, possibly both the 1816 and 1835 models were used in the first battle of the U.S.-Mexican War. The reason was that a new musket model was introduced to peacetime units only after regimental supplies of their serviceable older model became unfit or were exhausted. Even individual companies, scattered as they were along the frontier, might have different musket models. Nonetheless, all American military muskets of the period had the same .69-caliber bore. This permitted a commonality of ammunition, if not of musket parts, among infantry units.[11]

Paradoxically, although the musket was the principal infantry weapon, it was not subjected to intensive scientific experimentation in this country until the 1840s. In his tests at the Washington Arsenal in 1843 and 1844, Captain Alfred Mordecai found that "for the musket, the variation now allowed in the diameter of the bore is . . . unnecessarily great. But for these arms, a much more important change is that of reducing the windage, by increasing the diameter of the ball. . . . I propose that balls for small arms shall be made by compression, instead of being cast."[12]

An American civil engineer, known only as Bosworth, conducted some independent experiments. A strong supporter of rifled arms, Bosworth had some harsh words for the smoothbore musket in his treatise of 1846. He noted: "In point of model, structure, and proportion . . . the musket for accuracy of ball-practice may be considered the worst. It is out of proportion in point of size, the caliber being too great for the weight of the piece. . . . A ball projected with a full war-charge, can not be relied upon for any kind of accuracy; and the recoil is too severe for the strength of an ordinary soldier. . . . It is conceded on all hands, that the musket-barrel is too light for its caliber."[13]

The efforts of Mordecai, Bosworth, and other like-minded individuals soon resulted in changes. Between 1845 and 1846, the Washington Arsenal turned out a million and a half pressed musket balls and a million pressed rifle balls. To improve the cartridge as a whole, the Ordnance Department in 1844 procured a quarter of a million tinfoil cartridges, but they did not work well in service.[14] Regardless of cartridge type, the musket used with it was of uniformly high quality by the beginning of the U.S.-Mexican War. But a military musket or any other gun performs no better than the soldier shooting it. In touching on this subject, Bosworth noted that the musket "is now all it ever has been, and in some points much improved. . . . In the hands of one who has studied its properties, [it] will throw a ball with an accuracy that would surprise a large portion of those who are in the habit of using it. What we seriously want is more knowledge among the soldiery, both of guns and gunpowder."[15]

Other small-arms ordnance experts of the period echoed Bosworth's comment, but it was not until after the Civil War that the American Army required detailed small-arms training.

SHOTGUNS

Some American soldiers used the common shotgun. Captain Reginald Melton of the First Dragoons, who was on the Missouri River in the summer of 1842, carried with him a "large Colt's pistol" and "my old Damascus double-barreled shot-gun." In fact, the Ordnance Department issued a total of forty-three "double barrel guns" in 1839–40; however, these may have gone to Florida for use against the Seminoles instead of to the West. During the U.S.-Mexican War, it was not unusual for officers to carry their personal shotguns into battle since they were very effective weapons in close-quarter fighting.[16]

HALL RIFLE

Within Taylor's command, one battalion from the 4th Infantry was used as skirmisher-sharpshooters, its members armed with the model 1819 Hall flintlock rifle.[17] The Hall employed a rectangular breech block, bored from the front with a chamber to accept a .52-caliber round ball and powder charge. Hinged at the rear, the breech block pivoted upward by a finger lever beneath the gun, exposing the mouth of the chamber for loading with either loose powder and ball or paper cartridges. The breech block was then lowered by the finger lever. Between 1819 and 1833, Hall rifles were flintlocks; between 1833 and 1844, the last years of their production, they were percussion, despite much opposition by hidebound ordnance officers. Also, a great many of the flintlock Halls were converted before the U.S.-Mexican War. It is possible, therefore, that some if not all the Hall rifles used at Palo Alto were percussion. The Hall design was advanced for its day, but the technology to make it genuinely functional and reliable did not exist. By the 1840s, most Hall rifles in service had somewhat worn-out mechanisms, allowing considerable gas and flame to escape at the junction between the barrel and the breech block. Extensive firing increased this defect to the point where it not only greatly reduced the power and service life of the gun but also created hazards to the shooter. For these reasons, American troopers did not favor the Hall in spite of its great superiority over muzzleloaders.[18]

Hall also manufactured a breechloading carbine specifically designed for the mounted trooper. The barrel was much shorter, the weight reduced, and, on the first two models, the cleaning rod changed into a rod-type bayonet with a triangular cross section. The model 1833 Hall carbine also has the distinction of being the first U.S. firearm with percussion ignition. Hall's first carbine model was produced as a .69-caliber smoothbore. This probably resulted from the conviction that mounted troops generally fought at short

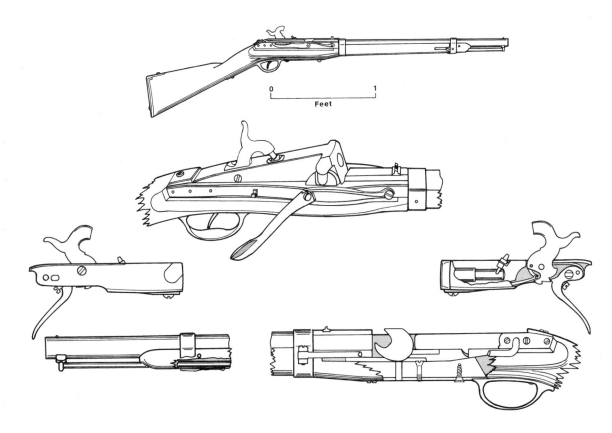

fig. 3.3. U.S. Hall-North
model 1843 percussion
carbine (adapted from
Hicks, Notes on United
States Ordnance, vol. 1:
Small Arms, 1776–1946).
Courtesy National Park
Service

range and that the larger-caliber smoothbore barrel could handle ball, buck-and-ball, and buckshot loads, thus favoring short-range power and flexibility over long-range accuracy. Later models 1836, 1838, 1840, and 1843 carbines (fig. 3.3) also included rifled .52-caliber barrels and .64-caliber smoothbore barrels. These later models used variations of the release mechanism that improved carbine use on horseback.[19]

All Hall percussion firearms had an unusual, advantageous feature that was probably not anticipated by ordnance officials who selected it for service. Since the chamber and all the lock parts were in the breech block, simply removing the breech block pivot screw and pulling out the block provided the trooper with an effective if somewhat clumsy pocket pistol, lethal at close range. A report of its use in Mexico is found in the picaresque autobiography of trooper Samuel Chamberlain of the First Dragoons. In relating some of his off-duty adventures in Monterrey in 1847, Chamberlain recalled, "When not on duty, I went into town day and night, armed with a Bowie Knife and the chamber of my Hall's Carbine, visited the fandangos, and gambling rooms, danced, gambled, drank wine and Muscal [sic], made love to the Senoritas, and with many a gold onza in my pocket staggered into camp at reveille." In one particular episode, Chamberlain had been carousing in a cantina with some of his companions, had fallen asleep in a

On the Prairie of Palo Alto

back room, and had somehow been left behind. When he awoke, he found that the place was now occupied by a party of Mexican guerrillas who were about to kill him. Chamberlain "thought my time had come, but resolved not to be rubb'd out without a struggle. With a bound I sprang behind a large table used as a bar, drew the chamber of my Hall's Carbine that I always carried in my pocket and stood cool and collected, at bay before those human tigers, guillers [sic]."[20]

WEAPONS OF THE TEXAS VOLUNTEERS

General Taylor's command included Walker's volunteer company of seventy-five Texas Rangers as mounted guides. Approximately twenty-five of them participated at Palo Alto. Firearms used by Texas volunteers during the war varied because it was a requirement that each man provide his own weapons. However, in 1840, the Texas government ordered 1,500 muskets of the U.S. model 1816 from Tryon of Philadelphia. This order proved too large for the Republic's treasury. Woefully short of funds, the Texans purchased only 860 of the Tryon smoothbores, each marked with the star of Texas. The American government eventually paid for the other 640. In 1843, Captain Philip Saint George Cooke and his dragoons overtook a large party of Texas freebooters on American soil, and among the arms Cooke confiscated were two Texas muskets. Besides their forty-seven rifles and two American dragoon carbines, the Texans were carrying various other types:

15 *English flintlock shot guns;*
3   *Tower [British musket] pieces;*
1   *Large American flintlock shot gun;*
2   *Double barrelled flintlock, stub and twist, shot guns;*
4   *Percussion lock, double barrelled, stub and twist, shot guns;*
1   *American musket;*
2   *Texas muskets [mentioned above].*[21]

The Texans did not use muskets strictly out of necessity. In describing the 1841 battle with the Mexicans at Mier, General Thomas Green of the Texas forces noted: "Some of the men [fell into] the water while crossing the river. One of the strongest objections to the rifle is the ease with which it is put out of order, and the difficulty of refixing it; if the powder should get wet, the difficulty of unbreeching is far greater than the drawing of a musket-load."[22]

The Texans' favorite weapons were Colt's Paterson Arms pistols and carbines, featuring the innovative revolving cylinder mechanism, and the model 1841 percussion rifle. The latter weapon was used primarily by the Mississippi Volunteers during the U.S.-Mexican War, hence its nickname the Mississippi rifle. In the hands of these volunteers, it proved to be a formidable weapon during the battle of Buena Vista. The model 1841 was manu-

---

factured during the 1840s by both the military and private contractors, but none is known to have been issued to Taylor's regular troops at any time during the war. It is debatable whether the Texas Republic purchased the model 1841 for its army.[23] It is possible, however, that some of the Texan volunteers at Palo Alto used this firearm as their personal weapon.

Other firearms used on the Texas frontier included the Jenks .64-caliber breechloading flintlock rifle and the Jenks .54-caliber flintlock carbine. In May, 1839, the Republic of Texas ordered 250 of the breechloading Jenks, but it is not known whether these were rifles or carbines. However, records indicate that the Jenks weapons saw service with Texan mounted troops and naval forces;[24] it is likely, therefore, that it was the musketoon and not the rifle that was purchased by Texas authorities. Texan volunteers during the U.S.-Mexican War also used a variety of shotguns in ten and twelve gauge, Kentucky flintlock rifles, and various captured Mexican firearms, possibly including the India Pattern musket. Taylor may have authorized issuance of the American army muskets, carbines, and pistols described above to inadequately armed Texans.

Colt's Paterson pistols were used experimentally during the Seminole War in the early 1840s, and veterans of that war were impressed with them. Consequently, in 1845, General Taylor urgently requested the purchase of 150 Colt pistols and carbines to equip some of his troops. At least a portion of this requisition reached the army depot at Point Isabel two weeks before the battle of Palo Alto. Revolvers were rare and valuable. Thus, thirty-two of these weapons, perhaps totaling the entire shipment, were issued to those most familiar with them—Walker's company. This action greatly irritated Taylor's regular officers, who apparently coveted revolvers as much for their prestige as for their firepower. Since 1839 the Texas Navy had been armed with Colt revolvers and, in 1844, the Texas Rangers had owned them as well. Several models were in Texas service by 1846, in both .31 and .40 calibers. Cylinders for pistols had five chambers; carbine cylinders had eight or ten. The depot officer at Point Isabel issued the thirty-two Colt pistols and carbines to Walker's company on April 20, 1846. Eight days later, Mexican guerrillas surprised thirteen of Walker's men in their encampment, killing or capturing most of the Texans. The guerrillas thereby obtained twelve Colt pistols, four Colt carbines, and three Hall rifles as well as boxes of percussion caps and cartridges.[25]

The Jenks breechloading firearms were far superior in design and performance to the Hall breechloaders issued to American troops. Nevertheless, just one hundred Jenks carbines and rifles were procured by the military in 1839 for limited trial use. Only the inferior Hall breechloader models were issued during the U.S.-Mexican War, despite strong recommendations to the contrary by army ballistics experts.[26]

Edged Weapons

BAYONETS

Combining the offensive firepower of the musket with the defensive qualities of the pike, bayonets were considered indispensable by both armies. Santa Anna, in his general orders for the Mexican attack on the Alamo in 1836, stated that "all armaments will be in good condition—especially the bayonets." A few months before Palo Alto, Mexican general Pedro de Ampudia referred to American soldiers in Texas as "those adventurers [who] cannot withstand the bayonet charge of our foot [soldiers]." On the day before the battle at Palo Alto, General Taylor reminded his infantry that "their main dependence must be in the bayonet." So important did both the United States and Mexico consider the bayonet that official ordnance returns of both countries divided serviceable muskets into two categories: "muskets complete" and "muskets without bayonets." To avoid the heavy casualties of a prolonged firefight, many tacticians advocated the immediate shock value of the bayonet charge. But charging an unshaken body of troops armed with muskets demands high discipline. As a result, commanders usually ordered bayonet charges against enemy units of apparent low morale. In such a situation, the sight of a yelling mass of men advancing with level bayonets would be sufficient to turn them to rout. Often it was the fear of the bayonet, not the bayonet itself, that decided the battles of this period. One American army surgeon noted that "bayonet and lance wounds were not common in Mexico. The brilliant charges of opposing columns in battle are almost always charges on paper."[27]

The India Pattern musket bayonet consisted of a triangular-sectioned blade fifteen inches long that was attached to a cylindrical socket and could be fixed to the mouth of the musket barrel. The bayonet was held in place by a right-angled slot passing over the foresight of the musket. Apparently, this was an insecure method since British soldiers used string and wire to prevent their India Pattern bayonets from being wrenched off by the enemy. The bayonet for the Baker rifle was designed so that it could also be used as a sword. The flat blade was twenty-three inches long, with one cutting edge. The brass hilt had a regular type of sword guard, shaped like a D, with a groove and catch in the side of the handle for attaching it to the rifle. The blade of the bayonet, positioned flat against the axis of the bore, had a tendency to catch the force of the explosion on the cross guard and on the flat of the blade, causing the rifle to whip to the right when fired. Only a few shots loosened the bayonet; after several firings, the bayonet was either badly bent or completely broken off. It had a relatively heavy weight of two pounds, which made the rifle difficult to hold steady.

The bayonets for U.S. models 1816 and 1835 muskets were triangular sectioned, with a fifteen-inch blade attached to a cylindrical socket. Unlike the India Pattern bayonet, however, the U.S. model 1835 had a clamping band that prevented slippage. Because of the American method of manufacturing interchangeable parts for firearms, one bayonet could fit any other musket of the same model. However, a bayonet made for one musket model could not fit onto the barrel of a different model. Considering the importance General Taylor placed on the bayonet, the interchangeable parts limitation may have encouraged greater uniformity among musket models within his command.[28]

LANCES

Mexican light cavalry units used the lance. Although there are no known accounts of American dragoons using this weapon during the U.S.-Mexican War, at least two squadrons of the Second Dragoons were trained as lancers while stationed at Fort Jesup, Louisiana, during the early 1840s. Mexican lances were nine feet long including point and socket. The point was shaped like a knife 8¼ inches long with three or four cutting edges separated by concave bayonetlike gutters. It also had a metal crosspiece at the lower end followed by a tube and two iron straps three feet long to screw on to the shaft as added reinforcement to protect against breakage from impact. The shaft was half an inch thick. Under the crosspiece of the blade hung a two-pointed pennant showing regimental colors; it functioned both as an ornament and to scare enemy horses by fluttering in front of their eyes. Mounted irregulars usually had lances of cruder design and quality. The lance was valued for its shock value, similar to that of a bayonet charge, and was especially useful for scouting and pursuit. A lancer, however, was defenseless once the lance point was deflected.[29]

SWORDS

Swords, like pistols, were intended primarily for use by officers and mounted troops of both armies. It is possible that regular troops in Mexican line regiments were also armed with infantry swords of French design, called *briquets*. Some swords were merely decorative or badges of office, but most were designed to be not only pleasing to the eye but functional as well. The pattern a Mexican officer might adopt was left more or less to his discretion. If he was following European custom, a Mexican infantry officer could have armed himself with either the straight-bladed sword or the curved-bladed saber. Special units, such as artillery, regimental bands, and sappers, were issued special sword patterns as an identifier. Noncommissioned officers also had distinctive sword patterns. All cavalrymen of the period traditionally used the saber, its curved blade being most appropriate for the mounted slashing-and-stabbing attack. It is likely that regulation-issue swords and sabers came mostly from British Army surplus stocks as well as from armories whose contents dated to the Spanish colonial period. Each enlisted man in the Mexican army usually carried his nonissue belt knife. Although a defensive weapon, it usually functioned as a tool for camp chores.[30]

American armed forces in 1840 adopted several new sword patterns, primarily copied from French and other European swords. The need for new styles of edged weapons was possibly inspired by the 1836–42 Florida Seminole War, although at the time there was an attempt to reequip U.S. soldiers in the European fashion. During the early 1840s, the American army adopted new swords for noncommissioned officers, musicians, and infantry as well as sabers for the dragoons. However, Taylor's command was partially equipped with previous models of edged weapons used in the Seminole War and earlier. The model 1833 dragoon saber was still issued during the U.S.-Mexican War. The heavier model 1840 dragoon saber, nicknamed "Old Wrist Breaker," was initially imported from Prussia; not until 1845 was it produced domestically in large quantities. The dragoon saber for enlisted men had a slightly curved, single-edge blade and a brass half-basket guard and pommel.[31]

The model 1832 foot artillery sword was a short, heavy weapon having a straight, nineteen-inch blade with grooves called fullers. The hilt was cast brass with a fish-scale pattern grip, and the pommel featured an American eagle and shield. Overall, the sword was reminiscent of the ancient Roman short sword. Infantry and artillery noncommissioned officers were issued swords with a straight, single-edge blade, a brass pommel, and leather-covered wooden grip. Since commissioned officers had to buy their own edged weapons, they were allowed some latitude and could choose from various styles and decorations. Infantry, artillery, and staff officers, however, usually carried straight-edged swords having a hilt with an ornate eagle motif.[32]

Cannon and Cannoneers

The United States and Mexico each had its own gun drill manual, which differed on certain details regarding numbers of gun-crew members and their duties. The general method of manning the gun, however, was fairly standard. It was strenuous work, requiring men with physical strength, dexterity, and intelligence. Crews of five to eight men per piece ran through their duties with continuous, quick teamwork. The senior gunner aligned the barrel using a tangent sight, gave the elevating screw a turn, motioned for the gun trail to be shifted right or left, and stood clear. A spongeman then swabbed out the barrel with a wet sponge, which was a rammer with a fleece nailed onto the head. While the sponging was in process a ventsman put his thumb, encased in a leather stall, over the vent to prevent ingress of air, which otherwise could cause smoldering material to blow back into the muzzle of the gun. Ammunition passers then brought up to the gun muzzle a fixed round, which was inserted into the muzzle by a loader using the rammer end of the sponge. The ventsman next positioned a pricker down the vent to puncture the flannel powder cartridge and filled the vent with either a length of quick-match or, more common by the early 1800s, a quill or paper tube of mealed powder. This established contact between the charge in the barrel and the spark that would ignite it.

After all the other crew members had moved clear of the gun, the firer then stepped forward to ignite the charge with a linstock or portfire, a length of burning slow-match in a holder. The more efficient friction primer was not officially adopted by American artillerymen until shortly before the end of the U.S.-Mexican War. Ignition of the gunpowder charge resulted in a loud explosion and billowing gunsmoke, which at the same time sent the projectile on its course and caused the gun to recoil sharply. The gun crew would have to shove it back again and realign the gun unless the enemy was at point-blank range.[33]

Rate of fire depended upon the time taken to re-lay the gun after recoil. A well-trained gun crew, such as Ringgold's horse artillery, could fire as many as four rounds per minute from a six-pounder gun under parade ground conditions. During battle, however, a slower rate of fire was maintained to compensate for the many uncontrollable and distressing factors on the battlefield. It was essential that the exact drill was carried out to avoid accidents, and the gunners were required to perform with a certain rhythm instead of extreme speed. Rate of fire was also affected by the dense, grayish-white clouds of smoke exuded by the powder charges. These clouds hung low, needed a brisk wind to disperse them, and usually obscured the front of any unit heavily engaged, which slowed the laying of the gun. Clouds of white smoke not only limited visibility but could also play tricks with the gunners' vision, sometimes making the target seem much closer and larger than it actually was. The gunners also would have been exhausted after several hours of pushing forward their heavy and unwieldy piece, rapidly sponging and ramming, and constantly hauling up ammunition. As a result, their efficiency would have suffered toward the end of a long battle.

Taking these considerations into account, a rate of fire of three rounds per minute for spherical case and shell, and two per minute for round shot and canister, could be expected. However, there is one report that Duncan's battery at Palo Alto fired eight rounds per minute during the last stages of the battle. If this is true, it would mean that his battery had eliminated some of the standard motions, such as sponging the bore between shots.[34] This was tempting fate because of the possibility of leaving smoldering remnants of cartridge bag and also because it allowed the piece to become dangerously hot. Of course, if enemy troops were about to overrun your battery, dispensing with the sponging to increase the rate of fire would be an understandable omission.

Smoothbore artillery did not allow indirect fire, which permits shooting from behind cover. Instead, gun positions had to be entirely in the open, in front of the lines of infantry, and in full view of the enemy if the weapons were to fire effectively. Although such artillery crews might have appeared quite vulnerable, they were in fact fearsome agents of destruction for a massed and charging enemy, cavalry as well as infantry. Natural cover reduced the effect of long-range artillery fire, so it often happened that reserve units not directly in combat were positioned behind screens of trees, low rises, and the like. At close range, however, both opposing forces had to be in sight of each other in order to inflict mutual damage.

Relatively static batteries of smoothbore cannon were more effective in defense than in attack, since charging infantry and cavalry always adopted compact formations that made them vulnerable to artillery fire. But the efficiency of such fire could only increase as the attackers came within closer range. Horse artillery, however, was ideally suited for taking the offensive since it did not wait for the enemy to come within effective range; instead, it brought such range to the enemy. Members of a horse artillery battery focused their whole energies on galloping to within a few hundred yards of the enemy's massed infantry, quickly unlimbering, and then letting loose with destructive blasts of canister and round shot. The unfortunate infantrymen on the receiving end simply did not have sufficient firepower to neutralize batteries.

Field battery ammunition used by both the United States and Mexico during this war consisted of four general types for all guns: round shot, canister, shell, and spherical case or shrapnel (fig. 3.4). Cannon ammunition is a significant category of artifact on the Palo Alto battlefield and warrants detailed discussion.

ROUND SHOT

Solid round shot was just what the name implies: a solid ball of cast metal. Most countries of the period usually made their round shot from iron, but Mexico used both iron and copper shot. Nineteenth-century tacticians considered round shot to be one of the most useful projectiles during the whole era of smoothbore ordnance; as such, it represented the largest proportion of ammunition found in artillery munitions chests. Round shot, and indeed all projectiles fired from smoothbore ordnance except mortars, were provided with a wooden bottom, or sabot. This was a circular plate of hardwood that fitted the bore and was fastened to the projectile with tin straps. The sabot was largely destroyed as it passed from the bore, but it prevented the shot from rolling or turning over and helped to seal the gases behind it.

Round shot was well suited for destroying walls, carriages, and wagons. It was also highly destructive when used against men or horses, particularly

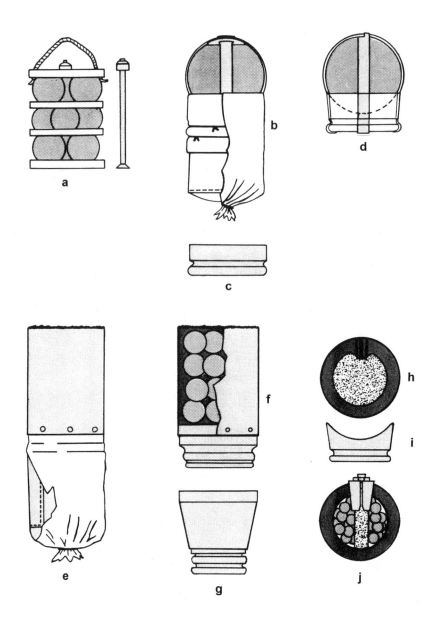

fig. 3.4. Ammunition for smoothbore artillery. a: Stand of grapeshot; b: shell, complete fixed round; c: wooden cartridge block for separate cartridge; d: round shot, tied to the sabot with tin straps; e: canister round, fixed; f: cutaway view of canister, showing iron shot; g: tapered sabot for howitzer round (the powder chamber for a howitzer was smaller than the bore); h: cutaway view of shell round; i: sabot for shell round and spherical case; j: cutaway view of spherical case round, showing lead ball shrapnel, wood fuse, and burster (adapted from an illustration in Coggins, Arms and Equipment of the Civil War). Courtesy National Park Service

when the target was in the open and en masse. The linear effect of round shot made it most effective if it could be fired either at its target at enfilade or in a sweeping line from end to end. Gunners always sought gun positions from which enfilade fire could be developed. This, and the soldiers' inability to fire over the heads of the infantry, led to the usual occupation of gun positions on the flanks of the troops being supported. Captain Duncan noted in his official battle report that, in addition to shell and spherical case, he also used round shot in his enfilade of the Mexican line. Duncan further noted that all three types of rounds he used were "so well directed, that the whole [Mexican] advance, horse and foot, fell back in disorder to the bushes."[35]

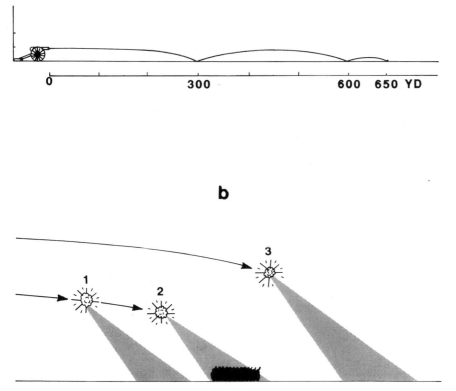

a

0   300   600   650 YD

b

1   2   3

fig. 3.5. Typical use and behavior of smoothbore cannon ammunition: a: Trajectory of a solid round shot fired from a six-pounder fieldpiece at zero degrees elevation; b: problems in firing spherical case shot. 1—trajectory correct, fuse too short; 2—trajectory correct, fuse correct; 3—fuse correct, trajectory incorrect (adapted from an illustration in Haythornthwaite, Weapons and Equipment of the Napoleonic Wars*). Courtesy National Park Service*

To produce its greatest effect, round shot had to arrive at its target with a high remaining velocity. The flatter its trajectory, the more devastating was its impact on either animate or inanimate targets. It was, therefore, normally fired from guns instead of from howitzers or mortars. Although the muzzle velocities of all smoothbore cannon were similar, the heavier the shot, the greater its speed upon reaching its target. This meant that heavy round shot was considerably more effective than light. At a thousand yards from its point of departure, an eighteen-pounder shot velocity is 840 feet per second (fps); for a six-pounder, 450 fps. Therefore, the heavier the shot, the greater its effect. As a result, a shot from an eighteen-pounder was three times more effective than a shot from a six-pounder.[36]

A round shot when fired fell steadily from the height of the muzzle until its "first graze," about three hundred yards for a six-pounder at zero degrees elevation. It then bounced up from its first graze until it hit the ground again—about six hundred yards for a six-pounder—at the "second graze." Finally, it usually bounced once more, usually around fifty yards for a six-pounder (fig. 3.5a). Since the entire trajectory was below human height, anything in its path would be struck down. As velocity and accuracy decreased with each bounce, it was ideal to have the first graze on the target, which could be achieved by elevating the barrel. Bounce was considerably reduced on soft ground; such surface conditions may have existed at Palo Alto owing to soggy soil at the time of the battle.

Round shot was a most fearsome projectile for those unfortunates on the receiving end. It was especially damaging to morale since the recipients could actually see these low-velocity objects approaching them but could not easily evade them during this era of close-order formations. Great carnage ensued once the round shot reached such a formation. Men and horses were sliced in half, and bodies literally exploded from the impact; this caused fragments of equipage and body parts to hurtle about in the ranks to kill and maim even more. Even when rolling along the ground like a bowling ball, round shot could strike off a limb in its path.

CANISTER

The effect of a solid projectile is naturally confined to a narrow line of fire, running from the gun to the target. Therefore, when engaging troops with round shot, artillerists always sought to fire it at enfilade. But round shot was not very effective against troops assaulting from a frontal position. For that situation, the canister shot was developed. As the name implies, this projectile consisted of an elongated tin container the same size as the bore. Inside the container were cast-iron balls packed in sawdust. By the time of the U.S.-Mexican War, the United States Ordnance Manual specified twenty-seven iron shot in six-, twelve-, and eighteen-pounder canisters. However, shot diameters for the three canister sizes were different: for the six-pounder canister, shot diameter was 1.15 inches; for the twelve-pounders, 1.07 inches; and for the eighteen-pounder, 1.68 inches.[37]

The canister held its contents together in the passage up the bore and prevented a too-wide spread at the muzzle. When the propellant exploded, inertia forced the balls to shatter the face of the container as they hurtled down the tube, producing a swathe of balls over the whole frontage of the gun position from which it was fired. The canister shot spread out rapidly at the muzzle, creating a roughly conical configuration whose diameter was approximately thirty-two feet per one hundred yards of range. This was most effective, but only up to its maximum range—for example, about three hundred yards for six-pounder guns—since the remaining velocity of the balls was not great enough to do damage beyond that distance. Much of this shot drove harmlessly into the ground or passed above the soldiers' heads and was thus not an efficient form of projectile. Since shot waste increased with range, canister was primarily a defensive type of round. However, there are many recorded instances of its use on the attack, such as by Duncan's battery at Palo Alto. Canister was a fearsome charge for infantry to face. Closely packed lines of charging men were particularly vulnerable to the shotgunlike blasts of such rounds, and it was also quite effective against the large targets presented by cavalry.

Two canisters could be, and often were, fired simultaneously from one gun or howitzer during the last stages of an enemy attack. There is a famous quote of General Zachary Taylor at Buena Vista when he supposedly gave the order, "A little more grape, Captain Bragg!" Alfred Pleasanton, who was there and overheard the actual conversation, reported that the order went something like this:

> "What are you firing, Captain?"
> "Canister, sir."
> "Double or single?"
> "Single, sir."
> "Then double it and give 'em Hell!" [38]

SHELL

Explosive shell, or shell, as it was usually called, was the forerunner of the modern and far more potent high-explosive round. It was a hollow projectile, with the cavity filled to about 90 percent capacity with black powder. The walls of the shell were of a thickness of about one-sixth the diameter of the shell. This ratio ensured that the shell contained as large a bursting charge as possible consistent with its ability to withstand the pressures of firing. The charge was ignited with a fuse lit by the flame of the burning propellant charge. If air bursts were required, a short fuse would be selected; if the shell was to explode on the ground, a longer one was used. Shells were most effective when fired from howitzers, siege cannon, and mortars since the stresses placed on shell were less with those weapons than with lighter fieldpieces. Because of the inadequacies of black powder as a military explosive, however, fragmentation of shell for a twelve-pounder field howitzer was limited to only four or five pieces, with correspondingly more fragments from an eighteen-pounder shell. But for all of its ballistic weaknesses, the shell round had definite psychological advantages over solid shot: it could unnerve men and horses by its noise and the flash of its explosion as well as by its destructive force.[39]

SPHERICAL CASE

Spherical case, or case shot, was a form of projectile invented by British general Henry Shrapnel in 1784. It was sometimes referred to by its inventor's name but more frequently termed case shot or case. It was hollow like a shell except the walls were not as thick; for example, a half-inch of thickness for a fieldpiece round. The cavity contained a number of lead musket balls held in a mass of melted sulfur or resin, a bursting charge of one ounce of powder, and a fuse to cause it to burst at the correct point on the trajectory. The United States Ordnance Manual of 1849 specified that a six-pounder spherical case shot should hold 38 lead balls; a twelve-pounder field howitzer case shot should hold 78; and an eighteen-pounder case shot, 120. Case shot was primarily an antipersonnel round and was used at distances beyond the maximum effective range of canister (for example, three hundred yards for six-pounders firing canister). The manuals of the day stated that case shot should be fused to explode fifty to seventy-five yards in front of the target and five to seven yards above it (fig. 3.5b). The resulting wide pattern of explosion compensated somewhat for miscalculation of the fuse length. For example, six-pounder shrapnel had a spread of about two hundred fifty yards at point-blank range to that of one hundred fifty yards at a distance of one thousand yards. Since shrapnel velocity dropped rapidly, the shrapnel thrown the farthest from the explosion might do little more than bruise.[40]

Tests conducted by the British during the early nineteenth century indicated that, on average, only about 10 percent of the shrapnel bullets were actually effective. However, those unfortunates who were massed directly below the explosion would have been killed or terribly wounded by high-velocity lead balls and iron shell fragments. Although spherical case shot was much less accurate than round shot, the resounding noise and confusion it produced on explosion was at least as significant as any real damage done. Case was most effective against cavalry in column by frightening the horses as well as destroying the morale of the men. One contemporary account of Wellington's peninsular campaign stated, "A single shell had been known to kill every horse in a gun team even at long range; and it was a really destructive projectile. The French hated it because they could not reply to it."[41]

By the 1840s, American artillerymen had adopted the use of paper fuses for their explosive rounds. This type of fuse consisted of a conical paper case two inches long containing the powder composition; its rate of burning was displayed by the color variant of the paper case. The gunner estimated the distance of the enemy from his position, then chose the appropriate fuse for the projectile to correctly explode (he hoped) just over the heads of the enemy. Paper fuses superseded wooden fuses, conical tubes of wood filled with powder composition. The wooden fuse was sawed to the correct length just before its use on the battlefield. If cut too long, the round might explode after it passed the proper point; if cut too short, there was a definite danger of premature burst, which might even occur in the bore of the piece itself. The use of paper fuses also eliminated saws, fuse-setters, extractors, files, and other implements needed for setting (and, if necessary, extracting) wood fuses.[42]

Grapeshot is mentioned by many writers of the period but is often confused with canister shot. Genuine "grape" for an eighteen-pounder cannon consisted of nine iron balls 2.4 inches in diameter packed around an iron column attached to a circular iron base. The whole of this was covered with painted canvas tied with string, giving the appearance of quilting. A twelve-pounder siege cannon fired grapeshot measuring about 2 inches in diameter. Since 1841, the United States Ordnance Department reserved grapeshot for naval and coastal cannon because it was not as efficient against troops as canister and because of the damage it caused to the bore of brass guns.[43] Since American eighteen-pounders were rated as both siege and coastal guns, however, grapeshot may have been present within the eighteen-pounder munitions chests at Palo Alto. The term *grapeshot* was informally used by nonartillerists during the muzzleloading period to describe the smaller shot within canister and spherical case rounds. One should not presume battlefield accounts are describing grapeshot as defined by artillery manuals of this period. Of course, since one's enemy presumably adhered to a different artillery manual, American soldiers may have occasionally experienced "the real thing."

AMERICAN ARTILLERY

American artillery dominated the battle of Palo Alto, and its dominance continued throughout the U.S.-Mexican War. At the outset of the war, the United States had an elite corps of artillery unexcelled anywhere in the world. This was achieved through a program that developed a whole new family of artillery pieces of the most advanced design. The artillery, in turn, was commanded by a new generation of professional officers provided by the United States Military Academy at West Point and the Artillery School at Fortress Monroe, Virginia. Undoubtedly, the horse artillery batteries at Palo Alto ensured victory for Taylor's small command. Large credit is due to Major Samuel Ringgold, who, years earlier, developed the tactic of rapidly deploying the new light artillery in support of infantry. Also, the unorthodox use of two eighteen-pounders in the forefront of battle, albeit slowly pulled by teams of oxen, contributed greatly to the battle outcome by decimating those Mexican infantry and cavalry formations beyond the normal range of the lighter six- and twelve-pounder field artillery.

United States artillery in 1845 was organized into four regiments with ten companies in each regiment. Ordinarily, each company occupied its own post. The posts, in turn, were widely scattered along the ever-advancing fringes of the frontier. Company strength varied, as did training and equipment, but disciplined career soldiers filled their ranks. A select few trained with the new, light six-pounder gun companies known as "flying artillery."[44]

These served apart from the rest of their arm, demonstrated by the way in which they were routinely identified in reports by their commanders' names instead of their regimental and company designations.

Field-service cannon consisted of (1) the gun, a long-barreled cannon firing projectiles at high velocities in a relatively flat trajectory; (2) the howitzer, a moderately short-barreled, light-weight cannon that lobbed a heavy projectile into an arcing trajectory for a moderate distance; and (3) the mortar, a short-barreled cannon firing projectiles for short distances in a very steep trajectory. Mortars were not used at Palo Alto by either army; however, they were present at Fort Texas and were used by Mexican forces during their siege of that fort. By 1845 the U.S. Army possessed various types and calibers of the newly developed field, siege, and garrison artillery. Seacoast artillery was not included in the new family of weapons but was part of the overall weapons system.[45] Of these varieties, only the six-, twelve-, and eighteen-pounder cannon are described below since they were present at Palo Alto.

The six-pounder gun served as the basic fieldpiece of the U.S. Army. A bronze smoothbore weapon with a maximum range of fifteen hundred yards, the tube weighed 880 pounds and had an outside tube length of 65.6 inches. The gun rode a standard two-wheel carriage with a box trail, featuring excellent maneuverability and a capability for rapid fire (fig. 3.6). The twelve-pounder howitzer served as the primary field howitzer of the U.S. Army. This was a bronze smoothbore piece that had a maximum range of approximately one thousand yards. Its tube weighed 785 pounds and had an outside tube length of 58.6 inches. The howitzer rode the same standard type of carriage as the six-pounder gun and had the same mobility with a corresponding firepower. The two eighteen-pounders within Taylor's train were intended for duty as siege, garrison, and coastal artillery pieces. These massive cast-iron weapons—each tube weighed 4,750 pounds—had to be hauled by a plodding team of either draft oxen or mules with civilian drivers. Their limited mobility normally meant that eighteen-pounders trailed a battle force in the baggage train. This is why it was such a novelty for them to be used at Palo Alto.

The artillery ammunition supply presented a logistical problem. Bulk quantities of this very heavy item followed the army in slow and unwieldy trains. On the battlefield, a caisson accompanied each field cannon, and limbers pulled by six-horse teams drew both the cannon and caisson. Each limber carried one ammunition chest, and each caisson carried two such chests. Prescribed loads, set according to the type of piece, filled the 600-pound ammunition chests. In addition, there was a traveling forge wagon for field repairs and horseshoeing as well as a battery wagon for extra supplies. In most pitched battles of the period, the artillery draught horses and support wagons stayed well to the rear once the guns had been brought up, with only the limbers and caissons moving to the front. Except for the drivers, most gun crews walked behind the heavy equipment to avoid overworking the horses, but they mounted and rode the limbers and caissons when rapid movement was needed. The exception by most accounts was Ringgold's Company C, 3rd Artillery. It was a true "flying" or horse artillery in that each man had his own mount. The other light companies with fewer horses were mounted artillery.[46]

MEXICAN ARTILLERY

The officers of the Mexican National Artillery Corps were mostly trained professionals. Many of its senior officers were foreign-born veterans of European wars, and most of the younger ones had trained at Chapultepec Military College. At Chapultepec they mastered the theoretical knowledge of artillery and perfected their gunnery. However, Mexican cannon tubes used by Mexico's Army of the North were of mixed caliber. Often old and obsolete and sometimes defective from long wear, they were potentially dangerous to operate. Three of the seven Mexican cannon tubes captured by Taylor's army at Resaca de la Palma have their year of manufacture molded onto

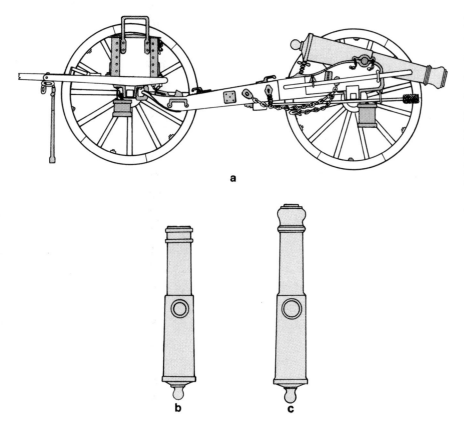

fig. 3.6. U.S. fieldpieces used at Palo Alto. a: Box trail-style gun carriage with caisson; b: twelve-pounder howitzer tube; c: six-pounder gun tube (adapted from illustrations in Coggins, Arms and Equipment of the Civil War). *Courtesy National Park Service*

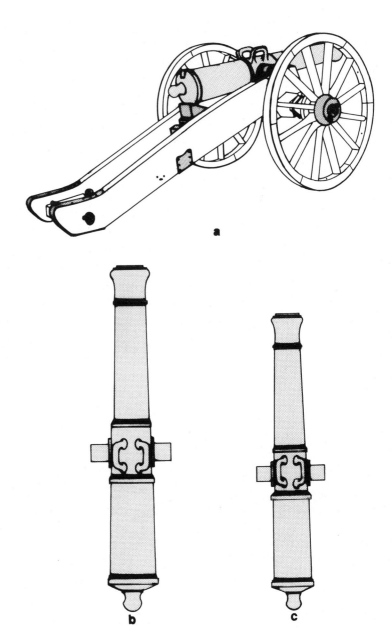

fig. 3.7. Mexican fieldpieces used at Palo Alto. a: Eighteenth-century-style double-bracket carriage (note the wedge or "quoin" used to hold the required elevation); b: eight-pounder gun tube; c: four-pounder gun tube (adapted from illustrations in Peterson, Round Shot and Rammers, *and Hay-thornthwaite*, Weapons and Equipment of the Napoleonic Wars). *Courtesy National Park Service*

them: 1766, 176- (exact year not discernible), and 1774. These dates indicate that their design and manufacture predated even the Gribeauval system, which was adopted by France in 1776. Gribeauval-type cannon likewise became obsolete during the early nineteenth century. By that time, the major European countries and the United States had adopted the lighter, maneuverable "box trail" system. It follows, therefore, that the Mexican gun carriages used at Palo Alto were probably of an antiquated, pre-Gribeauval design as well (fig. 3.7). Although serviceable, such gun carriages would have been at least twice as heavy and consequently far less maneuverable than the U.S cannon.[47]

On the Prairie of Palo Alto

Mexican-manufactured gunpowder for cannon as well as muskets was generally of inferior quality and often propelled projectiles far short of their intended targets. Mexican artillerists attempted to compensate for the poor performance of their gunpowder. An unnamed Mexican artillery officer who had fought at Palo Alto noted that their eight-pounder guns had to be greatly elevated like howitzers in order to obtain an arcing trajectory sufficient to reach the American lines. The same officer also described their four-pounders as "ridiculous." Another weakness of Mexican field artillery was its poor logistical support and insufficient mobility. To move ammunition and ordnance, civilian carts and drivers were hired or impressed as needed. Because the drivers were unacquainted with artillery drill and tactics, battery evolutions were awkward at best and moved slowly, if at all, during an engagement. Only the lightest of Mexican artillery pieces—those that supported cavalry units as "galloping guns"—could be maneuvered about the battlefield. The corps had disbanded its brigade of true horse artillery in 1833, since its workshops were underfunded and unable to provide the necessary special equipment. With such limitations, Mexican generals normally deployed their artillery in relatively static positions, thus restricting their usefulness to defensive warfare. Given all these matériel and logistical problems, it is no wonder that the Mexican artillerists at Palo Alto "fired only 850 cannon shots, while the [American forces] had let off more than 3000."[48]

At Palo Alto, the Mexican army used twelve cannon of the four- and eight-pounder sizes, which were grouped into batteries. They fired both iron and copper solid shot and antipersonnel rounds, the latter consisting of small copper canister shot encased in cloth or in rawhide shrunk tightly around its contents. The Mexican use of copper shot was a curiosity to American soldiers and war correspondents. Gullible Americans believed copper, supposedly unlike iron and lead, could poison the wounded victim—why else would Mexicans use a metal that, in their experience, was more costly than iron? In fact, copper was an abundant by-product of Mexican silver mines. One observant American soldier noted a predominance of copper shot at battles fought within the intensively mined Mexican interior. In contrast, all of the Mexican shot used along or near Mexico's coastline was imported and thus made of iron.[49] In light of this, use of both iron and copper shot by the Mexican army at Palo Alto conceivably reflects the places of origin of their various military units.

Uniforms, Accoutrements, and the Soldier

UNITED STATES ARMY

The 1841 Regulations for the Army of the United States are of little value in describing what the regular soldier wore during the U.S.-Mexican War. Instead, details of such dress come from a variety of War Department publications and archives as well as the few photographs and paintings by contemporary artists who followed the armies. Unless otherwise noted, the following descriptions are by Colonel John R. Elting.[50]

For fatigue wear in ordinary weather and for all services in 1846–47, infantry enlisted men were issued a jacket and trousers of a sky-blue, lightweight coarse wool called kersey. The infantry jacket had fifteen small white metal or pewter buttons decorated with the American eagle; uniform buttons for artillerymen and dragoons were made of brass with the American eagle design. Except for rank identifications, sergeants wore the same uniform. A dark-blue cloth forage cap went with this uniform, used by all branches and manufactured in several styles. No insignia or colored bands were known on infantry forage caps. Infantrymen wore a white buff leather belt over the left shoulder on which was secured at the center of the chest a lead-filled, brass circular plate showing the American eagle. Another white belt circled the waist, secured with a brass plate on which "U.S." appeared in raised lettering. A black leather bayonet scabbard was attached to the waist belt either by a short sliding sheath called a "frog" or on a shoulder belt. Certain noncommissioned officers used a double frog on a shoulder belt as a sword scabbard.

Knapsacks were nonrigid and made of canvas or India rubber, painted black, and marked with the regimental number in white. Both officers and enlisted men carried white cotton haversacks. Their flaps were marked in black to show the wearer's regiment, company, and (for enlisted men) their number. In these sacks the soldiers carried their food. Army-issue canteens were made of tin or wood, India rubber with a brass spout, or sewn leather. All of them held from 2.5 to 3 pints. Mexican gourds were preferred to American-issue canteens because they kept water cool on the hottest days.[51]

The cartridge box, suspended on the shoulder belt, was black leather and fitted to carry forty paper cartridges in tin dividers. On its flap was a round, lead-filled brass plate with a raised eagle. The waist belt was an oval brass plate, also lead-filled, with raised "U.S." lettering. Percussion caps, if they were carried at all, were transported in special cap pockets on the jackets or in cap pouches. Each soldier, if armed with a flintlock, wore a small brush and a wire vent-pricker suspended from a button on the front of his jacket or from his cartridge-box belt. Infantry line officers in campaign uniform wore a dark-blue single-breasted frock coat, sky-blue trousers, and the same forage cap as the enlisted men. While on duty with the troops, a crimson silk sash was always worn. Shoulder straps edged in silver lace indicated rank, and all officers' buttons were silver plated.

Because of their elite status, each of the light artillery companies had special-issue uniforms, at least at the beginning of the war. For example, Ringgold's Company C was dressed in a dark-blue "coatee," a short, close-fitting coat with tails, red facings, shoulder knots, yellow lace, and buttons; sky-blue trousers worn over short boots; and the "Ringgold cap," which was a shako with red cords and a horsehair plume. By June, 1846, these uniforms had worn out, thus replaced with the less flashy, general-issue uniforms. The field uniform for dragoons consisted of a dark-blue woolen jacket, blue-grey woolen trousers, and a visored, dark-blue wool forage cap. Yellow braid decorated the collar and shoulder straps. Officers wore a deep orange sash. Just before the U.S.-Mexican War, both dragoon regiments were reequipped with the new Ringgold saddle. Pistols were carried in covered holsters on either side of the pommel; extra clothing in a valise behind the cantle; and spare horseshoes, nails, and grooming equipment in small pouches that hung from the cantle. The rolled "great-coat" was fastened over the pommel.

THE AMERICAN SOLDIER

Except for a few Texas volunteers, Taylor's force at Palo Alto consisted of Regular Army professionals. Army muster rolls during the U.S.-Mexican War reveal that the average American regular was approximately twenty-five years old upon enlistment and was usually from one of the northern Atlantic cities or adjacent interior towns. Recruiters went where they hoped to find prospects. Although the ideal recruit might be a sturdy young farmer, they took what they could find, mostly laborers and newly arrived immigrants who concentrated in northern cities. Approximately 40 percent of regular soldiers were foreign-born, many of whom had yet to become culturally assimilated. One captain, complaining that fully one-half of his company did not understand English, observed, "They never could comprehend the difference between the command to 'charge' their muskets, 'charge' the enemy, and 'charge' the United States for services rendered."[52]

Men enlisted for a variety of reasons: some to escape entangling domestic problems or their creditors; others to support themselves through the army until the period's economic recession ended; and still others, mainly immigrants, to learn the language and customs of their new country. The xenophobic riots sweeping American cities during this period forced many immigrants into the army for their own safety. A study of soldiers' letters, journals, and reminiscences by one historian reveals a desire for personal glory and adventure as well as a need to avenge deaths incurred during the Texas Revolution and subsequent hostilities between the republics of Texas and Mexico. There were also those who entered the service with the sole purpose of making the government pay for their transportation to the frontier. Once there, these men deserted.[53]

Usually, however, desertion resulted from the rigors of war and camp life. During the entire U.S.-Mexican War, 2,850 men, more than 14 percent of the regulars, deserted. Hundreds of these deserters even embraced the Mexican cause. The punishment meted out to deserters was set by the courts-martial that tried them, and army regulations gave considerable latitude to the courts. Branding, when it was employed, was not normally done with a hot iron but instead as a tattoo. The mark of a "D" was placed on the deserter's hip or up under his arm so that if he ever tried to reenlist, the examining physician would see the tattoo and refuse to accept him. Forty of the captured American traitors-deserters that had fought with the Mexican San Patricio Battalion received an especially harsh sentence: they were hung. Their leader, John Riley, did not join them on the gallows since he had deserted before the declaration of war. Instead, Riley received fifty lashes well-laid with a bull whip and was then branded twice on his face with a hot iron.

Probably the main reason why soldiers deserted was the harsh treatment meted out "at the hand of young snot-nose and tyrannical officers" and "ignorant and brutal officers." To immigrants who had recently left the British army, it seemed incredible that "conceited Yankee subalterns should be free to strike enlisted men at the slightest provocation and inflict painful, humiliating punishments." Regular soldiers, unlike most of the volunteers who arrived after Palo Alto, were well drilled and relatively well disciplined. When possible, most career officers adequately attended to the welfare of their men. As a result, the rate of fatalities stemming from diseases caused by unsanitary conditions was significantly lower for regular soldiers than for the later volunteers.[54]

Even so, medical care and sanitary standards would not have presented a pleasing sight to a physician of today. Within Taylor's camp at Corpus Christi, the care of food and water and the disposal of wastes were conducted in a primitive manner or else generally ignored. Surgeon John Porter, 3rd Infantry, considered the camp at Corpus Christi "a vast hospital," with few men escaping debilitating attacks of diarrhea caused by amoebic dysentery and rancid food. Treatment of wounds was equally primitive, with recovery dependent largely on the stamina of the wounded and not a little luck. Just before the battle began, surgeons and those detailed to assist them took their positions in the rear of their assigned regiments. Surgeon Porter recalled that, at Palo Alto, Mexican cannonballs ricocheted over the ranks and fell thickly around him, and "soon our men began to fall and the medical officers had plenty to do. . . . The surgeons were busily employed with our own and the Mexican wounded left upon the field."[55]

Surgeons collected the wounded with the aid of untrained enlisted men pulled from the ranks. The usual method of treating battle-damaged limbs was amputation, although one surgeon of the U.S.-Mexican War declared that this operation was done with less abandon than during the Napoleonic era or even the Civil War. Ether had just been introduced as an anaesthetic by Massachusetts General Hospital a few months before the battle of Palo

Alto, and progressive army surgeons were already using it during General Scott's Veracruz campaign in 1847. Unfortunately for the amputees at Palo Alto, ether was apparently not available, and Porter was a strong opponent of its use anyway. Relatively less dangerous wounds were indifferently cleaned and covered with a dressing of lint, then tightly bandaged. Poultices of cornmeal, slippery elm bark, or sometimes even crushed cactus pads were employed as part of the healing process. The all-too-common presence of foreign substances in the "cleaned" wounds inevitably led to protracted suppuration; gangrene, then death, would almost certainly follow if not treated immediately.[56]

The day following the battle at Palo Alto, all of the wounded were taken via empty supply wagons down the bone-jarring dirt and mud road to Point Isabel, where regimental hospitals had been prepared. Surgeon Porter believed the wounded of Palo Alto and Resaca de la Palma did better than those of the other battlefields in Mexico, partly because the "infirm and worthless troops" had already been culled from the army and left, dead or alive, at Corpus Christi. The regimental hospitals at Point Isabel probably offered little in the way of comfort for the wounded. Regarding the U.S.-Mexican War, Porter recalled:

> For these [military hospitals] there was almost no provision, either in personnel or material. Hospital furniture, clothing, bedding, even cooking utensils were lacking. . . . Usually there was such urgent need for men of battle that few or no able-bodied men could be spared for the service for the hospitals; and at times the surgeons were obliged to organize their entire personnel from the patients. . . . The surgeons went from patient to patient, cleaning (?) all wounds with the same sponge, and infection was expected as a matter of course. The mortality of the wounded was 12 to 15 percent.[57]

At the time of the battles of Palo Alto and Resaca de la Palma, most of the senior officers assigned to the regiments were absent because of age or illness, some of them incapacitated for years but still holding field-grade positions in a regiment (that is, colonel, lieutenant colonel, or major). Nevertheless, veterans of the War of 1812 held key leadership positions. For example, Taylor was sixty-two years of age; McIntosh, fifty-nine; Twiggs, fifty-six; Worth, fifty-two; and Worth's second-in-command, Lieutenant Colonel William Belknap, also fifty-two. None of these commanders had attended West Point. Also present and in significant numbers, however, were lieutenants, captains, and young majors who were products of West Point and seasoned by years of fighting Indians or serving in some frontier garrison. The pride and determination of these young officers were expressed in letters, diaries, and autobiographies. They were resolved to prove the merit of a small professional army in combat against a similarly organized enemy. Furthermore, victory had to be achieved before they could be overwhelmed by volunteers who, they believed, would receive credit for any succeeding victories. Lieutenant George G. Meade was worried that they would not get into action fast enough. "We are all anxious to give [the Mexicans] a sound thrashing before the volunteers arrive, for the reputation of the army; for should we be unable to meet them before they come, and then gain a victory, it would be said the volunteers had done it, and without them we were useless."[58]

THE MEXICAN SOLDIER

Authentic pictorial material on the appearance of the Mexican soldier during this period is scant. Unless otherwise noted, the following information was taken from A. Nieto et al., who compiled it largely from texts on dress, equipment, armament, and accoutrements. Drawings associated with uniform decrees and contracts were no longer available for these authors to use as guides.[59] Also, one should realize that such uniform decrees specified the ideal. Mexican troops frequently had to be raised by arbitrary methods and were hastily organized and equipped with insufficient funds.

Many of the principal organizers and leaders of the Mexican military were former officers of the Spanish Army, as was General Mariano Arista. Under their influence, the Spanish and British tactics and drills utilized during the Napoleonic era prevailed. As previously noted, these tactics were very similar to those employed by the American army during the U.S.-Mexican War. However, uniforms and equipage adopted by the Mexican army evoked styles more in keeping with Napoleon's *Grande Armeé* circa 1812. The result was an army that was "picturesque but somewhat outmoded." The Mexican uniform regulations of 1841 specified distinctive uniforms for regular and light infantry as well as artillery and cavalry units. Infantry uniforms consisted of a tailcoat with cloth facings in a combination of distinctive colors different for each of the twelve line and three light regiments. All standing militia companies shared the same uniform design of blue tailcoat, red collar with embroidered company initials, and white pants.

Varying colors of bars or piping, indicating regiment and rank, were displayed on collars, lapels, and cuffs. Uniform regulations specified that regimental numbers be embroidered on collars and stamped on all buttons, yet none of the Mexican buttons found at Palo Alto during the 1992 and 1993 field seasons was numbered. Likewise, no Mexican buttons recovered to date from Texas Revolutionary sites have numbers, and only very few of the excavated buttons have the Mexican snake-and-eagle crest. The latter were probably reserved for officers. A brass "o" was also recovered from the Mexican battle line at Palo Alto, an artifact identified as a portion of a regimental uniform insignia for the Mexican 10th Infantry. This object was possibly worn on a shako. All ranks in the Regular Army wore plain white canvas pants in the summer and dark-blue wool pants in the winter. Boots, if worn, were sometimes covered by buttoned gaiters.

The active militia regiments had been in the field so long that there was virtually no difference between them and the regulars. They were ordered in 1842 to wear dark-blue coats with red collars, cuffs, and lapels, all outlined with yellow piping. Trousers were sky-blue with red piping, and the Regular Army shako was to be worn. Mexico's northern frontier was defended by companies of *presidiales*. These soldiers, including those that fought at Palo Alto, wore blue wool coats with low red collars and narrow cuffs. Their trousers were blue, hats black and broad brimmed. Cartridge boxes were plain brown, and their bandoleers had the *presidio* name embroidered on them.[60]

The dress regulations describe the military headgear of the U.S.-Mexican War in very general terms. Contemporary illustrations show at least twenty different models of shakos, helmets, caps, and hats in use. A typical infantryman shako was a visored black leather cylinder at least seven inches high, with a colored pom-pom, silver cord, and tricolor cockade. It was fronted by a brass shield stamped with a regimental number and had a chin strap of metal scales fastened by a pair of decorative metal pieces. Typical headgear for a cavalryman was a combed helmet of brass or leather with a long horsetail and fronted with a silver Mexican eagle. Soft cloth forage or barracks caps were issued to all army branches and ranks.

Line cavalry wore standard sky-blue coatees with scarlet collars, cuffs, piping, and epaulets; plain white metal buttons; and the regimental number inscribed on collars. Foot artillery soldiers were dressed in blue tailcoat and pants, and their collar was crimson with an embroidered exploding bomb. Engineers, sharpshooters, medical professionals, musicians, and other specialized units each had their own uniform colors and styles, usually sporting more brass emblems than those worn by ordinary enlisted men. All officers ranked colonel and below wore the same regimental colors as their units, but they also had fringed and embroidered epaulets, gilded buttons, and colored silk sashes. The decorative excesses stipulated for earlier officer uniforms were prohibited by 1841. Generals, however, were allowed such field-dress fineries as gold epaulets with heavy bullion fringes, intricate gold and silver collar embroidery, and jeweled medals.

Uniform accoutrements for the regular infantryman included a hide or canvas knapsack that held spare clothes, rations, musket flints, and the like; a strapped burlap blanket; a cross belt supporting a forty-round tin cartridge box and bayonet scabbard; and a canteen of either wooden drum or tin style. Gourds were also used as nonregulation canteens in both Mexican and American armies. A cavalryman was issued a belted saddle roll, bandoleer, pistol holsters, cartridge box, canteen, riding gauntlets, and various horse furniture, including a canvas sack with horse-grooming accessories.

The uniforms and accoutrements were generally supplied only to relatively small, elite corps because they were difficult to supply to the entire armed forces. The complaints of General Ciriano Vázquez from Jalapa, written in 1842, were also typical of the Mexican Army during the later war with the United States.

> The greater part of the rank-and-file of the 2nd Active Battalion, 7th Regiment, are short of overcoats, blankets or any heavier garment that could serve them as cover on rainy and cold nights or when asleep in their quarters, it being necessary for them to go to sleep dressed, with the result that the only uniform issue they possess is quickly destroyed. To avoid this damage and provide them with an indispensable item that will make their service more bearable . . . have the kindness to inform His Excellency the President about the great necessity of providing them at least with one coarse frieze blanket each.

Three months later, Vázquez received one canvas uniform per man, which consisted of a shirt, jacket, stock, trousers, and barracks cap. However, he was told that it was impossible to obtain the regulation one wool and two canvas uniform sets per soldier.[61]

The average Mexican enlisted man was an Indian or mestizo of small build with a height averaging five feet two inches. He was drafted into the army by a lottery held each year toward the end of October—not coincidentally, perhaps, just before the Feast Day of the Day of the Dead—or was possibly forcibly impressed at any given time during the year. A list of exempt professions excluded many from the draft; as a result, those at the bottom of the Mexican socioeconomic ladder ended up in the ranks. A substitute system existed for those who could afford to hire a replacement. Conscripts served ten years, whereas volunteers served eight. The ranks also numbered conscripts taken en masse from prisons as well as unmarried men without influence. Some were unlucky enough to have been caught in one of the yearly dragnets while in dance halls, streets, and other public places. Those of mestizo heritage and proven competence could conceivably become noncommissioned officers and even reach officer rank.[62] At Palo Alto, the Mexican army was made up of line regiments, sapper battalions, guard units, *presidiales*, and auxiliaries. All came from various Mexican states, which reflected the diverse cultures, language groups, and split loyalties found within nineteenth-century Mexico.

Since pre-Conquest times and up to the 1930s, a Mexican army was almost always followed by a ragtag mob of women, some with children in tow. Although at the very bottom of this army's pecking order, paradoxically the women, termed *soldaderas*, were an absolute necessity: without them, most of the men would have deserted. Soldaderas marched with soldiers for various reasons. Most were wives or mistresses of soldiers while others had been abducted or were forced to work as army cooks and laundresses. Armies

On the Prairie of Palo Alto

in Mexico usually did not issue rations to their soldiers. Instead, a soldier would turn his pay over to a soldadera, who would use it to purchase food and personal supplies. A soldadera's other duties might consist of carrying supplies, nursing, smuggling, and spying. Although the primary role of soldaderas was that of domestic servants, the nature of warfare often placed them in the thick of battle. A tough and resourceful lot, some of the soldaderas fought in the ranks alongside the men. There are several accounts of selfless acts of courage exhibited by soldaderas during the U.S.-Mexican War. Significantly, a Mexican mass grave at the battle site of Resaca de la Palma included the remains of four women.[63] Given this physical evidence, it is almost certain that soldaderas were present at Palo Alto and may have fought there as well.

If the recruit was an Indian he may have had an imperfect understanding of Spanish, and his entire service time was usually spent in an alien region far from home. The desertion rate within the Mexican Army as a whole was understandably high. When caught, deserters generally received additional service time for the first offense. For the second offense, the deserter spent his service time in one of the fever-ridden garrisons along the coast—essentially a variant on the death sentence. Pay for common *soldados* was fifteen pesos per month, from which clothing and food allowances were drawn. The elite *cazadores* and *grenaderos* received sixteen pesos. There also existed so-called *puro* volunteer organizations, such as the Active Commerce Regiment, whose officer corps and ranks were drawn from the professional community as volunteers and whose men contributed to a unit fund that paid for their weapons and uniforms. Foreign soldiers were an exception. Excluding the San Patricio Battalion raised during the U.S.-Mexican War, there were not large numbers of Europeans or North Americans in the ranks. The San Patricio Battalion, with its Europeans and U.S. Army deserters, made up the largest single grouping of non-Mexicans to serve.[64]

The Mexican Medical Health Corps consisted of over two hundred professional officer-surgeons, who were assisted by noncommissioned "meritorious" medical students. Ambulance companies were formed at a proportion of eight stretcher bearers for every one hundred combatants. These companies of enlisted men were trained by the medical officers to gather the wounded and manipulate stretchers as well as form escorts for sanitation equipment in the field or en route. What exactly this equipment consisted of is not known, but it is interesting to note that no similar equipment is known for the U.S. Army of 1846. Upon hearing the bugle call "hospital," stretcher-bearer attendants assembled at the main ambulance tent located to the rear of the battle line and near headquarters. At the bugle call "open fire," the attendants assembled their stretchers while the medical officers passed up and down the line to render assistance.

Like their American counterparts, members of the Medical Health Corps were expected to attend equally to the needs of both friend and foe, nationals and foreigners. Unlike his American counterpart, however, each Mexican surgeon was required to provide spiritual services as well. He informed his patients when they were mortally wounded so that army chaplains could prepare them for death and make out their testaments. Mexican surgeons were also responsible for vaccinating every soldier and visiting all sick and wounded every morning. Medical instruments, a wide variety of medicines, bandages, and so forth, were standardized and boxed for field use. The items found in a typical Mexican medical baggage were comparable—perhaps even superior in some particulars—to American Army medical paraphernalia.[65]

The Mexican officer corps was incredibly disproportionate in size to that of the rank and file. By 1847, the Mexican Army had 24,000 officers yet only 20,000 enlisted men. Many of the senior officers were politicians with virtually no formal training or practical experience in the military profession. Regional chieftains and their semiprivate forces provided a significant portion of the Mexican Army. Officers of such units, however, rarely possessed the training and discipline needed to conduct a successful campaign. When the British minister to Mexico wrote home in April, 1846, he described such officers as "the worst perhaps to be found in any part of the world. They are totally ignorant of their duty."[66] Mexico did have Chapultepec Military Academy, founded in 1833, but the academy produced only one hundred cadets every three years, if that. Nevertheless, this small cadre of officers provided the underlying structure of professionalism and competence for the Mexican Army during the 1846–48 war.

Between 1835 and 1843 the Mexican Army experienced several organizational changes, in large part because of rapid successions in governments that usually pitted one Army faction against another. By around 1845, however, Army organization had more or less stabilized—just in time for the U.S.-Mexican War. The structure of Mexican battalions was inherited from the Spanish Army following its restructure by the British peninsular campaign during the Napoleonic War. Battalions were organized into eight companies consisting of some eighty soldiers each—yet rarely were the battalions at full strength since companies averaged around forty effectives. One company was designated as *cazadores*, an elite unit of light infantry used for skirmish duty. A second elite unit, the *grenaderos*, consisted of veterans normally used as a reserve. The other six companies were the *fusilero* or line companies, which did the bulk of the fighting for the battalion. The 1839 Army reorganization called for local militias to be made into battalions, which, along with the various coastal guard units, were supposed to serve as garrison troops. Actually these troops often fought as field regiments (for example, the Tampico Coastal Guards at Palo Alto). In 1841 Mexico created *ligero* or light infantry regiments, which supposedly functioned as skirmish troops. Usually, however, light infantry regiments during the

U.S.-Mexican War fought as regular infantry in order to make up for losses in the line regiments. In 1843, a new drill manual by Captain Juan Ordoñez was adopted. A year later, Lieutenant Colonel José López Uraga translated the French bayonet drill for the Mexican Army.[67]

Mexican infantry regulations detailed a variety of relatively complex tactical maneuvers performed to perfection by elite veteran units. Less was expected from soldiers in line regiments, who were drilled to march in simple column formation and dress ranks on the firing line. Musket drill was a simplified version of contemporary European armies, and live-round musketry practice was virtually nonexistent. It was once observed that a Mexican soldier's first experience at firing a musket was at his first battle. The Mexican infantryman had to overload his musket to compensate for the notoriously bad gunpowder that contained too much sulfur and charcoal. To protect himself from the resulting heavy recoil he often fired from the hip, thus causing the musket ball to fly on a high trajectory well over the heads of the enemy ranks. In light of this, it is not surprising that Mexican generals placed their faith in the bayonet charge.

The level of preparedness of Mexican cavalry was better relative to the infantry arm. This was a result of the Mexican legacy of horsemanship, which also explains why their cavalry units contained large numbers of skilled horsemen. Both regular line cavalry units and the irregular *ranchero* auxiliaries were armed with a great variety of weapons including various models of short-barreled carbines, pistols, sabers, short swords, lariats, and the lance. Most of Mexico's cavalry units were "light" (that is, small men on small horses) and were the type of Mexican cavalry that fought at Palo Alto. The *Tulacingo Cuirassiers*, created in 1842, were the only true heavy cavalry regiment in Mexican service. The uniform of this particular unit strongly evoked the appearance of Napoleon's personal Horse Guard, and its members were carefully picked for their superior height and dashing appearance. But elite units such as the *Tulacingo Cuirassiers* were utilized by Santa Anna both to protect his person and to overawe the citizenry of major cities. They were rarely seen in the hinterlands, such as along Mexico's northern frontier.[68]

Tactics

Strategy is that aspect of military science dealing with the planning and directing of projects and campaigns. It involves the mass handling and movement of troops, artillery, and equipage for waging war within a theater of operations. Tactics, "the armored fist of strategy," represent the means by which the field commander achieves the goals of the strategy planners. Attack and defense, deployment of soldiers in an advance or withdrawal, patrols and skirmishes, commitment of additional troops—all are elements of tactics. At the time of the U.S.-Mexican War, the authorized tactical infantry manual for the United States was General Winfield Scott's three-volume *Infantry Tactics*. Its counterpart was the Mexican tactical manual *Instrucción para la infantería ligera del ejército Mexicano*.[69]

In general, American tactical doctrine and principles of warfare followed French-style tactics as they existed after the Napoleonic wars. At West Point, both staff and students carefully studied Napoleon's strategy and tactics; the instructors and cadets also formed a Napoleon Club where they discussed the emperor's methods. Mexican tactics were perhaps more reminiscent of those used by Wellington and introduced to the Spanish during the peninsular campaigns of the early nineteenth century. Nonetheless, American and Mexican infantry formations were not radically different. Theoretical tacticians of the time emphasized the open frontal assault over the defensive, as exemplified by bayonet attacks and close-order formations. Attack maneuvers required units of men to be compressed and well-ordered in their advance, to bring them to up the opposing line for a concentrated volley, and, finally, to make a determined bayonet charge.[70]

As such, both Mexican and American armies were governed by the linear formation, a tactic used as an integral aspect of European-style warfare since the late seventeenth century. Innovative modifications to line formation tactics had occurred during the Napoleonic wars, and many European countries had adopted these modifications as standard practice for their armies. Using these tactics, troops marched to the place of battle in columns consisting of two or more files of men covered by two or more companies of skirmishers, the latter seeking to disrupt the enemy line by use of aimed fire. The columns would then form a firing line or deliver a bayonet charge according to circumstances. By forming the line in two ranks, the frontage and resulting firepower of a battalion increased by one-third. The firepower could shrink, however, when gaps caused by casualties were closed by men moving in toward the center of the line. As a result, spaces could appear between battalions or even between companies of a battalion; if they became too great, these spaces could cause a weakness in the battle line. It is likely that the terrible artillery pounding inflicted on the Mexican army at Palo Alto caused this very situation to occur along their linear formation.

U.S.–Mexican War tactics required the delivery of musket fire in several ways: by a massed volley of the entire battalion, which was not popular because the line would be undefended until all had reloaded; by ranks, requiring one rank to be loaded at all times; or by subdivision, either by company or platoons, so that musketry would be issuing from some part of the line at all times. This sometimes was termed a "rolling volley," as alternate companies or platoons fired in succession from one end of the line to the other. Loading and firing was done in precision by word of command. With bayonets fixed, the attacking force advanced with some form of musical assistance. In an American army it was played using fifes, drums, and bugles;

a Mexican army had large regimental brass bands "beside a horde of trumpeters and buglers."[71]

Noncommissioned officers kept the alignment of ranks straight or evenly spaced, if necessary using wooden canes or the flat sides of their swords on the backsides of the recalcitrant. Flanks of the outermost ends of a line were most vulnerable to an attack delivered at right angles to the line. As a result, Great Britain and France, as well as the United States and Mexico, adopted three basic formations to secure the flanks: (1) a company at the extreme end of the line could be "refused," or remain in line but be thrown back at an angle to cover the flank; (2) it could be deployed in column on the flank; or (3) in the case of a long battle line, an entire battalion could be arrayed in column-ready formation to form a square if threatened by cavalry. In this kind of warfare, rate of fire became more valuable than accuracy. Speed and precision had to be combined with discipline, needed factors for the soldiers to continue loading and firing "among the heaped-up bodies of their motionless or writhing comrades."[72]

Effective infantry fire required intensive training so that the routine of loading and firing would become mechanical. For instance, in loading, the soldier armed with a flintlock musket had to be careful to first prime the pan with cartridge powder, and next put the remaining powder into the musket barrel followed by the musket ball. If he mistakenly put the ball in first the powder naturally could not ignite, requiring the laborious extraction of the ball in the middle of a firefight before the soldier could reload correctly. Since the bayonet was usually fixed, he had to be careful not to spike his hand or wrist while using the ramrod. Occasionally, some overexcited soldier would forget to withdraw the ramrod from his musket barrel, thereby losing this critical piece of equipment when the weapon was fired. The musket had to be held tightly against the shoulder when fired, or its kick could knock him to the ground into the ranks behind him.

It was dry, exhausting, adrenaline-pumping work. Every time a soldier's musket priming sparked, he got a small shower of half-burnt powder grains and flint particles in his face. At the same time, his musket gave a shoulder-wrenching kick. A great deal of jostling occurred in the ranks as a result of the constant kicking of muskets. There was a cacophony of noise, with musket and artillery fire being the loudest and most pervasive. Other contributory noises were bullets and shrapnel striking the blades of swords and bayonets to create a weird harmonic vibration, the whistle and sigh of projectiles overhead, and the beating of drums and the blare of bugles. Orders had to be shouted or even screamed since one could hardly hear what was said by the adjacent person. Damage to hearing was not unusual for those who had spent an entire day with their ears only inches away from the muzzles of the rear ranks. Gunpowder smoke burned in everyone's eyes, there were anguished sounds of pain from wounded comrades and horses, and, at one's feet, lay smashed equipment, round shot, pools of blood, body parts, and the dead. Many in the ranks would have been suffering from diarrhea, and, since none could leave the ranks while the army was deployed, sufferers would have had to relieve themselves even while they stood and fired. Biting cartridges dried out the mouth and throat, but there was no time to take a drink—assuming any water was left in a one-quart canteen. A veteran might be able to shoot three, or possibly four, rounds a minute as the battle began. Later, only two rounds a minute at most was possible as men became exhausted and muskets grew foul.[73]

COLUMN FORMATION

An army arrived on the battlefield in groups of battalions—during this period one full-strength battalion consisted of approximately four hundred to six hundred men—in march formation, then formed into lines of battle or columns of attack. There was a difference in formation between a column in march and a column of attack. A column in march had a frontage of perhaps six or eight men and an immense length; in attack, a column's frontage was usually greater in length than depth. Its purpose was to deliver a decisive impact at the point where the head of the column struck the defending line. But a columnar formation essentially disarmed the majority of soldiers confined within it. Although an attacking column was mobile, the only muskets it used were those of the first two or three ranks of the leading company.

Effective firepower of an attacking column was limited to those at the very front and along the margins; those in the interior could not raise their muskets to fire even if they had a glimpse of the enemy. With so few muskets effective at the head of a column, the attacking battalion was obviously at a disadvantage against a line formation that could bring all its muskets to bear simultaneously. Thus, if the defending line remained steady and unshaken, its concentrated musketry directed against the head of the attacking column could virtually destroy the leading ranks of the latter. Also, since its depth and mass were greater than the ranks in line formation, an attack column was especially vulnerable to artillery fire. Because of the inaccuracy of the smoothbore musket, the attackers were relatively free of casualties until they reached a point eighty to one hundred yards from their objective. The final phase of the battle demanded that the soldiers on the attack hold their fire until their unit had advanced to a point about fifty yards from the enemy line. The officer of the American Revolution who reportedly exhorted his men, "Don't fire until you see the whites of their eyes," was not making a statement for posterity but giving a necessary order. Here at point-blank range, the order to fire was given. At the moment of impact, as it closed in upon its opponent, the attacking force turned to the bayonet.[74]

On the Prairie of Palo Alto

A skirmish line of men, often armed with rifles by the mid-nineteenth century, had the freedom of movement to fight in front of the main body in order to protect the initial column deployment. They delivered their fire not in volley but "at will" and aimed at specific targets, such as officers and artillerymen. Their proper performance required skirmishers to avoid coming into close quarters with the enemy. Nevertheless, this type of fire could cause disorder in the ranks of the enemy line, which was largely powerless to reply. Musketry delivered in volley at skirmishers would cause few casualties since the targets were not in line formation, and artillery fire was less effective against skirmishers because they were not tightly packed as a line or column. Another function of skirmishers was to screen the advance of attack columns behind them. If this was correctly done, the attack columns would burst upon the enemy line with a degree of surprise, especially if delivered with the rapid pace that columnar formation allowed. The bayonet, a shock instrument, was expected to carry the assault at the final moment of the attack.[75]

SQUARE FORMATION

Infantrymen in line were extremely vulnerable to an aggressive cavalry charge. If the cavalry could catch a unit in line, especially from a flank, a massacre could ensue as the line was "rolled up" and trampled beneath the charge. The square formation was the solution to the cavalry threat. Forming a square, actually more of an oblong, required precision and considerable discipline under fire since any foul-ups in its execution would be sure to be exploited by enemy cavalry. Squares could be formed from column or from line by any company. With a ten-company battalion in line, three companies would stand fast, the remainder falling back at right angles and the flanks turning at right angles again to close the rear of the square (or more commonly an oblong formation). Sides were normally four deep, necessitating some contraction from a two-deep line. The square was almost invariably hollow, with officers, musicians, colors, and baggage in the center. Each side faced outward to present an almost impenetrable, bristling hedge of bayonets.

It took nerve for cavalry to charge such a defense against which it was powerless. The exception to the rule would be an attack on a square formation by lancers, who could spear the infantry without getting within reach of the bayonets. Yet, even in this situation, volleys of fire from the faces of the square could easily thwart an attack by lancers. Very few examples of cavalry breaking a square exist, and then only if the infantry were demoralized. The weakness of the square was its vulnerability to artillery fire, enforcing the dictum that cavalry attacks should ideally be accompanied by horse artillery. Otherwise, a square was almost invulnerable.[76]

During the U.S.-Mexican War, both American and Mexican troops used these tactical formations in a manner that would have been familiar to European armies of the period. At Palo Alto, American troops deployed from column into line while flanking regiments formed into squares to counter Mexican cavalry. Mexican troops during this battle were arrayed into a two-line formation that was interspersed by artillery, its flanks anchored on natural obstructions as well as protected by companies of light cavalry. At Resaca de la Palma, fought the following day, the junglelike terrain forced American infantry to go into action in open order against Mexican units in linear formation. At Monterrey, American assault columns, covered by light infantry skirmishers, rushed the city's defenses. Close-order formations, deployed lines for firing, and columns for maneuver and assault had to be employed since armies of the period were constrained by the limitations of their smoothbore weapons.

How effective was the smoothbore musket, not only as a weapon but as a determining force on the battlefield of linear tactics? Colonel George Hanger, a British officer during the Napoleonic wars, had this to say about the regulation firearm of this period:

> A soldier's musket, if not exceedingly ill-bored (as many of them are), will strike the figure of a man at eighty yards; it may even at 100; but a soldier must be unfortunate indeed who shall be wounded by a common musket at 150 yards, provided his antagonist aims at him; and as to firing at a man at 200 yards with a common musket, you may just as well fire at the moon and have the same hopes of hitting your object. I do maintain and will prove, whenever called on, that no man was ever killed at 200 yards by a common soldier's musket, by the person who aimed at him.[77]

Ulysses S. Grant noted in his *Memoirs* that "a man with a musket at a range of a few hundred yards might fire at you all day without you finding it out." Major Luther Giddings, a colonel of a volunteer regiment during the U.S.-Mexican War, said, "In vain did we caution our men not to fire until commanded. . . . [M]ost of them discharged their guns as they obtained a good aim, but when the enemy was too distant to secure the most satisfactory results."[78] Yet, despite its limited effective range and other shortcomings, the musket was an adequate weapon given the tactics of the times. Although individual musket fire was inaccurate, when delivered in concentrated volleys it could be powerful within its range.

Of course, at Palo Alto, neither army employed the culminating bayonet charge demanded by linear tactics. Instead, the Americans simply battered the Mexican battle line from a safe distance with their artillery, and most of the Mexican infantrymen never came within four hundred yards of their adversaries. This tactic was something of an innovation since up until then American field artillery, in its offensive role, acted only as a support to the all-important and culminating infantry assault. A few years later, the Civil War–era rifled musket made obsolete the Napoleonic-era tactics of wheeling light field artillery batteries in front of infantry advances to blow a hole in the defensive line. Linear tactics were practical only as long as the primary weapon was the smoothbore musket. This tactic became outmoded after the acceptance of the rifle as the standard infantry arm.

Topographic
and Documentary Analyses

A key to success on the battlefield is the ability to use the landscape to gain advantage over one's opponent. A screening of trees and undergrowth, subtle dips and rises of the ground, open spaces, bodies of water and marsh, roads, and trails: these and many other topographic features will determine the tactics chosen by the combatants. This was especially true during the era of smoothbore muskets and artillery when visual contact was necessary to strike at the enemy. Artillery had to be positioned in the open for effective sighting and firing. If possible, attack columns avoided uneven or obstructed ground in order to maintain a tight formation and massed firepower. In contrast, cover from enemy view was a valuable asset to skirmishers and defenders, for whom even a small bank of earth might provide considerable protection. Lacking natural cover, troops on the receiving end of an artillery attack might find some protection by simply lying low.

To construct an archaeological interpretation of Palo Alto, one must correlate Napoleonic-era weaponry and tactics with topographic features of the battlefield. Stated another way, we must visualize Palo Alto as it appeared on May 8, 1846. To do so, we place ourselves in the roles of soldiers who made tactical decisions based on how the battlefield appeared. An artillery officer who positioned his battery on the edge of the Palo Alto prairie had to determine what obstructions might affect his fire and whether his gun carriages would get bogged down in the prairie muck. A cavalry commander who led his unit on a flanking attack had to quickly decide if the prairie brush could sufficiently screen his movement and if the marsh ahead would impede rapid maneuvers. An infantryman in retreat might have wondered whether the levee ahead would provide sufficient cover to protect him from an artillery barrage. To "read" the battlefield, then, we need to understand the parameters set by the physical environment, which restricted both the movement and the visibility of the combatants. Once these topographic parameters are identified, we may then conjoin this information with eyewitness accounts and period battle maps. Our ultimate goal is a determination of likely locations of artifact patternings.

The prairie at Palo Alto was an ideal setting for a Napoleonic-style battle, in which a clear view of one's opponent was essential. Located within the delta region of the Rio Grande, its topography, like that of the surrounding flood basin, is monotonously flat. Elevations range between eight and twenty feet above sea level, permitting ample opportunity to see and be seen. The monotony of the lowland is relieved somewhat by innumerable inactive meander scars and tributary channels abandoned by the ever-shifting Rio Grande. Periodic hurricane flooding and consequent soil deposition eventually turned these channels into boggy wetlands that support such water-loving plants as cattails and sedges. Old river channels that still retain water most of the year are locally termed *resacas* instead of oxbow lakes, the term commonly used in other regions of the United States. The word *resaca* derives from the Spanish *resacar*, meaning "to take back," in the sense that the water is taking back its old riverbed location. The resaca that figured as a flanking obstacle to the Mexicans during the battle is named, appropriately, Resaca de Palo Alto.

The battlefield is also marked by a number of natural depressions that hold water of varying depth during the rainy season. The two largest depressions cover at least thirty acres each, and both figured prominently during the battle. Palo Alto Pond was a relatively deep depression that served as a source of fresh water to American troops as well as a logical place to park the wagon train. An unnamed marshy expanse lay between the Mexican and American battle lines. Within the last fifty years, these two depressions have lost much of their water to the excavation of cattle tanks at their centers. If these earthen tanks were filled in today, it is likely that the depressions would revert back to their water-retaining and tactically significant characteristics of circa 1846.

Just a slight change in elevation on the battlefield, even when measured in inches, can affect its vegetation. This phenomenon is reflected by Palo Alto's two major vegetation zones: brushland and salt prairie (fig. 4.1, map 6). The lowest elevations of the Palo Alto battlefield have the poorest drainage, hence the greatest salt build-up. Its vegetation zone is termed a salt prairie and comprises 77 percent of the battlefield. It can support very little woody vegetation, although a few scattered mesquite and yucca are locally common. Cordgrass (*Spartina* sp.) is the dominant plant species in this zone. If not burned off, clumps of cordgrass can grow several feet high, providing cover for a variety of fauna and smaller flora. This species of coastal grass can greatly torment anyone on foot since its stiff, extremely sharp, spine-tipped leaves can poke through even the toughest of clothes. In his *Memoirs*, Ulysses S. Grant recalled, "Where we were the grass was very tall,

fig. 4.1. Mixed salt-borrichia prairies, near the Mexican battle line, looking southeast. The brushland-covered clay dune that is Arista Hill is on the horizon. Pinflags mark the locations of artifacts. Courtesy National Park Service

reaching to the shoulders of the men. It was very stiff, and each stock was pointed at the top, and hard and almost as sharp as a darning needle."[1] It was also demonstrated on the day of the battle that cordgrass has the peculiar ability to burn readily while still green.

Approximately 98 percent of the Rio Grande delta has gone under the plow or else was altered in some fashion. Although the salt prairie of Palo Alto has largely escaped this fate, a portion of salt prairie in the middle of the battlefield nevertheless still shows the scars of circa 1960 row plowing, which appear as a series of evenly spaced bands. These bands are the result of unsuccessful field trials to plant nonnative grasses that are more palatable to cattle than cordgrass. It is indeed fortunate that the salinity of Palo Alto prairie soil is especially high; otherwise, this fairly pristine patch of native vegetation would have gone the way of the rest of the delta, thereby compromising battlefield topography and associated artifact patterning.

Brushland covers about 23 percent of the battlefield. It is found primarily along the resacas, especially on both levees that demarcate Resaca de Palo Alto. This vegetation zone is dominated by mesquite (*Prosopis glandulosa*). Within the northern one-third of the battlefield are found stands of mesquite that are virtually impenetrable, especially where there is also a dense understory of prickly pear and yucca. Such brushland probably has changed little since 1846. Cattle grazing within the last sixty years, however, has contributed to the invasion of herbaceous plants, and clearing of brush

On the Prairie of Palo Alto

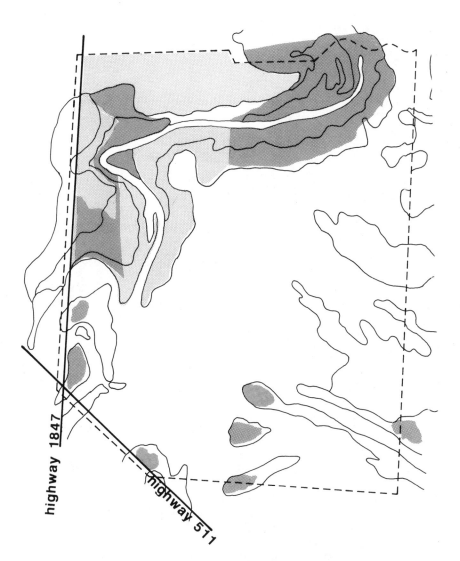

map 6. Dense brushland (dark shading) on the higher levee soils, which are adjacent to Resaca de Palo Alto and older meander scars. Plowed areas (light shading) are potential revegetation areas that should grow brush. Salt prairies (unshaded areas) dominate. Courtesy National Park Service

in some places for crop production has reduced its former extent even more. Brushland also covers the few clay-based aeolian dunes found at Palo Alto. These dunes, locally termed *motitas*, originally formed along saline lakes, lagoons, and tidal flats. Mesquite and shrub-covered *motitas* are significant from a military standpoint because of their relative height, rising as much as ten feet above the surrounding salt prairie. One battlefield *motita* is named Motita de Arista, in the local belief that General Mariano Arista viewed the battle from its lofty height.

Traversing Palo Alto's sharp-pointed cordgrass, almost impenetrable mesquite forest, water-filled resacas, boggy meander scars, and depressions can be quite difficult even with the modern conveyances of today. It would have been much worse in 1846, when all travel was accomplished by foot, horse or other livestock, and wagon. The spring rainy season sometimes

fig. 4.2. Aerial photograph of Palo Alto Battlefield National Historic Site. Significant areas of the battlefield are denoted A–G: Area A, Palo Alto Pond; Area B, Resaca de Palo Alto; Area C, possible tracings of the Matamoros–Point Isabel wagon road; Area D, marshy area between battle lines; Area E, Arista Hill; Area F, lomas tendidas, the wooded levee; Area G, the road that connected Palo Alto with Tanques de Ramireño. Courtesy National Park Service

On the Prairie of Palo Alto

brings an overabundance of water. During such times the *motitas* can become veritable islands, the resacas and depressions transformed into boggy hazards difficult to cross by man and animal, especially by wagon. Several accounts indicate that the spring of 1846 was wetter than usual, which meant that the only practical way to cross the salt prairie of Palo Alto was via the alternate and more circuitous wet-weather route of the Point Isabel–Matamoros Road. At Palo Alto, the wet-weather route extended in part along the crest of the levee of Resaca de Palo Alto, taking advantage of its natural drainage and thus relatively drier surface. The levee skirted the water-filled resaca to the north and west as well as the treacherous, sticky-when-wet clayey prairie soils to the south and east. The road between Palo Alto and Tanques de Ramireño used by Arista's army on the day of the battle would also have followed any ground that was elevated relative to the adjacent salt prairie, resacas, and depressions.

The Palo Alto battlefield has largely escaped agricultural alterations that have transformed much of the Lower Rio Grande Valley, such as the destruction of native vegetation, the flattening and removal of *motitas*, and the filling of resacas. Because of this fortunate circumstance, we believe the topography of the Palo Alto terrain of today can be correlated with most of the natural and man-made features described on the day of the battle. These features include Palo Alto Pond, the resaca that figured prominently on the west side of the battle, a segment of the Point Isabel–Matamoros Road where the Mexican left flank bisected it, the marshy area between the battle lines, the *motita* that anchored the Mexican right flank, the approximate location of the *lomas tendidas* (low rises) that extended east of the initial Mexican battle line, and the Tanques de Ramireño road. Refer to fig. 4.2 and map 7 for the following discussion of these features.

Palo Alto Pond (Area A)

Although presently drained by a stock tank, Palo Alto Pond is nevertheless visually prominent on the aerial photograph. Several battlefield accounts noted that the American army obtained water from this pond, located just west of the wagon road they followed, before their final advance toward the Mexican army.[2] Also, the southeastern portion of the pond may be the approximate location of Worth's Camp, where the American army, under the temporary command of Colonel William Worth, had encamped March 24–27 and where the wagon train on the day of the battle formed into defensive position. Recognition of Palo Alto Pond permits an educated guess regarding the location of the original battle line of the American army. Also, various defensive maneuvers of the U.S. 3rd, 5th, and 8th Infantry regiments were conducted to the east and west of this pond to protect the wagon train. It is possible, therefore, to deduce the estimated locations of these regiments during this phase of battle.

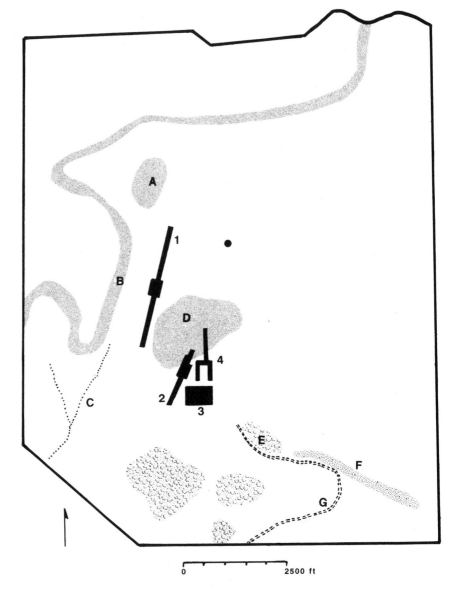

map 7. Palo Alto Battle-
field National Historic
Site, areas of investigation.
Area A, Palo Alto Pond;
Area B, Resaca de Palo
Alto; Area C, possible
tracings of wagon road;
Area D, marshy area
between battle lines; Area
E, Arista Hill; Area F,
"lomas tendidas"; Area G,
the road that connected
Palo Alto with Tanques de
Ramireño. Also shown are
the locations of Search
Areas (SAs) 1–4. The
filled-in circle • denotes the
approximate location of
Captain Duncan's battery
toward the end of the
battle, as indicated by
artifact patterning.
Produced by Charles M.
Haecker

Resaca de Palo Alto (Area B)

A number of battle accounts emphasize the tactical significance of a resaca
where it bordered the west side of the above-mentioned wagon road.[3] These
"woods and marshes difficult to overcome"[4] anchored the Mexican left flank.
Undoubtedly this is Area B. We suspect Torrejón's cavalry carried out its
flanking attempts within the area bounded on three sides by a loop of this
resaca. It was also within this region that we believe the U.S. 3rd and 5th
Infantry regiments, Ridgely's battery, and Texan volunteers took their defensive positions when they thwarted the Mexican flanking attack. Approximately half of Area B, including its levee, has been cleared of its native

On the Prairie of Palo Alto

vegetation and leveled for crops and pasturage. Both the American 3rd and 5th Infantry regiments executed square formations near Resaca de Palo Alto. To accomplish this, the Americans would have needed fairly open ground, their views unobstructed by the dense mesquite forest that would have bordered the resaca.

Matamoros–Point Isabel Wagon Road Segment (Area C)

This feature segment appears on the aerial photograph as an anomalous linear configuration typical of abandoned roads. A ground check before its survey revealed that this is an area of disturbance vegetation that extends within the park boundary for about one-half mile and averages around fifty feet wide. Close inspection of the photograph also shows a fork in the now-abandoned road. We suspect this fork in the road is the same one illustrated on period battle maps. If correct, then the cavalry and light infantry units that comprised the left wing of the Mexican army were initially stationed just to the north of the fork and, to their left, the resaca labeled Area B. Following this line of reasoning, Torrejón's cavalry units were placed to the immediate east of the fork, with the Mexican 4th Line Regiment positioned a few hundred yards east of the cavalry. During the final phase of battle, Churchill's eighteen-pounder battery would have been positioned on this road approximately where Torrejón's cavalry had been stationed; that is, near the fork in the road. Also in this vicinity were the American Artillery Battalion, the 4th Infantry, and Captain May's squad of dragoons.

Marshy Area (Area D)

One battle report describes a broad, marshy area separating the two opposing battle lines.[5] The only likely candidate for this topographic feature is Area D. This terrain has a slight depression supporting several species of water-tolerant shrubs and succulents. At present there is a drainage stock tank located more or less at the center of Area D. If the stock tank was filled, this seemingly innocuous portion of the battlefield would undoubtedly revert back to its pristine, boglike state. Area D, therefore, would have been avoided by both sides as a tactical hazard.

Motitas and Arista Hill (Area E)

Given the fact that there are no other low rises in this area of the battlefield, we believe Area E is the same topographic feature described by the Mexicans as *loma de Motisas* [sic].[6] Local tradition has named these two low hills *las motitas de Arista* in the belief that General Arista placed his field headquarters here. Regardless of where Arista pitched his tent, the *motitas* provided a natural albeit meager anchor for the Mexican right flank. Also, the Mexican supply wagons were reportedly placed behind the *motitas* to exploit their relative protection. The westernmost *motita* additionally may have provided some minimal shelter and drier ground for the Mexican field hospital, reportedly stationed about three hundred *varas,* or roughly nine hundred feet, south of the Mexican battle line.[7]

A line running east-west between Area E and the fork in the road of Area C should then represent the approximate location and axis of the initial Mexican battle line. The distance between these two defined areas is a little less than a mile. One Mexican document noted that their battle line at Palo Alto consisted of 3,300 men (it is not clear if this included cavalry units) "two men deep, without secondary lines, nor reserves, nor any concentration of troops whatsoever." This would mean two lines of men, each line thus consisting of some 1,650 men with each man allotted "two paces," or about five feet of linear space, the regulation spacing between Mexican soldiers. Such a formation would have resulted in a Mexican battle line approximately one and one-half miles long. Additional space for artillery pieces between the units would have extended the line a bit farther, and Mexican cavalry on the flanks would have stretched the battle line even more.[8]

Lomas Tendidas (Area F)

Several American and Mexican battle accounts[9] note the presence of *lomas tendidas,* or low rises. These rises were covered by a mesquite thicket that extended eastward from the extreme east end of the Mexican right flank. It was this thicket that the Mexicans used as a screen for their final flanking attempt and also possibly to obscure their retreat and encampment following the battle. Today there are no clearly demarcated traces of the low rises: like the surrounding salt prairie, Area F is covered by cordgrass instead of mesquite.

We believe this area, in 1846, was a levee several feet high that once bordered an ancient river meander, the latter still visible from the aerial photograph. Fortunately, biologists have identified within Area F a linear deposition of silty clay and loamy soils typical of levees in the region. Such alluvial soils would have supported the type of brushland that existed here at the time of the battle, but only with enough elevation to permit runoff. Apparently the levee, along with its mesquite brushland, disappeared over the last 150 years. This was the result of natural erosion, mechanical land flattening, or a combination of the two. Nonetheless, vestiges of this topographic feature are sometimes delineated for a short period following heavy rains, when the lower-elevation lands surrounding the old levee are inundated.

Tanques de Ramireño Road (Area G)

This unpaved ranch road is probably an actual segment of the old Tanques de Ramireño Road, the route taken by the Mexican army when it entered Palo Alto prairie on the day of the battle. A ground check revealed that this is still the most practical route when one approaches the open prairie of Palo Alto from the south. A more linear, direct approach is impractical because of two meander scars, both visible on the aerial photograph. These scars can become quite marshy when heavy spring rains drain into them, as may have been the case on May 8, 1846. The road follows a barely discernible levee remnant. Although only inches higher than the adjacent meander scar, the remains of the levee still provide an elevated surface that drains into the adjacent low areas. In 1846, when it was several feet higher, the levee would have been at least marginally attractive to foot, livestock, and wagon traffic.

Battle Maps

A simple 1:1 overlay of period battle maps of Palo Alto onto United States Geological Survey (USGS) topographic maps and aerial photographs does not provide a reliable reconstruction of the battle lines. The standards and scaling of period maps were not at all accurate as compared to USGS quadrangle maps of today, nor were the period maps expected to be that accurate. This situation prevents precise correlation of Palo Alto battle maps with modern maps of the battlefield. Reasonably accurate battle interpretation requires synthesis of selected and weighted information obtained from various historical maps and battle accounts. Only then can such data be correlated in conjunction with topographic maps, aerial photographs, and artifact distributions.

Historic maps and eyewitness accounts of the battle are subjective constructs of their authors, whose observations were possibly influenced by nationalistic biases or faulty powers of observation. Some eyewitness reports of the battle of Palo Alto disagree on specifics, perhaps a result of confused memories when written many years later. Recorded observations of battle events might conflict owing to various fields of vision, which was probably obscured at times by the literal "fog of battle." Soldiers often recollect a battle as "a half-remembered blur, a mosaic somehow fragmented and haphazardly reassembled."[10] U.S.–Mexican War historian Justin Smith noted that many misrepresentations, both intentional and accidental, existed in official military documents of the war:

> It was legitimate for a general, bearing in mind that probably his statements would soon become known, to consider their effect on the officers concerned, the army in general, the government, the public at home, the enemy, and the world at large. . . . To gain these ends more or less misrepresentation was needed. . . . General Taylor received great credit for his reports, but they were written, in fact, by the assistant adjutant-general of his army, W. W. S. Bliss, who was a finished artist in discreetly omitting and sagaciously emphasizing. Bliss never lied and never told the truth, one may almost say.[11]

Yet objective battlefield data, such as aerial photographs, topographic maps, and archaeological evidence, have their interpretive limitations as well. As previously noted, various alterations in topographic and vegetative configurations have occurred at Palo Alto. Some changes are obviously man-made, or are known as such through informants; others are the result of natural erosion and deposition ongoing since the battle. Thus, one cannot presume that every natural feature described at the time of battle has the same configuration today or, for that matter, still exists. For example, one could mistakenly assign historical significance to a present-day marshy area not in existence at the time of the battle. Furthermore, the "true" marshy region may have long since dried up or filled with soil without leaving any visual trace.

Assigning artifact concentrations to a specific battle event, such as a historically documented Mexican flanking maneuver, has its interpretive hazard as well. Battlefield plundering by relic collectors has compromised pattern interpretation to an unknown degree since artifacts have been both selectively and intensively removed from accessible areas. Our survey of Palo Alto indicated that areas lacking thick vegetation cover were usually devoid of both surface and subsurface artifacts. It is possible, therefore, that a concentration of artifacts exists not because a specific battle event took place there but because a covering of cordgrass has protected it from the collectors.

Greater weight attends battlefield data that hold up best under the following four criteria:

(1) *Closeness.* Some sources of information derive from actual observers and participants of the battle. Fortunately, there are a number of such sources. There are also sources who provide hearsay accounts, or accounts recorded many years after the battle took place.

(2) *Competence.* Of the above sources, those are considered competent if they are capable of understanding and describing the battle. The best-detailed descriptions of battle events were written by educated individuals who could make exacting, dispassionate reports regarding their observations.

(3) *Mutual support.* Certain eyewitness sources gave congruent descriptions of specific battle events and topographic features, thereby strongly supporting their validity. This is especially true if the sources were opponents since there is much less chance of one such informant influencing the other.

(4) *Impartiality.* Impartial sources are those with the least to gain from distorting battle events; for example, a soldier whose career would not be enhanced or jeopardized by providing a true account of what he observed. In a sense, this criterion also includes archaeological data. Such data provide artifact patterns that form a dispassionate record of battle events: it is the interpreter of that record who might lack impartiality.

Thus, the ideal sources of evidence would be highly competent and impartial observers whose written observations are mutually supportive. Realizing such sources for Palo Alto research is, unfortunately, comparable to Diogenes' search for an honest man.

Historic Maps

Historical interpretations of Palo Alto greatly depend on period maps illustrating the placement of military units and their various tactical maneuvers. Of equal importance are the topographic data such documents provide. Unfortunately, for whatever reason, U.S. topographical engineers on Taylor's staff did not prepare official battle maps of Palo Alto and Resaca de la Palma as they did for all the rest of the major battles south of the Rio Grande. Several contemporary American battle maps of Palo Alto were produced by unknown or obscure individuals who may well have used superannuated, nonauthoritative battle accounts to produce their maps.[12]

A somewhat different problem exists vis-à-vis the battle map of Palo Alto prepared by an officer of the Mexican army. In this instance, two semi-official battle map sketches (figs. 4.3 and 4.4) were produced by General Mejía's adjutant, Captain Jean Louis Berlandier, a colorful character with an interesting background. Berlandier was born around 1805 in Fort-de-l'Ecluse, France, near the Swiss border. The son of poor parents, Berlandier traveled to Geneva and apprenticed himself to a pharmacist. He taught himself Latin and Greek, and his persistent drive brought him to the attention of the Swiss naturalist A. P. Candolle, who took him on as a student at the Academy of Geneva. Berlandier's first publication, a monograph on gooseberries, was published in 1826. He continued to publish and present papers before learned societies until Candolle decided to send his prize student to Mexico to collect plants. Candolle corresponded with Mexican politician Lucas Alamán and, through this connection, arranged to have Berlandier attached to the Mexican Boundary Commission, then operating along the Río Bravo (later named the Rio Grande).

By 1828 Berlandier had resided in Mexico for some time. During this period, he fell out of favor with his mentor, who charged his student with neglecting his responsibilities. It is likely, however, that both shared the blame, since the Swiss naturalist had little idea of the hardships involved in collecting and preserving plants within Mexico's northern provinces. Berlandier eventually became a physician in the town of Matamoros, although he continued to collect specimens. Here he probably met General Mariano Arista, who during the 1830s and early 1840s was the military commander of the area. Berlandier's travels very likely made him familiar with the region around Palo Alto, and he was thus useful to Arista during his campaign in this region. Berlandier, an educated and talented man, certainly meets our

fig. 4.3: Berlandier's first sketch of the battle. Courtesy Library of Congress

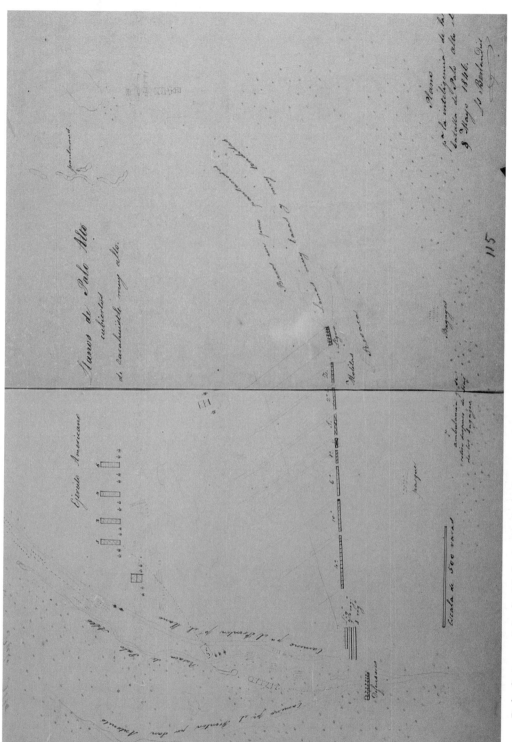

fig. 4.4. Berlandier's second sketch of the battle. Courtesy Library of Congress

criteria of closeness to the event and competence. Yet, as discussed below, Berlandier's battle map sketches are not without their own peculiar problems.

The Berlandier Sketches

Primary research conducted by National Park Service historians resulted in the discovery of Berlandier's two sketch plans of the battle, drawn shortly after the struggle took place. Presumably fig. 4.3 is Berlandier's first sketch attempt since its page number is 55; the second sketch, fig. 4.4, is paginated 78. Essential battle data noted on both sketches include the initial position of the Mexican army between the Point Isabel–Matamoros Road and the western terminus of the low rises to the east; orders of battle for both armies; the various maneuvers of both armies; the approximate spacing between the two opposing forces; the location of the road to Matamoros; and the general positions of resacas, ponds, low rises, and mesquite thickets.

Berlandier noted on his first sketch the presence of two or three marshy areas, centered more or less between the two opposing forces. He apparently then decided to group them together on the sketch as simply one large marsh. In addition to this marsh, he delineated another smaller marshy area, located directly in front of his placement of Captain Duncan's battery during

fig. 4.5. Published Mexican map of the battle of Palo Alto (map A) (from Alcaraz et al., Apuntes para la historia de la guerra entre México y los Estados Unidos, trans. and ed. Albert C. Ramsey). Courtesy National Park Service

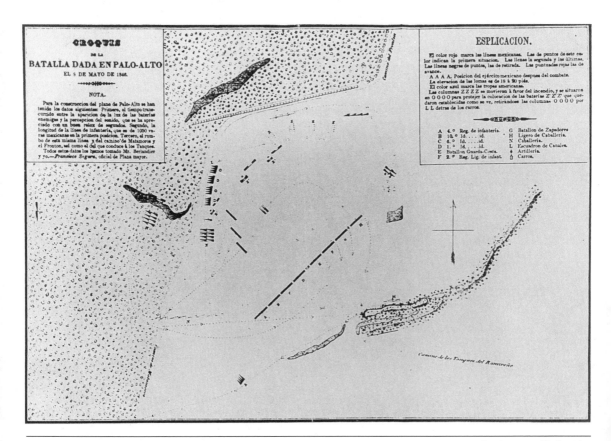

On the Prairie of Palo Alto

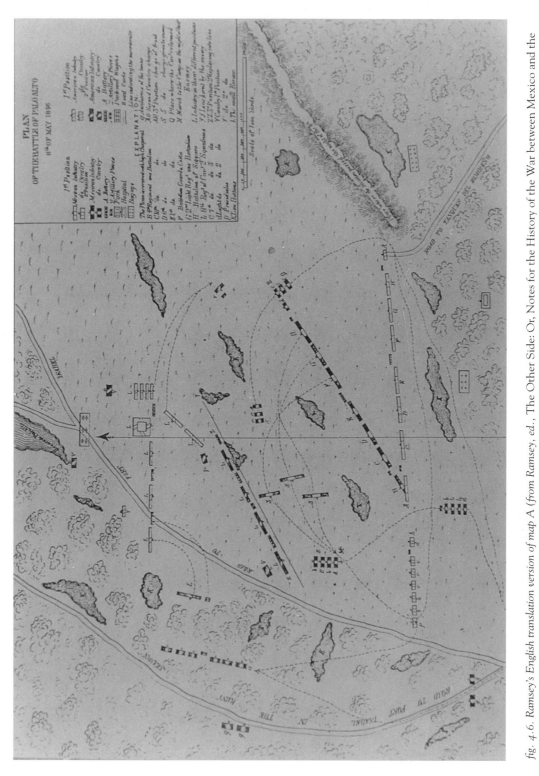

fig. 4.6. Ramsey's English translation version of map A (from Ramsey, ed., The Other Side: Or, Notes for the History of the War between Mexico and the United States). Courtesy National Park Service

the final phase of battle. Both of these marshes are present on the second sketch, but their delineations are faint, as if they had been erased.

The earliest-known published battle map of Palo Alto appeared in *Compaña contra los Americanos, mayo de 1846* (fig. 4.5), which was printed within a year after the battle. Hereafter, this battle map is referred to as map A. Berlandier produced map A, his sketches undoubtedly used to provide the information described on this map. Map A was a significant source of information for several historians who wrote about the battle. For example, it was published in a Mexican account of the war, then recently concluded; in an American translation of this book, edited by Albert C. Ramsey (fig. 4.6); and by J. W. Stewart in 1887 (fig. 4.7). Stewart, however, significantly revised Mexican troop movements during the second phase of battle.[13] Hereafter, Stewart's edited version of map A and Ramsey's map will be referred to as map B.

Unlike Berlandier's first sketch showing one large marsh between the two armies, Ramsey's map depicts five marshy bodies widely scattered between the two forces. These marshy areas are described as "low bottoms" on the map legend. Also, Mexican troop movements noted on map A reveal that these low bottoms hindered the advance of the Mexican right flank during the final phase of battle. Apparently, a marshy obstruction of some tactical significance existed between the two armies. This obstruction was perhaps one reason why significant troop movements at Palo Alto occurred only on the flanks. Any major assault toward the center of the opposing army might have literally bogged down, inviting destruction of the stalled attackers.

Map A and Berlandier's sketches show the relatively high ground that demarcated the southern and eastern boundaries of the battlefield. The second sketch presents the most detailed information regarding the high ground, described as *lomas muy baxas y muy tendidas*, or "hills that are very low and very spread out." This formation was probably the low levee (Area F) that still borders the present-day resaca. Fronting the northern sides of this probable levee were *baños un poco pantandos*, or "a few stagnant ponds."

Berlandier also identified a resaca at the southern end of the dune series, as well as *motitas*, or low rises, situated directly behind the extreme right flank of the Mexican army. Berlandier's sketches and map A show a cover of thick vegetation south of the Mexican position as well as the approximate locations of the Mexican field hospital and wagon park.

Curiously, on his second sketch, Berlandier lightly drew in a large detachment of Mexican cavalry and light infantry at the northern end of the above-described dunal formation—almost a mile away from the Mexican right flank. Neither his first sketch nor map A illustrated such a phantom and forlorn detachment, which raises some doubt as to its actual placement—

On the Prairie of Palo Alto

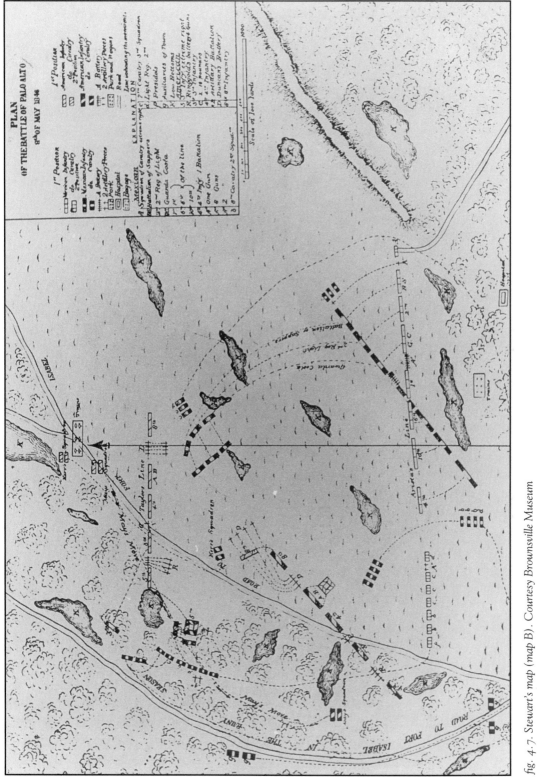

fig. 4-7. Stewart's map (map B). Courtesy Brownsville Museum

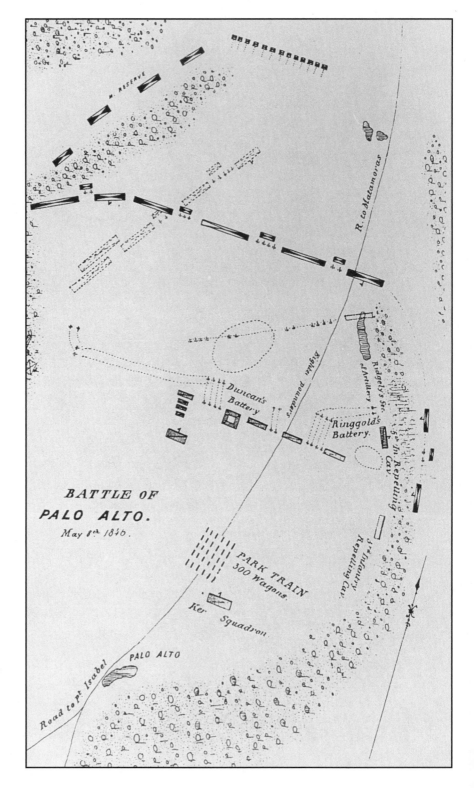

fig. 4.8. Captain Henry's map (map C) (from Henry, Campaign Sketches of the War with Mexico). Courtesy National Park Service

or possibly even its existence—on the battlefield. Yet this isolated Mexican detachment also appears on Captain Henry's map of Palo Alto, or map C (fig. 4.8), discussed below.

In his first sketch, Berlandier detailed the battle positions held by the various American battalions and batteries toward the end of the day. Yet map A illustrates these American positions in a different battle line configuration. Of some note is the fact that Berlandier's first sketch best approximates what the American officer Lieutenant Scarritt observed and sketched for the final phase of the American battle line.

Taken as a whole, Berlandier's two sketches, map A, and Ramsey's version of map A portray a Mexican army that protected its flanks with topographic obstacles and cavalry, a defense strategy that was not especially innovative but adhered to the basic principles of line battle tactics; conducted several aggressive cavalry and light infantry attacks on the enemy's flanks, including a final, thirty-five-degree counterclockwise swing of the entire Mexican line toward the Americans; and held the American army at bay. The latter was shown to have stayed at least 150 yards from the Mexican left flank. If this was true, it means the Mexican army did *not* retreat from its strategic position on the Matamoros road.

The American Maps

The following two American battle maps conflict with Berlandier's sketches on certain details: map C, presented by Captain W. S. Henry and first published in 1847; and map D (fig. 4.9), drawn by Lieutenant S. D. Dobbins of the 3rd Infantry and published in a pamphlet a few months after the battle of Palo Alto. The latter map was later reproduced, with minor changes, in three other histories of the war.[14]

Captain Henry joined Taylor's command some months after the battle of Palo Alto. In his book, *Campaign Sketches of the War with Mexico*, Henry stated that he depended on official dispatches and personal written accounts to describe events at which he was not present, like the battle of Palo Alto. Lieutenant Dobbins was an officer with the 3rd Infantry, the regiment at Palo Alto that moved to the American right/west flank in defense of the wagon train. From this position, Dobbins would probably not have been an actual observer of the fighting east of the Matamoros road. Thus, to produce his map, Dobbins would have had to obtain much of his information from official documents and from other knowledgeable battle participants.[15]

Instead of a Mexican advance pivoting on their 4th Line Regiment, both maps C and D show a *retreat* of the Mexican left flank while only their right flank advanced. These American maps, however, portray the Mexican *center* as their pivot point during the second phase of battle. Also, maps C and D show the final Mexican battle line as extending along an almost

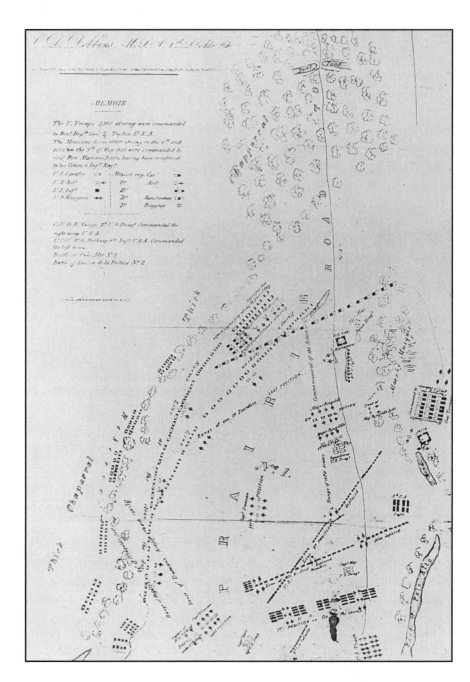

fig. 4.9. Lieutenant
Dobbins's map (map D)
(from Life and Public
Services of Gen. Z.
Taylor). Courtesy
National Park Service

north-south axis, which represents more than a seventy-five-degree shift
from its original position. In contrast, both Berlandier's sketches and map A
reveal a counterclockwise shift in the Mexican line of about thirty-five degrees. Maps C and D also portray the retreat of the Mexican left flank as an
abandonment of its initial position on the Matamoros Road; this is a significant contradiction of map A, Ramsey's map, and Berlandier's sketches.

Maps C and D, unlike the Mexican map and sketch versions, identify the presence of Mexican reserves behind a belt of thick vegetation (presumably the higher ground illustrated on both of Berlandier's sketches and on map A) and provide greater detail on the various positions taken by the American light field pieces. Interestingly, map C shows the Mexican *rancheros*, or mounted irregulars, on the Mexican right flank. In all written accounts, the Mexican irregular mounted unit, led by General Canales, was positioned well to the west of Palo Alto and did not participate in the battle.

Map C identifies a marshy area between the original battle lines, as do the Berlandier sketches and map A. However, map C shows the second U.S. battle line position partially within this marshy area, suggesting that the swampy terrain may not have been an especially significant tactical obstacle. Note that the orientation for map C has "south" at the top of the page and no scale.

Map C shows the American supply train about equidistant between Palo Alto Pond and the initial position of the U.S. army. This version also portrays the train in a defensive, compacted formation by the time the battle began. In contrast, Berlandier's sketches and map A depict the train as an unformed, essentially defenseless string of wagons. Ramsey's map, however, reveals the wagons in their postbattle defensive position: just south of Palo Alto Pond and in defensive formation.

Map D shows American and Mexican positions in three phases: their original battle lines; a later counterclockwise shift in linear positions; and a final phase, in which American eighteen-pounders faced almost due east. During the final phase, the Mexican line appears to extend along an almost north-south axis in front of a belt of chaparral on the eastern limits of the battlefield. Presumably, the chaparral corresponds to the "very low hills in a series" noted on Berlandier's sketches and on Ramsey's map. Map D also depicts the last location of Duncan's artillery pieces. At this point, the distance of his pieces from the Mexican line is two hundred yards. Finally, Stewart's map B shows the retreat of the Mexican army from its defensive position on the road. This suggests that map B was based largely on information gleaned from maps C and D.

Lieutenant Scarritt's Sketches

Lieutenant J. M. Scarritt was the officer in charge of the fortified wagon train the day after the battle. Four days later, Scarritt wrote a letter to Colonel J. G. Totten of the Topographic Engineers in which he described the battle. In the margins of his letter, Scarritt provided three sketches showing the battle phases and various unit maneuvers conducted by both armies (figs. 4.10, 4.11, 4.12). A fourth sketch depicts a plan view of the defensive earthworks for the wagon train (fig. 2.15). None of the sketches includes a

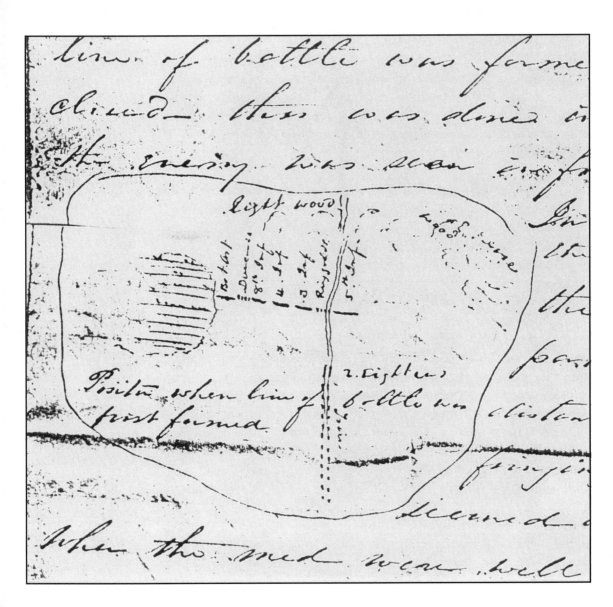

fig. 4.10. Lieutenant
Scarritt's first sketch, initial
order of battle of the U.S.
Army. Courtesy National
Archives

scale or north arrow. Figure 4.10 is Scarritt's first sketch, showing the "[U.S.] position when line of battle was first formed." According to the text of the letter, this line of battle was formed "when about 15 miles from Point Isabel and one mile this side of the position called Worth's Camp. . . . This was done in consequence of the report of our advance that the enemy was seen in front and appeared to be advancing. . . . The force advanced until it came to the water hole at Gen. Worth's camp. . . . From this position the enemy were distinctly seen distant about two miles."[16]

Besides labeling the various American units, Scarritt also noted the following features on the first sketch: a broad, marshy area to the immediate left (east) of the Artillery Battalion, the latter positioned on the extreme

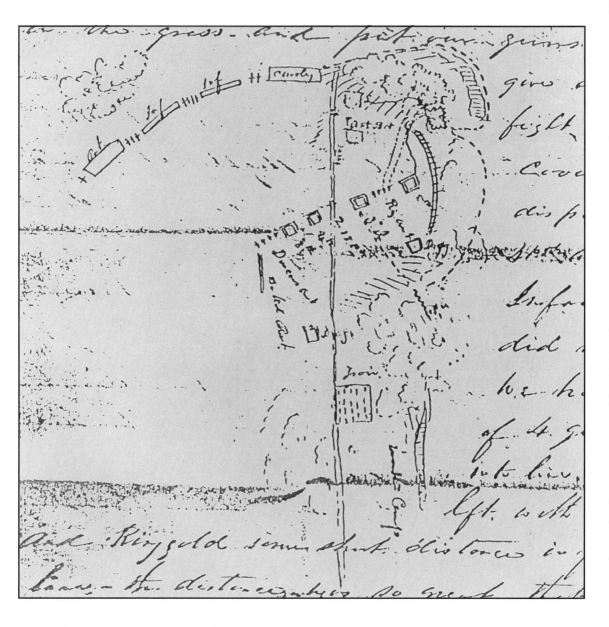

left flank of the American army; the road leading to Matamoros, as well as the wagon train strung out on the road and behind the army; and "light wood" and "wood resace [*sic*]" to the north and west of the army, respectively. Figure 4.11 is Scarritt's second sketch, which shows both armies' unit positions at the commencement of the battle. Although it has no attendant scale, the text of the letter states that the American right flank "came within one half mile of [the Mexican] left."[17] The sketch also shows the following: that the U.S. train had, by then, assumed its defensive formation at Worth's Camp, a clearing between the road and Palo Alto Pond that had been occupied by the Mexican army just a few days before the battle; the Mexican

fig. 4.11. Lieutenant Scarritt's second sketch, showing the first phase of the battle. Courtesy National Archives

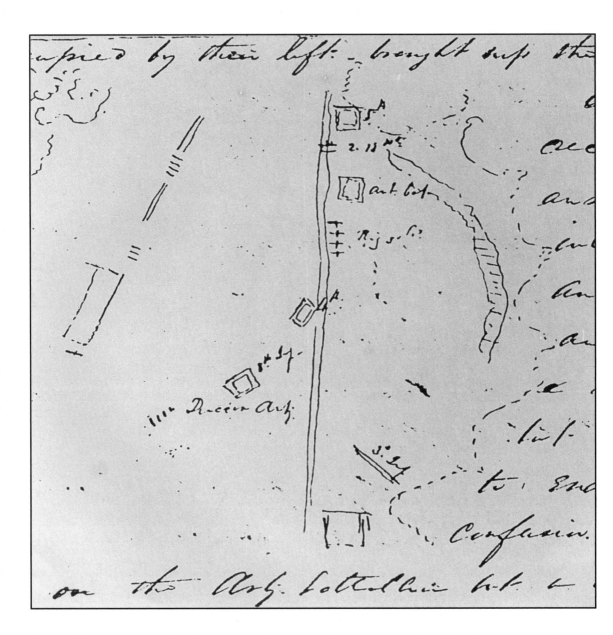

fig. 4.12. Lieutenant Scarritt's third sketch, the final phase of the battle. Note that the U.S. Fifth Infantry, the eighteen-pounder battery, the Artillery Battalion, and Major Ringgold's battery are shown aligned along the wagon road. Courtesy National Archives

battle line extending across the prairie in a broad arc formation, with a total of ten cannon interspersed between the Mexican units; and the Mexicans' initial flanking attempt, a maneuver thwarted by the American right flank.

Figure 4.12 is Scarritt's illustration of the final phase of battle. It reveals the right flank of the American army more or less aligned with the road and "advanced . . . to the place [once] occupied by [the Mexican] left";[18] Churchill's eighteen-pounders and Ringgold's six-pounders, both batteries aligned perpendicular to the road to face the final Mexican battle line now positioned to the east of the Americans; and Duncan's battery in its final position to enfilade the oncoming Mexican right flank.

On the Prairie of Palo Alto

In summary, Scarritt's sketches, Henry's map C, and Dobbins's map D agree that the Mexican line extended along an almost north-south axis during the last phase of battle, presumably as a defensive reaction to the final American position situated in part on the original Mexican battle line and in rough alignment with the Matamoros road; and, as a result of this new location, the Americans forced back the Mexican left flank. Thus, the illustrations of Scarritt, Henry, and Dobbins meet the criterion of mutual support. Stewart's map B seems to be a hybrid of earlier maps, which combined information obtained from both Mexican and American versions of the battle.

But what of Berlandier's sketches, map A, and Ramsey's version of map A? These maps show that the Mexicans accomplished an orderly, almost clockwork-precise pivot *advance* toward the Americans, an interpretation sharply at odds with the contemporary American maps and sketches described above. Yet we consider Berlandier to be part of the select group of competent eyewitnesses. In fact, some of his sketch notations, such as the marshy area between the battle lines, orders of battle, and various other maneuvers of both armies, receive mutual support from certain American map versions. At this juncture, one must consider the possibly overriding criterion of *impartiality* (or lack thereof). Perhaps it was politically wise for Berlandier to illustrate an aggressive Mexican advance of their entire battle line during the final phase of battle instead of a collapse of their right flank, which is what happened. Justin Smith's earlier-quoted assertion regarding official American Army equivocations during the war would certainly have applied to officers of the Mexican Army as well.

It is also possible that Berlandier's tactical observations were simply the result of an honest mistake; he, too, must have experienced some obfuscation and confusion amidst the fog of battle. One can never ascertain the underlying psychological motives that directed the observations of any of the participants, including Berlandier, nor do we desire to impugn the integrity or competence of those who can no longer defend their actions. However, one can evaluate and compare the ultimately subjective qualities of battle maps and eyewitness accounts with aerial photographs, conjoined with the patterned material results of the battle. The above hypotheses are not offered as "truth" or "fact." They are simply possible explanations, open to continued testing and revision upon the discovery of new facts. Additional investigation is required from both written documents and the physical evidence obtained from the battlefield. The latter is within the purview of archaeology, which is discussed in the following chapter.

5

The Physical Evidence
of the Battle

In 1992, the project director for the Palo Alto Archaeology Project developed a research design that described his proposed survey plans of Palo Alto Battlefield National Historic Site (NHS). The goal of the 1992 survey was to locate both American and Mexican battle lines, thereby facilitating land purchases toward the development of the park. The research design used recommendations made thirteen years earlier by Texas A&M University archaeologists after their completion of a reconnaissance-level survey of the battlefield. Only twenty battle-related artifacts were recovered as a result of this survey. These artifacts, although few in number, presented a broad pattern of distribution that apparently confirmed what was then known of the battle: the American army had occupied the northern end of the battlefield; the Mexican army, the southern end.

Survey Methodology

The 1992 fieldwork consisted of two phases: orientation and inventory. Orientation began with the placement of a grid of fifty data-control points spaced 1,600 feet apart. The grid was oriented relative to Farm-Market Road 1847, which is the western boundary of the proposed park. These control points were then paneled to facilitate the taking of aerial photographs of the entire 3,400-acre park area. The grid also provided data reference points during the inventory phase. The resultant aerial photos were then used to plan survey strategies. Orientation also included teaching volunteers about the history of the battle, artifact identification, and the various methods of archaeological recordation.

The typical dimension of a survey unit was 500 by 100 feet. In some instances, boundaries of these units were contiguous. For example, Search Area (SA) 308 consisted of six contiguous units, which resulted in a surveyed strip of land measuring 100 feet wide and 3,000 feet long. All of the units were placed in a manner that would ensure a sample of each of the three sectors of the battlefield where battle documents indicated troop deployments had occurred. These sectors included the presumed scene of action where both American and Mexican cavalry units attempted flanking maneuvers on the western side of the core battle area; the initial combat position for the Mexican left flank and preattack staging area for the Mexican cavalry units mentioned above; and the area north and east of Arista Hill, where the Mexican army tried to outflank the American army toward the end of the battle.

The survey also encompassed reconnaissance-level metal detector sweeps. This survey method involved one or more metal detector operators walking over informally or topographically defined areas, such as pastures and resaca levees. Use of this approach could quickly determine the presence or absence of significant clusters of artifacts within a given sector of the battlefield. This in turn provided guidance on the placement of survey units and indicated areas for future battlefield investigation. Such reconnaissance-level sweeps, representing an estimated 5 percent of a given target area, could be completed by one or two surveyors in a few hours. Using this approach, an artifact cluster, if such existed within the target area, would initially appear as a widely spaced distribution of a few artifacts. This reconnaissance method, however, has its limitations: it cannot provide data allowing for relative comparisons of artifact cluster densities, nor can it furnish a comprehensive list of artifact type(s) within a given cluster. Such data would only be gained via the intensive metal detector sweeps of formally defined sample units.

If necessary, the sample units were first mowed, thereby permitting the use of metal detectors (fig. 5.1). The inventory of the survey units included three sequential operations: survey, recovery, and recording. The survey crew consisted of volunteer metal detector operators working under the direction of National Park Service archaeologists. The crew members, aligned at about ten-foot intervals, then proceeded in line down the long axis of each survey unit (fig. 5.2). When metal was detected, its location was marked by a pinflag. A follow-up recovery crew then excavated the artifacts. Approximately 2 percent of the artifacts were found on the surface, with the remainder usually lying at a depth no greater than six inches below the surface. Screening for artifacts was not required since a metal detector was used to pinpoint the artifact during the recovery process. Once exposed, an artifact was then left within its excavation hole for later recordation and collection by the field curation crew (fig. 5.3). The final step was the precise mapping of each artifact location, using an electronic transit set over one of several data grid points.

Using the above field methods, the 1992 field season yielded 426 battle-related artifacts from fifty-four acres. The southern half of the battlefield

fig. 5.1. Metal detector survey of Search Area 308, after mowing its covering of cordgrass, looking north. Courtesy National Park Service

fig. 5.2. Metal detector survey in a vegetated field, looking west. The mesquite forest on the horizon demarcates Resaca de Palo Alto. Courtesy National Park Service

produced most of these artifacts, including Mexican musket fragments, uniform buttons, and personal items, intermixed with American shrapnel and canister shot. American and Mexican canister shot, cannonballs, and shrapnel were the dominant artifact types found within the central portion of the battlefield, which separated the two armies. The northern part of the battlefield, however, contained few American-related artifacts. We believe this paucity of artifacts is largely explainable by the relatively few American casualties, compared to what the Mexican army had suffered. Also, land leveling within this portion of the battlefield would have destroyed any artifact patterning that might have existed here at one time.

    On the Prairie of Palo Alto

It was gratifying to recover so many artifacts. However, there was a total absence of artifacts in the vicinity where the wagon road forked. According to Mexican battle maps, the fork in the road anchored the Mexican left flank: at least some items should have been found here. Concentrations of Mexican-related artifacts, including badges of the Mexican 4th and 10th Line Regiments, were found within several of the survey units. These collections, however, were situated more than one thousand feet east of where Mexican battle maps placed these two regiments. We began to suspect that Berlandier's portrayal of certain events might not be entirely correct.

The researching of documents continued up to the beginning of the 1993 field season. This research located several battle maps that had been created by American officers. Essentially, the American battle maps challenged Berlandier's interpretation as to the final phase of the battle. Nevertheless, it was still possible that physical remains of the

fig. 5.3. In situ Mexican cannonball. Courtesy National Park Service

Mexican 4th would be found somewhere between the wagon road and the artifact concentrations discussed above. The 1993 survey consequently included sampling this sector of the battlefield. Virtually nothing was found there until our survey units extended up to where Mexican artifacts had been discovered in 1992. We then focused on this area of the battlefield, hoping that its artifact patterning might yet provide a clue as to the orientation of the Mexican battle line. Fortunately, it did.

One survey unit, measuring 700 by 500 feet, contained Mexican-related items deposited in a linear pattern some 500 feet long. Significantly, this linear patterning extended along an almost north-south axis. Here was conclusive evidence that the American version of battle events more closely approximated what had actually happened. Additional sampling of the Mexican battle line produced numbered badges representing each of the four Mexican line regiments. These diagnostic artifacts were all found within a three-acre area, suggesting that the Mexican battle line had become compacted during the course of the battle.

Mexican-related artifacts were also found farther to the north and east of this concentration but widely dispersed. We interpreted this dispersion as a reflection of the rapid movement of Mexican troops over a broad area and within a short time span. In fact, this type of movement had occurred during the final flanking attempt by the Mexican right flank. Both American and Mexican accounts agree that this final maneuver was a costly failure. Mexican cavalry and light infantry, crushed by an enfilade of American canister and round shot, collapsed onto the Mexican line regiments to cause great confusion and, ultimately, a disordered retreat of the entire Mexican army. Essentially, the archaeological evidence challenges the validity of the Mexican battle maps concerning the final phase of the battle.

The 1993 field season recovered 525 artifacts from the battle. These artifacts derived from 15 acres that had been intensively surveyed and from 210 acres that had been subjected to reconnaissance-level sweeps. Thus, both field seasons combined yielded 951 battle-related artifacts from a 17 percent sample of the estimated 1,200-acre core battle area, or an 8 percent sample of the proposed 3,400-acre park.

Artifacts Description and Analysis

The 1992 and 1993 archaeological investigations of Palo Alto Battlefield NHS resulted in the recordation of 1,061 artifacts: 951 from the battle, 109 from postbattle discard, and one artifact—a stone projectile point—dating from aboriginal times. Battle-related artifacts are grouped and described under the following categories: artillery and firearm ammunition, which includes the subcategories lead balls, spherical case and shell, shot, and cannonballs; firearm parts; edged weapons; buckles; buttons; uniform brass and accoutrements; personal possessions; farriery and horse tack; hardware; and human bone. The section on artillery and firearm ammunition receives special emphasis because of the critical role artillery played during the battle as well as being a reflection of the great abundance of artillery-related ammunition recovered from the battlefield. English measurements of caliber, inch, and pound are used to describe all American ammunition since this was the measurement applied by English-speaking ordnance manufacturers of the period. For the sake of comparison, English measurements are used for Mexican ordnance as well.

Artillery and Firearm Ammunition

LEAD BALLS

Relatively few examples of the millions of lead balls manufactured for American regulation muzzleloaders exist today. Here and there specimens can be seen in museums and collections and are occasionally still held in storage at government arsenals. Very little work has been done, however, toward compiling information on these once-important objects. Fortunately, most of the major varieties of lead balls have quite distinctive physical characteristics that can provide some useful information on their manufacture and use on the battlefield.

During the American Revolution, the only small arms that approached standardization were those of the French and British Armies. These were various models that dated back, in many cases, to the French and Indian wars. Specifically, the .75-caliber British "Brown Bess" used a ball supposedly standardized at caliber 0.688, weighing 1.14 ounces. From examination of seventy musket balls found at British campsites, it appears that Brown Bess musket balls of Revolutionary War vintage varied from 0.687 to 0.700 caliber, with an average caliber of 0.694 and a weight of 1.14 ounces. The difference between the diameter of the musket ball and that of the barrel is termed *windage*. It was standard practice to make the ball caliber .050 smaller than the caliber of the musket barrel for which it was intended. This clearance was needed to take care of three inaccuracies: molded musket balls were not perfectly round and varied in diameter from mold to mold; the barrels were not uniform in the inside diameter or *bore*, either from one end to the other in a single musket or from musket to musket; and the inside of the barrel accumulated fouling from firing with greatest buildup just forward of the chamber. Beginning with the model 1795 musket, its design based on the French model 1763, regulation U.S. muskets had barrel bores of .69 caliber. Because of crude manufacturing techniques of the period the dimension was not precise, but good barrels generally ranged from .690 to .705 caliber, or a spread of .015. Up through the U.S.-Mexican War, the standard American musket ball was .640 caliber, with an approximate weight of .9 ounce.[1]

An 1840 American tactics manual states that buck-and-ball cartridges were standard by this time and apparently continued in use for at least another thirty-five years. Such a load was considered of great value for guard duty, Indian fighting, and operations in brushy country. Buckshot was .310 caliber and weighed 0.09 ounce. The ball for Hall rifle models, first introduced in 1819, was .525 caliber and weighed .5 ounce. These were the regulation calibers and weights used by the U.S. Army during the U.S.-Mexican War. Shortly after the war, however, a slightly larger, 0.65-caliber, ball weighing .94 ounce was adopted. The improved "swage" process of manufacturing musket balls by compression instead of by casting allowed for the decrease in windage, thus producing a slightly better seal of the expanding gases and a concomitant increase in projectile velocity.[2]

American arsenals and armories have traditionally been ammunition procurement centers. In 1812, the commissary-general of ordnance wrote the secretary of war that "in the making of musket cartridges, children of 12 or 14 years of age can be employed as usefully or even more so than men." Army regulations published in 1814 provided for three laboratories or arsenals, stating, "At these workshops shall be . . . prepared all kinds of ammunition for garrison and field service." In 1825, the Saint Louis Arsenal was authorized to supply troops on the western frontier. By 1841, the Frankford Arsenal in Pennsylvania was the principal manufacturer of military gunpowder. The latter arsenal eventually became the center of government ammunition development and manufacture. The American soldier did not manufacture his own musket balls at the time of the U.S.-Mexican War. Instead, these essential items were provided to him ready-made and in paper cartridge form.[3]

In 1846, presumably because of the U.S.-Mexican War, lead ball compression or swage machines were set up at the Frankford Arsenal. Such machines could manufacture balls at the rate of forty thousand per worker per day. Similar machines were eventually installed for the Saint Louis and Watervliet Arsenals. Balls made by this method were "more uniform in size and weight, they were smoother, more solid, and give more accurate results, than cast balls."[4] In this method of manufacture, lead bars were fed into a machine that cut off a part sufficient for one ball. This portion was then transferred into a die that formed the ball. The balls were trimmed by hand with a knife, then passed through a cylinder-gauge for proper sizing. Buckshot was either made in a similar manner or else purchased from private shot works.[5]

In lieu of the compression method, the arsenal manufacture of musket balls involved first melting lead in kettles, then pouring the molten lead into gang molds, and finally removing the cooled lead balls from the molds and trimming their *sprue* (the knob of waste metal formed in the mold hole). Regulations required first castings to be thrown back into the kettle since they were imperfectly round owing to the cold mold. Periodic measurements of ball samples and a thorough cleaning of lead buildup in the molds was necessary. Molds that yielded imperfect balls were either repaired or destroyed. Balls were smoothed by rolling in a barrel for several minutes, then run through a gauge-screen. Balls not falling through the screen were recast.[6]

As previously noted, musket balls used as shrapnel filling for spherical case rounds were also manufactured at the arsenals. The 1849 U.S. Ordnance Manual specified 38 lead balls in a six-pounder case shot; an eighteen-pounder spherical case round contained 120. Other than having a different delivery system, lead ball shrapnel should have the same caliber and weight and should have passed the same quality controls as those shot from a musket. At present, very little is known or documented about the Mexican method of supplying troops with ordnance, including musket balls. Yet it is known that Mexicans did not maintain as efficient an arsenal system as did the Americans in 1846. Machinery in Mexico's only quality small-arms arsenal had been in disrepair since at least 1834.[7] Thus, Mexican lead balls were conceivably made using molds by ad hoc details of soldiers and by relatively small, civilian-operated "cottage industries." Under such a system of dispersed manufacture, quality control may have been difficult to maintain. Significant numbers of delivered musket balls would have been out-of-round because of cold, misaligned, or poorly maintained molds; others would have had their sprue only partially removed; and there would have been a lack of overall smoothness because of the elimination of the final manufacturing stages of barrel rolling and gauge-screening.

One thing to consider regarding the manufacture of Mexican musket balls was the substandard grade of metal parts and correspondingly low tolerances characteristic of muskets used by many of their soldiers. Most Mexican troopers were armed with the British India Pattern musket, produced in vast quantities during the Napoleonic wars. To increase its rate of production during those wars, even less-exacting tolerances for viewing and proof (that is, bore caliber and chamber pressure, respectively) were allowed for this stop-gap musket model. In 1833, the British had 440,000 of these then-obsolete weapons, of which 264,000 were condemned as unserviceable. Britain sold muskets to Mexico primarily, if not exclusively, from its stockpile of condemned muskets during the 1830s.

This suggests that an unknown number of Mexican soldiers at Palo Alto would have been armed with muskets having barrel bores of substandard calibers. Thus, a soldier who had a musket with a bore that was too small (for example, .71 caliber instead of the standard .75 caliber) would have found it extremely difficult, if not impossible, to ram a standard-issue musket ball down the tight barrel. In fact, at several investigated Civil War battlefield sites, archaeological evidence indicates that soldiers on the battle line discarded about 5 percent of their Minié balls because they were incorrectly manufactured: either poorly cast or having calibers greater than what was required for their firearm.[8]

The Mexican armed forces used a poor-quality gunpowder that contained too much charcoal and not enough potassium nitrate; this meant that the soldiers needed unusually large powder charges for their muskets to obtain sufficient ball velocity. Such charges would have produced an unusually thick buildup of residue in the barrel. Barrel bores may have become so fouled after several firings that it became extremely difficult to ram down the musket ball, necessitating a thorough cleaning of the barrel to make it serviceable again. In contrast, American gunpowder was of superior quality. Actual tests of U.S. gunpowder used during this war demonstrated that it was in fact considerably better than what was specified in government contracts.[9]

Lead Balls from Palo Alto Battlefield

For the purpose of this report, the generic term *lead ball* is adopted instead of *musket ball* since items in this category were used as ball shrapnel for U.S.

spherical case shot and as Mexican canister or bag shot as well as projectiles for rifles, pistols, and muskets. A total of 359 lead balls were recovered. Of all artifact categories this is numerically the largest, representing approximately 40 percent of the total collected artifacts. Lead ball analyses involved monitoring calibers and weights as well as the presence or absence of sprues, mold seams, gouges, cuts, and cloth imprints; and detecting out-of-round characteristics resulting from impact (that is, faceting and flattening). Lead balls were also checked for powder flash, an attribute occasionally present if the object was used as a firearm projectile. Monitoring these characteristics was expected to identify nationality of origin, method of manufacture, and manner of use on the battlefield. Together with its exact provenience data, the resulting information could identify and delineate specific events both within battle lines and in areas of intense combat between the lines.

Caliber measurement provided identification of the national origin of a lead ball. If it measured between .630 and .670 calibers inclusive, it was identified as American (fig. 5.4g); if between .671 and .750+ calibers, it was Mexican (fig. 5.4e–f). Lead balls of around .620 caliber were ammunition for a British-made Baker rifle used by the Mexican army (fig. 5.4c). One lead ball of .525 caliber was classified as ammunition for the American Hall rifle (fig. 5.4h). Many lead balls were out-of-round; therefore, their caliber could not be monitored. In such instances, weight was used to assign national origin. The median weight for caliber-measured American lead balls was .86 ounce; for Mexican lead balls, 1.16 ounces. Some error in assigning national origin may have occurred since muskets of both armies could conceivably use lead balls ranging between .67 and .68 calibers or between .88 and .95 ounces. Fortunately, only 8 of the total 359 lead balls fall within these caliber and weight ranges. Thus, we assume most of the lead balls are correctly assigned, an assumption supported by patterned groupings based on these assignments.

The point provenience of all 359 lead balls indicates significant distributions of this category of artifact within various search areas (SAs). The greatest concentrations of lead balls lie within the Mexican battle line, and attribute analysis reveals that these balls are both Mexican and American in origin. In addition, pattern analysis of lead balls shows that they are found both in relatively dense clusterings and as more or less isolated occurrences. Overall artifact patterning within SA 3 was especially informative. Virtually all of the artifacts discovered within this search area fall within two major clusters, designated Clusters A and B (map 8). These clusters are approximately one hundred fifty feet apart, with very few artifacts found between them. Possibly the clusters reflect General Arista's order toward the end of the battle that his soldiers advance "twenty varas," about sixty feet, so they should not be near "the first to fall, hearing their moans."[10]

Cluster A has a pronounced linear distribution that extends about five hundred feet along an almost north-south axis. This cluster consisted pri-

On the Prairie of Palo Alto

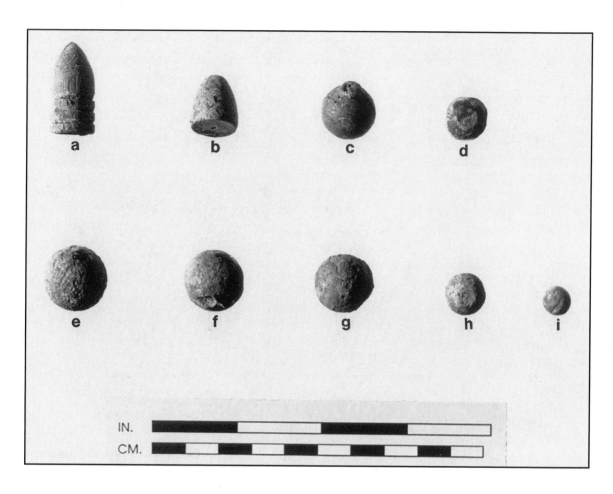

marily of American lead shrapnel balls as well as a few U.S. spherical case shot fragments and iron balls from six-pounder canister rounds. Several Mexican items—a sword hilt, belt stud, brass cap, gun part, and button—were also present within this cluster. An explanation for such a remarkable linearity is that it reflects the final position of the Mexican battle line. The ground detonation of an American spherical case round may have propelled a cone or fan of shrapnel an indeterminate distance, with a line of human targets acting as a break to the forward motion of the shrapnel. Some shrapnel would have flown harmlessly over the heads of the intended victims and landed hundreds of feet away; some would have been carried off the battle line inside the wounded and killed; and some shrapnel would have hit the human targets but not penetrate them. This latter shrapnel would have fallen to the ground, thereby creating a linear pattern. We believe the widespread scattering of unfired Mexican lead balls within the cluster was the result of cartridge loss, part of the general deposition of Mexican equipment stemming from such an artillery attack.

The term *artifact concentration* was applied to an artifact patterning wherein three or more relics were found within a four-square-foot area. Four

fig. 5.4. Lead balls. a: .58-caliber Minié ball, Civil War era; b: .54-caliber conoidal bullet; c: .62-caliber ball for a Baker rifle (note sprue); d: .50-caliber ball shrapnel from a model 1897 cannon round (note facets); e: .75-caliber musket ball for an India Pattern musket; f: ball with teeth marks; g: .69-caliber ball shrapnel from a U.S. spherical case round; h: .52-caliber ball for a Hall rifle and carbine; i: .30-caliber buckshot.

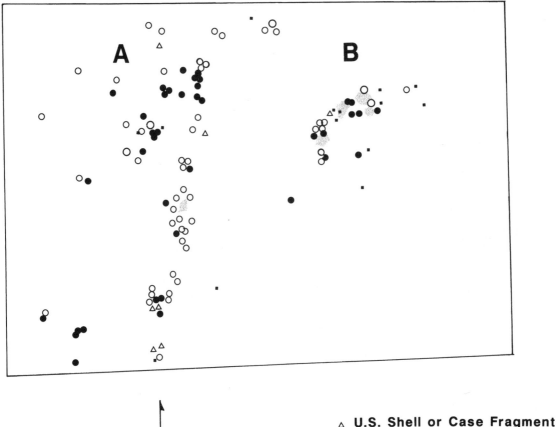

△ **U.S. Shell or Case Fragment**
○ **U.S. Canister Shot**
○ **U.S. Lead Ball (Shrapnel)**
● **Mexican Lead Ball**
 Mexican Lead Ball Cluster
. **Mexican Equipage**

map 8. Search Area 3, artifact distribution. Pattern A exhibits a linear patterning of the Mexican battle line. Pattern B suggests the position of at least four Mexican soldiers, as revealed by the four clusters of Mexican lead balls. Produced by Charles M. Haecker

relatively compact concentrations of lead balls were discovered within Cluster B. All of these collections consisted entirely of Mexican lead balls; furthermore, all of them are round (that is, they do not exhibit the flattened surfaces caused by having been fired). We believe such nondeformed lead balls represent unfired and lost paper cartridges, with each concentration probably representing spillage from a single cartridge box. If this is correct, then Cluster B illustrates the position of at least four Mexican soldiers, each one of whom left the contents of his cartridge box on the battlefield. Also present within Cluster B was a more widespread scattering of both Mexican and American lead balls, the latter probably derived from an eighteen-pounder spherical case round. A shell fragment of such an ordnance type was within a collection of American lead balls along with some Mexican accoutrements such as buttons, a buckle, and a metal fitting of a Paget carbine. It is conceivable, then, that the scattered remnants of this American explosive spherical case were the undoing of these four Mexican soldiers.

Thirteen of the total forty-seven Mexican lead balls from SA 3 are faceted, perhaps a result of hitting against other lead balls inside a soldier's ammunition pouch. If so, then at least some Mexican soldiers were issued not paper cartridges that protected the lead balls from battering but, instead, balls in loose form. This would also mean that their gunpowder was issued in loose form as well and stored in a powder horn or flask. It is less likely the faceting of Mexican lead balls is the result of their striking each other upon detonation of a spherical case round since, at Palo Alto, the Mexican army did not use this type of explosive ordnance. Two Mexican musket balls, however, are flattened from impact. This raises a question: from where were they fired? If Mexican soldiers fired toward the Americans, one would expect their musket balls to have landed somewhere *away* from their own line, not where they stood. One explanation is that some muskets were unintentionally fired when both weapons and soldiers were hit by American shrapnel, which caused some balls to be deposited nearby. It is also possible that these lead balls had been fired from an earlier Mexican battle line position. In effect, SA 3 may indicate a mixing of two artifact depositions resulting from battle events at different times.

SA 2, also located within the area of the Mexican battle line, yielded 173 Mexican and 29 American lead balls (map 9). Most of these American lead balls are faceted as is expected for lead shrapnel. Yet, unlike Area A within SA 3, the American balls here fell in a pattern that is far more dispersed. It has been noted that a nineteenth-century spherical case round exploding in midair results in a spread of shrapnel 250 yards in diameter when the round is fired at point-blank range.[11] We believe the widespread patternings of American lead balls within SA 2 resulted from overhead ordnance detonation. SA 2 also contained Mexican lead balls, and most of these were found within three concentrations. Once again, these collections probably resulted from spilling cartridges and loose lead balls out of their respective cartridge boxes or pouches.

Finally, the following lead balls found within this area of the Mexican battle line are worthy of special note: a .30-caliber ball (fig. 5.4*i*); a .52-caliber ball (fig. 5.4*h*); and a .68-caliber ball with teeth marks (fig. 5.4*f*). The .30-caliber ball is appropriate for buckshot in buck-and-ball rounds. However, American infantrymen presumably never came within effective musket range; that is, a hundred yards of the Mexican center. It is possible that this projectile came from a small-caliber, nonregulation pocket pistol. The .52-caliber ball is suitable for Hall rifles and carbines used by American skirmishers and dragoons, respectively.

Unlike all the other lead balls, the one with teeth marks possesses a certain poignancy. Bitten and chewed musket balls are occasionally found

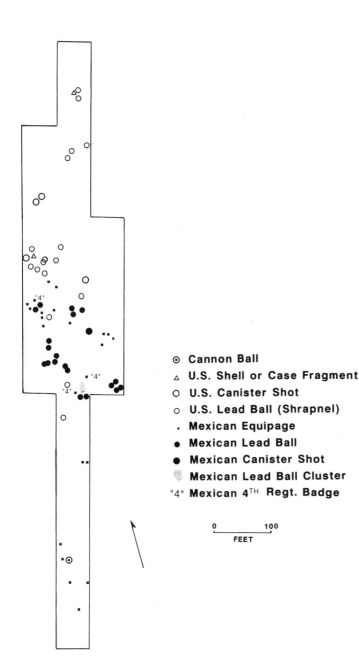

at military encampments of the period. Several such bullets were found on a Revolutionary War site; their discoverer theorized that they "were given to culprits in the army that they might chew them to ease their agony while being flogged."[12] This particular lead ball, of Mexican caliber and found on the Mexican battle line, may well have been bitten by a wounded Mexican soldier while he received some medical attention, or chewed on to relieve tension.

Lead balls were also found in the following battlefield areas: near the western edge of the resaca (Area B); the region bisected by the Point Isabel–Matamoros Road (Area C); alongside the marshy area between the two battle lines (Area D); and the eastern half of the battlefield, bounded to the south and east by chaparral-covered low rises and dunal ridges (Areas E and F, respectively).

Only five American and four Mexican lead balls were recovered from Area A, the portion of the battlefield largely, if not exclusively, occupied by American troops. The paucity of lead balls from this area was understandable because the American army incurred only a few casualties from Mexican firearms.

⊙ **Cannon Ball**
△ **U.S. Shell or Case Fragment**
○ **U.S. Canister Shot**
○ **U.S. Lead Ball (Shrapnel)**
. **Mexican Equipage**
● **Mexican Lead Ball**
⬤ **Mexican Canister Shot**
▨ **Mexican Lead Ball Cluster**
"4" **Mexican 4**TH **Regt. Badge**

0 ——— 100
FEET

map 9. Search Area 2, artifact distribution. Produced by Charles M. Haecker

Also, since the Americans occupied this area, evidence of spherical case rounds should be minimal. All of the lead balls found within SA I are American in origin. Their widely dispersed scattering stemmed from a spherical case round that prematurely exploded in midair—probably uncomfortably close to those who fired it. Several fragments of spherical case were also recovered from these search areas. The presence of Mexican lead balls within Area A may have been the consequence of their failed attacks on the American right flank. One of the Mexican balls recovered from Area A is .62

caliber, meaning that it was fired or dropped by a Mexican rifleman. One .70-caliber Mexican lead ball was found on the west side of the resaca. Its caliber and location suggest that it was dropped during General Torrejón's flanking attacks in this vicinity of the battlefield.

Twelve American and seven Mexican lead balls were found along the southeastern perimeter of Area D. American lead balls derived from Area D are all flattened or faceted, resulting either from musket fire or from spherical case rounds directed at the Mexicans. In contrast, all but one of the Mexican lead balls are unfired, implying that Mexican soldiers occupied this position at least for awhile during the battle.

The 1992 and 1993 surveys recovered twenty-three lead balls from the sixteen search areas that sampled the eastern half of the battlefield and north of Arista Hill. Of these, twenty are identified as Mexican, three as American. In addition, relic hunters in 1990 collected at least another sixty-five lead balls from this area. The exact proveniences, calibers, and other physical attributes were not monitored by the collectors; therefore, these artifacts cannot be incorporated into the 1992–93 lead ball data.

Other lead balls reclaimed from this portion of the battlefield include a .54-caliber conoidal, flat-based bullet (fig. 5.4b); a .58-caliber Minié-type bullet (fig. 5.4a); and two .62-caliber balls (fig. 5.4c). The .54-caliber conoidal bullet may have been deposited during the battle because, in 1842, the American Army began experimenting with variously shaped firearm projectiles. Ballistics tests conducted during the early 1840s included the firing of .54-caliber conoidal bullets from model 1841 percussion rifles. Although American regulars were not armed with this rifle, some Texas volunteers present at Palo Alto may have owned them and consequently may also have fired conoidal bullets. The .58-caliber Minié-type bullet was adopted by the American Army in 1855; therefore, this kind of bullet definitely postdates Palo Alto. Mexican sharpshooters were armed with the British Baker rifle, which used a .62-caliber ball.[13]

Finally, a comparative analysis of the attributes of lead balls shows a general trend concerning the various methods and standards for their manufacture. The following data are pertinent to lead balls intended for standard musket types used by the Mexican and U.S. armies. It does not include data from the six lead balls having .30, .52, .54, and .62 calibers. The eight lead balls with .67 and .68 calibers are also excluded from the ensuing discussion because they could have been fired by either Mexican or American muskets.

Of the 70 lead balls definitely identified as American, 2 have both sprue and mold seams and 3 have mold seams only; therefore, 7 percent of American balls are out-of-round. Of the 281 lead balls identified as Mexican, 70 are out-of-round owing to sprues and mold seams. Two additional balls are inadequately cast, possibly because of a cold mold. Thus, around 25 percent of all Mexican lead balls are out-of-round.

Sixty-three American lead balls are flattened or faceted, which meant their calibers could not be determined by measuring diameters. Fortunately, the caliber of a whole lead ball can also be determined by weight. It was found that all American lead balls are within the narrow range of .64–.65 calibers, a variance of only .01 caliber. In contrast, Mexican lead balls fall within the relatively broader range of .680–.770 calibers, or .09 calibers in variance. This range for Mexican balls is far greater than noted for British-made lead balls of the Revolutionary War era, which had a range of .687–.700 calibers.

Of the total 281 Mexican lead balls, 23, or 8 percent, have calibers greater than .730. These balls would be difficult to ram down a correctly bored and cleaned barrel of a .75-caliber India Pattern musket, and they could not be used at all if the musket barrel itself had an incorrect bore of less than .750 caliber. As previously noted, approximately 5 percent of the Minié balls recorded from several Civil War battlefields were discarded on the battle line because they were misshapen or too large for the barrel. Apparently, the discard rate of Mexican musket balls at Palo Alto was considerably greater than the American rate of lead ball discard during both the U.S.-Mexican War and American Civil War. Finally, significant numbers of out-of-round lead balls also support the stated hypothesis regarding Mexican methods of manufacturing lead balls, including their corresponding lack of quality control.

The above data suggest that most American musket balls varied little in caliber. Interestingly, several measurable lead balls are .65 caliber; this diameter was supposedly not adopted until *after* the U.S.-Mexican War. The presence of American-molded lead balls also suggests usage of spherical case ordnance produced before the changeover by arsenals to the swage method. Since Palo Alto was the first battle of the U.S.-Mexican War, very likely some ordnance manufactured before the 1846 changeover would have been in General Taylor's supply wagons. But at least one spherical case round contained swage-manufactured lead balls: the American lead balls found in linear distribution within SA 209 all lack mold seams and sprues, and all are .64 caliber.

SPHERICAL CASE AND SHELL

A total of forty-three iron fragments of shell and spherical case were recovered (fig. 5.5j–k). Analysis of this artifact type included a thickness measurement since its thickness determines both the type of explosive round and its poundage. The following information is from a U.S. artillery treatise of the period:

fig. 5.5. Cannon shot, shell, and spherical case fragments. a, b: Mexican copper shot, 1.05- and 1.0- inch diameters; c: Mexican lead shot, .95-inch diameter; d, e: Mexican copper shot, 1.3- and 1.25- inch diameters; f: copper shot joined by sprue; g: U.S. iron grapeshot, from an eighteen-pounder coastal/siege gun; h: U.S. iron shot, from a six-pounder gun; i: U.S. iron shot, from a twelve-pounder field howitzer; j: eighteen-pounder spherical case shell fragment (note portion of the fuse hole); k: twelve-pounder shell fragment. Courtesy National Park Service

18-pounder spherical case round wall thickness	.47–.52 inches
18-pounder shell wall thickness	.86–.94″
12-pounder spherical case round wall thickness	.42–.47″
12-pounder shell wall thickness	.66–.74″
6-pounder spherical case round wall thickness	.33–.38″

A six-pounder shell was not manufactured.[14]

The arc of an explosive ordnance fragment was also monitored to best determine poundage. This was necessary because of the thickness overlap for twelve- and eighteen-pounder spherical case rounds of .47 inch as well as some postdetonation expansion of the fragment owing to ground salt absorption. The arc of a fragment was compared with arcs of three circles having diameters of 5.17, 4.52, and 3.58 inches. These are the diameters of eighteen-, twelve-, and six-pounders, respectively.[15]

Using the above parameters, ordnance fragments were identified as follows:

18-pounder spherical case	*10 examples*
18-pounder shell	*5"*
12-pounder spherical case	*1"*
12-pounder shell	*9"*
6-pounder spherical case	*1"*
Indeterminate	*17"*

The presence of twelve-pounder ordnance is especially significant since some sources state that Duncan's and Ringgold's batteries consisted exclusively of six-pounders, a conclusion presumably based on reliable documents. One such document may have been Lieutenant Scarritt's letter dated May 12, 1846. The lieutenant wrote that, for defense of the wagon train the day after battle, "the 12-pdrs. on truck carriages were got out of the waggons [*sic*] and placed at my disposal." Also, in his history of the battle, Cadmus Wilcox noted that "the trains of Taylor remained during the 9th parked as on the 8th; with them were four guns, the two 18-pounders that had rendered such good service the previous day, *and the two 12-pounders that had not been used* [emphasis added]."[16]

The above information would suggest that twelve-pounders played no active role during the battle. In a letter he wrote shortly after the battle, however, Ulysses S. Grant said the Americans, in addition to the eighteen-pounders, had "three or four 12-pounder howitzers and four or five 6-pounder howitzers." Incidentally, Grant was mistaken in calling the six-pounders "howitzers"—they were guns. Assuming Grant's memory was correct, his statement indicates that one or two others existed besides the two twelve-pounders Scarritt used the day after the battle. Possibly Scarritt was referring to twelve-pounder siege guns, a much heavier class of cannon than the lighter, mobile, twelve-pounder field howitzers. Siege guns normally traveled with an army's supply train and required draft oxen or mules with civilian drivers.[17] Presumably, the two twelve-pounder siege guns were already with the train and thus used in its defense, along with the two eighteen-pounder siege or coastal guns employed on the battlefield the previous day.

Inside Cullum Hall at West Point there are fifteen cannon barrels used during the U.S.-Mexican War. On the first floor and mounted onto the wall are seven barrels from Mexican artillery pieces captured at Resaca de la Palma. On the stairway wall leading to the second floor are cannon barrels belonging to the batteries of Captain James Duncan and Major Samuel Ringgold. All four of Ringgold's cannon barrels are six-pounder guns. Duncan's cannon barrels consist of three six-pounder guns and one twelve-pounder howitzer. This latter fieldpiece may have been added to Duncan's battery later in the war; however, the archaeological evidence suggests that at least one twelve-pounder field howitzer was used at Palo Alto.

Fragments of American spherical case and common shell were recovered from the following areas of the battlefield: Area C, the Point Isabel–Matamoros Road segment; west of Area B, the resaca; the major portion of the Mexican battle line, situated east of Area C up to the low rises or *motitas* of Area E; and the eastern portion of the battlefield, north of Area E.

Four fragments were found in Area B: one twelve-pounder spherical case, two eighteen-pounder spherical case, and one unidentified fragment. Since this area of the battlefield was occupied largely by American forces, it is logical that only a few American ordnance fragments were found here. A possible explanation for their presence is premature midair detonation, a not-unusual event with nineteenth-century explosive ordnance.

Three fragments were discovered west of Area B: two are identified as eighteen-pounder spherical case, and one is from a six-pounder spherical case. These fragments may reflect the American defensive use of cannon to foil Mexican flanking attempts in this area of the battlefield. During this action, the left flank of the American 5th Infantry was protected by two six-pounders firing canister rounds.[18] The presence of eighteen-pounder spherical case fragments suggests that these heavier cannon contributed to flank defense as well.

Sampling of the Mexican battle line produced twenty-two eighteen-pounder spherical case and shell fragments as well as fragments of twelve-pounder shell. These ordnance fragments were found both widely scattered and in relative concentrations. A wide dispersal of ordnance fragments suggests a midair detonation of explosive ordnance, while concentrations probably resulted from ground detonation. In one instance, fragments of a spherical case round were found intermixed with a concentration of American lead ball shrapnel. It is possible that this particular round became partly buried on impact and then exploded, which scattered shrapnel of its unburied portion only.

All four ordnance fragments found in the eastern portion of the battlefield are of widely scattered pieces of twelve-pounder shell. These remnants probably reflect Duncan's successful defense of the American left flank toward the end of the battle.

CANISTER SHOT

Following the terminology of nineteenth-century ordnance manuals, *shot* refers to the metal ball shrapnel that filled canister. Shot should not be confused with grapeshot; the latter term was reserved by artillerymen of the period to describe larger-diameter iron balls fired in clusters of nine. From an archaeological standpoint it is fortunate that the Americans used only iron shot, the Mexicans only copper and—to a lesser degree—lead shot. We can, therefore, determine the approximate locations of the opposing battle lines. A total of 343 iron, copper, and lead shot was recorded, with over 90 percent of these found within two concentrations: one 700–1,000 feet east of the resaca, or Area B; and the other within the eastern portion of the marsh, Area D. Canister was most effective when used against infantry and cavalry in massed formations and when the target was no greater than 1,200 feet from the cannon that fired it. Thus, it is likely the cannon(s) responsible for the two canister shot concentrations were no more than 1,200 feet away from them.

Search Area 1, located about seven hundred feet east of the resaca, clearly reveals that this portion of the battlefield was, at least for awhile, "no man's land"—the contested area that separates battle lines. Map 10 illustrates the distribution of American iron and Mexican copper shot within this search area. Note the majority of iron shot clusters toward its southern end, with the Mexican copper shot clustering toward its northern end. A mixing of both shot types occurs within the central portion of the surveyed strip. This patterning corroborates our belief that toward the end of the battle, the American battle line was more or less aligned with the wagon road where it bordered the resaca. Similarly, the Mexican battle line extended from a position east of their initial position on the wagon road and up to the marshy area between the two armies.

American iron shot. The following canister shot diameters in inches are from Gibbon's *Manual*, which provides the basis for identifying American shot:

6-pounder shot, large gauge,	1.17 inches (fig. 5.5h)
6-pounder shot, small gauge,	1.14"
12-pounder shot, large gauge,	1.08"
12-pounder shot, small gauge,	1.05" (fig. 5.5i)
18-pounder grapeshot, large gauge,	2.46"
18-pounder grapeshot, small gauge,	2.36" (fig. 5.5g)[19]

map 10. Search Area 1, artifact distribution. Produced by Charles M. Haecker

△ **U.S. Shell or Case Fragment**
○ **U.S. Canister Shot**
○ **U.S. Lead Ball (Shrapnel)**
▣ **U.S. Equipage**
● **Mexican Canister Shot**
✳ **Human Bone**

0   400
FEET

A total of 167 iron shot and 3 grapeshot were recovered. Of these, 86 have either all or a sufficient amount of original surface, permitting accurate gauging. The remaining 84 shot are now missing entire original surfaces because of exfoliation (the flaking away of the initial surface due to oxidation and other natural causes). An exfoliated shot, therefore, was assigned to the proximate, larger-sized gauge category. For example, an exfoliated shot having a diameter of 1.37 inches after conservation was identified as an eighteen-pounder shot, or within the range of 1.67–1.70 inches. Of course, since actual amounts of exfoliation cannot be quantified, an error in gauge determinations may have occurred. Fortunately, when exfoliated shot are factored out, there is no significant change in the percentages distribution of shot gauges.

By far the greatest concentration of iron shot lay within the eastern half of Area D. A metal detector sweep of this area resulted in a noncollection recording of 110 shot, representing 65 percent of all noted iron shot. Because of relatively moist conditions within Area D, over 70 percent of these shot are moderately to severely exfoliated. In fact, several are little more than iron crumbs that could not be measured, only provenienced and then reburied. Diameters of measurable shot indicate that these all came from canister fired from six-pounder guns. The overall shot patterning suggests that Mexican troops massed to the south and east of the marsh barrier, providing a tempting target for American field batteries. In contrast, 10 of the 13 shot found on the Mexican battle line south of Area D came from eighteen-pounder canister. This pattern apparently reflects an American artillery tactic practiced during the battle: using the greater range of the eighteen-pounders to destroy Mexican troop concentrations beyond the normal reach of American light batteries. These batteries, in turn, converged on front-line Mexican troops to the immediate south and east of Area D.

A dense concentration of six-pounder and twelve-pounder canister shot, including two eighteen-pounder grapeshot, is found just within the extreme southwestern limits of Area D. Given its location on the battlefield, this collection might be the result of American cannon fire directed at the Mexican cavalry, when the latter attempted to destroy the eighteen-pounders toward the end of the battle. If this is correct, the cavalry units probably originated from a sector of the battlefield just south of Area D. The eighteen-pounder battery had to reposition itself in order to repel this attack, and the maneuver was accomplished just in time to discharge rounds of canister, case, and common shell at the oncoming cavalry. In his account of the battle, Taylor mentioned only the Artillery Battalion in support of the eighteen-pounder battery during this attack.[20] The archaeological evidence suggests that at least one of the two horse-artillery batteries likewise provided fire support.

Nine shot and one grapeshot were recovered from the eastern portion of the battlefield. All but two of the ten ball shrapnel are the eighteen-pounder size, and most were north of Arista Hill. The presence of American ordnance here, together with Mexican-related accoutrements such as uniform brass and gun parts, provides additional data for the hypothesis that eighteen-pounders aimed for Mexican troops beyond the effective range of American light artillery. Negative information supporting this hypothesis is the comparative scarcity of American ordnance from light artillery within this area of the battlefield. The American *Ordnance Manual* of 1841 required that grapeshot be used only by naval, seacoast, and siege guns.[21] Thus, one should not expect to find American grapeshot on battlefields after 1841. Yet three iron balls of 2.10-, 2.15-, and 2.20-inch diameters were recovered from the battlefield (fig. 5.5g). Using the method of assigning ordnance described above, these three artifacts are small-gauge eighteen-pounder grapeshot. An explanation for their presence is that eighteen-pounders, in their dual capacity as seacoast artillery, would have had stands of grapeshot in their munitions chests and supply wagons. Perhaps the gunners of the eighteen-pounders resorted to using grapeshot when their supply of spherical case, shell, and canister was running low.

Mexican cuprous and lead shot. A total of fifty-nine cuprous and four lead shot were recovered (for examples, fig. 5.5a–f). Cuprous shot is Mexican in origin since several American accounts note the use of copper in the manufacture of Mexican cannonballs and shot.[22] Mexican shot served the same function as its American counterpart. Besides the cylindrical tin canisters used by the Americans, Mexican shot could also be packaged in cloth bags or rawhide, the latter dried to shrink tightly around the contents.

The Mexican shot has ten groupings, which are based on diameters. The average diameters, in inches, are as follows: .85, .90, .95, 1.0, 1.05, 1.12, 1.25, 1.30, 1.35, and 1.45. The greatest concentration of copper shot lay primarily to the east and northeast of Area D, and all but the shot with a diameter of 1.45 inches are represented in this area. The presence of Mexican shot here may reflect their response to Captain May's dragoon attack on the Mexican left flank. May described this action as follows: "About half an hour before sunset I received orders to proceed to the enemy's left flank, and drive in his cavalry. In execution of these orders . . . the enemy concentrated the fire from his batteries upon us, killing six of my horses and wounding five men. I succeeded in gaining a position on the enemy's left, with a view of charging his cavalry, but found him in such a force as to render ineffectual a charge from my small command."[23]

Colonel McIntosh, commander of the 5th Infantry, described May's attack toward the end of the battle. "While in this position [held by the 5th Infantry] a cannon shot struck into a squadron of Dragoons *moving through a marsh in front of us* [emphasis added], killing some horses and disabling one man."[24]

Toward the end of the battle, the American 5th Infantry faced an easterly direction roughly parallel with the wagon road. Taking this new position into account, the above-mentioned marshy area was probably Area D. The movement of May's squadron through Area D implies that the Mexican left flank by this time was anchored on the southeastern side of this natural feature (see fig. 4.2 and map 7). It is, therefore, plausible that Mexican copper shot found west and north of Area D is the cannon shot described above by Colonel McIntosh.

The physical characteristics of Mexican shot suggest at least four different manufacturing sources for this type of ordnance. Some of the balls are almost egg-shaped and pitted, with the sprues partially intact; some are faceted due to filing off of the sprue and other out-of-round imperfections; mold seams are strongly evident on others; and a few are almost perfectly spherical with a relatively smooth surface. One of the shot indicates its method of manufacture (fig. 5.5f): two shot joined by a channel sprue, a result of nonseparation of the shot from a gang mold.

The four lead shot found on the Mexican battle line are presumed to be Mexican for the following three reasons: (1) only iron is mentioned for the manufacture of American shot; (2) the diameters of the lead shot (1.0–1.03 inches) correspond to one of the diameter ranges employed for Mexican copper shot; and (3) the lead shot display other distinguishing characteristics similar to those found on some of the recovered copper shot, such as a slight nonalignment of ball hemispheres owing to a shot mold in need of repair (fig. 5.5c).

SOLID SHOT (CANNONBALLS)

Although "solid shot" is the correct nineteenth-century technical term for this ordnance, the more popular term of "cannonball" will be used in the following discussion to avoid confusing it with the much smaller ball shot used in canister rounds. Twelve iron and four cuprous cannonballs were recorded during the 1992 and 1993 surveys (fig. 5.6). Most of the iron balls have deteriorated because of oxidation and absorption of ground salts, which causes exfoliation. As a result, their present weights and diameters do not correspond closely to those of their earlier days, when in pristine condition. The cuprous cannonballs, however, have not deteriorated; as a result, their present measurements are presumably the same as on the day of the battle.

When in pristine condition, cannonballs for American six-pounders measured 3.58 inches in diameter and weighed 6.16 pounds. Twelve-pounder field howitzer cannonballs were 4.52 inches in diameter and weighed 12.30 pounds.[25] None of the recovered cannonballs apparently was fired by a twelve-pounder howitzer. However, measurements of two of the iron balls come close to what is appropriate for American six-pounders. One of these can-

fig. 5.6. Cannonballs. a: U.S. six-pounder iron cannonball; b: Mexican four-pounder copper cannonball; c: alloyed metal nose fuse from a model 1897, 75-mm cannon round. Courtesy National Park Service

nonballs derives from an area where we suspect the Mexican field hospital was located.

As previously noted, seven Mexican cannon tubes captured at Resaca de la Palma are on display at West Point. Five of these tubes have a bore of 3.50 inches, and one has a bore of 4.25 inches. The bore of the seventh tube cannot be measured since it is imbedded in the wall. Brass cannon tubes made during this period have a difference in windage averaging around .20 inch.[26] The cuprous cannonballs described above, therefore, were likely fired from those tubes with a bore diameter of 3.50 inches. In light of this, one of the recovered iron cannonballs was possibly fired from the same Mexican cannon tube at West Point with a bore of 4.25 inches. Unfortunately, because of exfoliation, the original caliber of most of the iron balls cannot be identified with assurance. All four of the copper cannonballs and nine of the iron ones, however, fell within a seventeen-acre area of the battlefield. A concentration of American accoutrements—a cartridge belt plate, a canteen spout, a spur strap buckle, and a spur sideplate—also occurred within this acreage. We suspect the American accoutrements reveal one of the positions held by Captain Duncan's battery, and the surrounding cannonballs reflect unsuccessful attempts by Mexican artillery to destroy this battery.

Firearm Parts

All of the firearm parts are Mexican-related (fig. 5.7), and they derive from either the Mexican battle line or the contested "no man's land" between

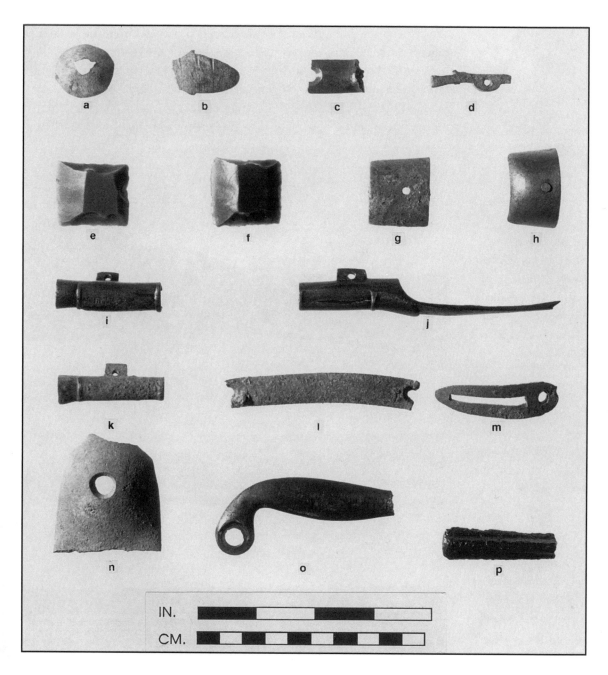

fig. 5.7. Firearm parts. a: Pistol butt cap; b: trigger guard upper finial; c: trigger guard; d: firearm spring attachment (?); e, f: gunflints; g: musket nosecap; h: carbine nosecap; i: second ramrod pipe; j: terminal ramrod pipe; k: second ramrod pipe; l: trigger guard tail, fragment; m: trigger plate; n: butt plate, fragment; o: sideplate; p: bayonet blade, fragment. Courtesy National Park Service

the battle lines. The presence of Mexican firearm parts from the latter area reflects the Mexicans' various attempts to outflank the American battle line. Most of the firearm parts are brass fittings of the India Pattern muskets (figs. 5.8–13). Recovered India Pattern musket parts include nosecaps (two), sideplates (two), a trigger guard, a trigger guard tail, a trigger plate, ramrod pipes (three), and a butt plate. The provenience of the butt plate is espe-

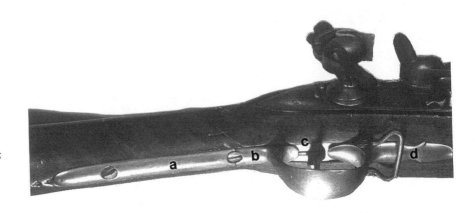

fig. 5.8. Trigger guard parts of an India Pattern musket. a: Trigger guard tail; b: trigger guard and guard tail; c: trigger plate; d: upper finial. Courtesy Samuel Nesmith

fig. 5.9. Detail of a Paget carbine. Note the nosecap and ramrod pipe. Courtesy Samuel Nesmith

fig. 5.10. Underside of the barrel stock of an India Pattern musket. Note the second pipe. Courtesy Samuel Nesmith

fig. 5.11. Terminal ramrod pipe, India Pattern musket. Courtesy Samuel Nesmith

On the Prairie of Palo Alto

fig. 5.12. Butt plate, India Pattern musket. Courtesy Samuel Nesmith

fig. 5.13. Sideplate, India Pattern musket. Courtesy Samuel Nesmith

cially significant: it was found just north of the marsh that separated the two armies.

This location suggests that elements of the Mexican right flank, in their final attempt to overrun the American wagon train, actually came well within a thousand feet of reaching their goal. The recovery of brass fittings for India Pattern muskets also supports the written record, which states that Mexico purchased great quantities of this musket model for its regular soldiers. Two other firearm parts came from the Mexican battle line: the nosecap for a Paget carbine, one of the types of firearms used by Mexican mounted troops; and a crudely made pistol butt cap. This latter artifact, fashioned from a piece of sheet copper that was then hammered into a crude cupule, reflects the type of repair work that can be found on well-used Mexican firearms of the period.

Two gunflints were found intermixed with a concentration of Mexican accoutrements and musket parts. The size of both gunflints meets the specifications required of a British carbine; however, this size can also be used on a musket. The morphological characteristics of both artifacts indicate that they derive from the flint beds of Brandon, England, an area extensively developed for gunflints since around 1790. The physical characteristics of the two artifacts are typical of the blade technology found in gunflints made in England since around 1775; that is, possessing two transverse flake scars, a beveled edge, a trimmed-off heel, cleanly broken sides, and characteristic demicones of percussion. The working edges of neither gunflint exhibits scars of use and wear due to firing; however, one of the gunflints has a series of flake scars along its other two sides, suggesting its use as a strike-a-light.[27]

Edged Weapons

A fragment of an American model 1816 bayonet was found roughly four hundred feet to the northwest of Area D. The provenience of the bayonet fragment provides a clue as to the approximate location of the American battle line. It should be noted that the model number of the bayonet does not necessarily mean it was used on a model 1816 musket, since between 1801 and 1840 U.S. bayonets did not change appreciably.[28]

A brass sword hilt, minus its knuckle guard, was found on the Mexican battle line. The hilt is hollow, with a graze indentation along one side that is presumably the result of shrapnel. The hilt derives from a short, curved infantry sword called a *briquet*, typically carried by infantrymen in the Mexi-

fig. 5.14. Briquet *sword hilt, recovered from the Mexican battle line. Courtesy National Park Service*

fig. 5.15. Intact briquet *sword hilt. Courtesy Samuel Nesmith*

can Army (figs. 5.14–15). The hilt was made in Mexico, its design based on that used by the French during the Napoleonic wars.

Buckles

Eighteen buckles were recovered and grouped into twelve types (fig. 5.16). These designations were based on buckle form and, where positive identification was possible, by function. There is a close relationship between form and function for the large American harness buckles. The smaller Mexican buckles were probably used on such personal gear as cartridge boxes, knapsacks, and belts (fig. 5.16a–c, Type 1); the larger buckles, as harnesses. All of the Mexican buckles are made of brass; of the four American buckles, two are ferrous (fig. 5.16m, Type 10) and two are brass (fig. 5.16n–o, Types 11, 12).

TYPE 1 (FIG. 5.16a–c)

Five examples: these are single-frame buckles made of cast-and-filed brass. None of the Type 1 buckle frames has tangs, which suggests the tangs were made of iron that rusted away. All Type 1 buckles derive from the Mexican battle line. The dimensions are comparable to clothing-related buckles found at the Spanish colonial site of Quiburi in Arizona. Type 1 buckles were recovered in the excavated Mexican mass burial at Resaca de la Palma. Within this burial site, two Type 1 buckles were found on the left pelvic region of the skeletal remains of a Mexican soldier. This position on the pelvis suggests that Type 1 buckles were used on Mexican cartridge boxes. Buckles of *fig. 5.16. Buckles. a–c: Type 1; d: Type 2; e, f: Type 3; g: Type 4; h: Type 5; i: Type 6; j: Type 7; k: Type 8; l: Type 9; m: Type 10; n: Type 11; o: Type 12. Courtesy National Park Service*

TYPE 2 (FIG. 5.16d)

One example: this is a single-frame buckle with brass tang. It is made of cast-and-filed brass. Type 2 was recovered from the Mexican battle line. An iron stirrup buckle from the late eighteenth or early nineteenth century of the same size and shape, but decorated, came from a site dating from the Spanish colonial and Mexican period in New Mexico.[30]

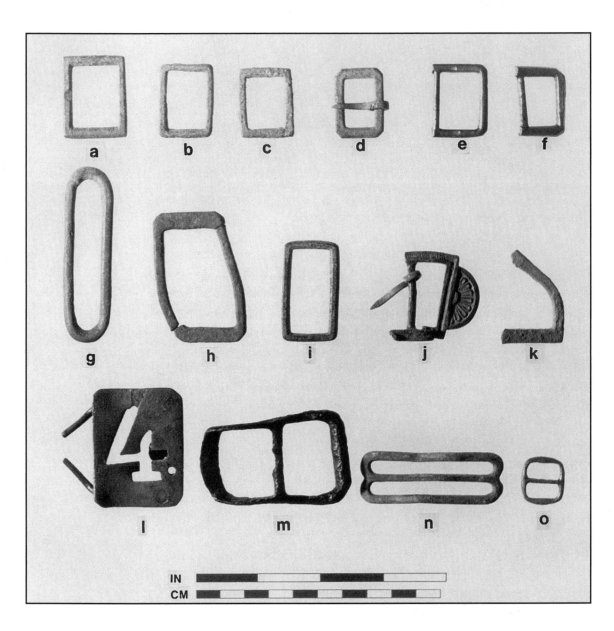

TYPE 3 (FIG. 5.16e–f)

Two examples: these are fragments of brass double-frame buckles. One of the buckles was found between the battle lines, about two hundred fifty feet west of Area D; the other Type 3 buckle was recovered from the Mexican battle line. If whole, the Type 3 buckles would be approximately 1.5–2.0 inches long. This would be comparable in size and design to a harness buckle found at Fort Stanwix, a mid-eighteenth-century British fort near Rome, New York. A similar double-frame buckle was recovered from the Spanish colonial site of Quibiri and identified as a bridle buckle.[31]

TYPE 4 (FIG 5.16 g)

Two examples: single-frame buckles made of cast brass, round in cross section. Both buckles are plain, elongated ovals, each without a tang. The specific function of Type 4 buckles is not known with certainty but their large size, relative to Type 1 buckles, suggests that they were used on Mexican horse tack. It is also possible that Type 4 buckles were used to suspend some of the equipment carried by Mexican soldiers.

TYPE 5 (FIG. 5.16h)

One example: single-frame buckle of cast brass, broken into two parts. It is rectangular, with rounded corners. There is no tang. Type 5 was found between the two battle lines, approximately two hundred fifty feet west of Area D. Based on its large size relative to Type 1, this buckle was probably used on Mexican horse tack. Its provenience suggests that this artifact was deposited during the Mexican cavalry attack on the American eighteen-pounders and Artillery Battalion.

TYPE 6 (FIG. 5.16i)

One example: this is a single-frame buckle made of cast-and-filed brass. Based on its large size compared to Type 1 buckles, Type 6 was probably used on Mexican horse tack. Its provenience between the battle lines (approximately) implies that this artifact was lost during the final Mexican cavalry attack.

TYPE 7 (FIG. 5.16j)

One example: this is a double-frame buckle of cast brass with a molded decoration. A tang is present. One of the frame bars is missing, and one side is broken apart and bent. A molded half-rosette decoration is on the belt-support flange, and stamped line rouletting is on the frames. Type 7 was found on the Mexican battle line. It is identified as an officer's sword belt buckle, which would have been a personal purchase and not regulation issue.

TYPE 8 (FIG. 5.16*k*)

One example (fragment): this is a single-frame buckle made of cast brass. Type 8 was probably five-sided when whole with one flat side, the opposite side coming to a point. Found on the Mexican battle line, its function is not known.

TYPE 9 (FIG. 5.16*l*)

One example: this is a Mexican waist-belt buckle made of cast brass. It is a rectangular plate with the number four cut out, in the same manufacturing style used on the cartridge-box belt plates of the Mexican 4th Regiment. Both American and Mexican enlisted men wore suspenders and not waist belts; therefore, we believe this buckle was used by either an officer or a rifleman (the latter required a belt to carry his extra equipment). Type 9 was found on the Mexican battle line.

TYPE 10 (FIG. 5.16*m*)

Two examples: these are double-frame buckles made of cast iron or steel. These buckles have one round end in cross section, the other end spatulate for accommodating the belt. Type 10 is identified as an American harness buckle of early- to mid-nineteenth-century design. Both buckles were found just south of Palo Alto Pond, thereby providing locational clues that aid in the delineation of the American battle line.

TYPE 11 (FIG. 5.16*n*)

One example: this is a double-frame buckle made of cast brass. The patination is tan, unlike the distinctive dark green of Mexican brass. There is no tang. The frames are ovoid and are joined by a center post. Type 11 was discovered about two hundred feet west of Palo Alto Pond, probably just behind the American battle line. An object of similar size and design, found at eighteenth-century Fort Stanwix near present-day Rome, New York, is described as a buckle for a sword baldric.[32] Type 11 is identified as an American officer's sword buckle.

TYPE 12 (FIG. 5.16*o*)

One example: this is a double-frame buckle made of cast brass. It is plain and rectangular with rounded corners. The tang is absent, but there is tang wear on both the center post and one of the frame sides, the latter slightly flattened to accommodate the strap end. Type 12 was found where we believe Captain Duncan's battery was located during the final phase of the battle. This type is identified as an American spur strap buckle.

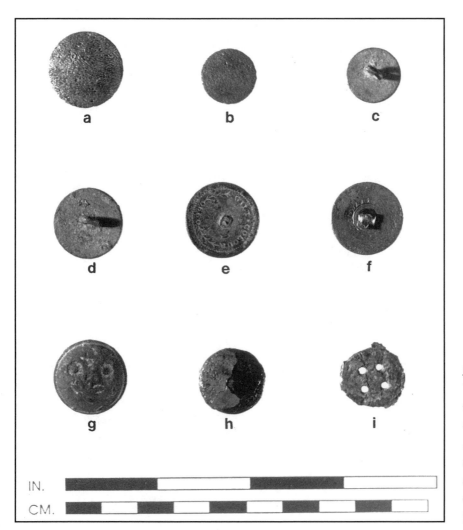

fig. 5.17. Buttons. a, b: Type 1, obverse; c: Type 1, reverse; d: Type 2, reverse; e: Type 3, reverse; f: Type 4, reverse; g: Type 5, obverse; h: Type 6, obverse; i: Type 7. Courtesy National Park Service

Buttons

All but one of the twenty-eight buttons recovered during the 1992 and 1993 surveys are from the Mexican battle line. Of the twenty-seven Mexican buttons, twenty-one are the standard-issue variety used on the Mexican enlisted men's uniforms. This button type is identified in this report as Type 1 (fig. 5.17). Types 2–6 are also found on the Mexican battle line. These buttons probably came from officers' uniforms since they either have superior physical characteristics when compared to Type 1 or have backmarks indicating gilding. Type 7 is the only example of an American button found within the approximate location of the U.S. battle line. None of the recovered buttons supplies information regarding nationality—such as the Mexican eagle and serpent or the American eagle—or specifies branch of service or regimental numbers.

TYPE 1 (FIG. 5.17a–c)

Twenty-one examples: this is a two-piece button consisting of a stamped brass disc that is flat or slightly concave and a brass, unfooted wire eye soldered onto the disc back. None of the Type 1 buttons has stamped designs or military insignias on the front, nor are there backmarks. Most of the recovered buttons have eyes separated from the discs, apparently due to the fragility of the solder. There are two sizes of this type: a button with a .75–.83-inch diameter (fig. 5.17a), used on the uniform coat front; and a button with a .59-inch diameter (fig. 5.17b–c), used on the uniform cuffs. Both Type 1 sizes have also been found in the Mexican siege trenches that fronted the Alamo and in the Alamo plaza. At Palo Alto, all of the Type 1 buttons were found along the Mexican battle line. The method used to make Type 1 buttons corresponds somewhat to a type of British-American button that was popular between 1725 and 1812. Unlike the Mexican Type 1 button, however, its British-American counterpart is made of cast metal, often has a stamped design or insignia on the disc face, and sometimes has a backmark.[33]

TYPE 2 (FIG. 5.17d)

One example: this is a two-piece button made of a cast-brass disc with a soldered brass eye shank. The shank is probably footed but hidden by the solder, which is more liberally used than on the Type 1 button. Type 2 has a plain face with no backmark. Its disc diameter indicates that it is a coat button. Type 2 is apparently an officer's button since it is better made, and therefore more expensive, than Type 1. Type 2 closely corresponds to British-American buttons produced after 1812.[34]

TYPE 3 (FIG. 5.17e)

One example: this is a two-piece button made of cast brass. The eye is missing. There is a backmark, stamped "Gilt Colour" in English Gothic letters, and "0660," the lettering and numbers separated by two wreath sprigs, also appears. The gilding is no longer present. Its disc diameter reveals this to be a coat button. Type 3 is probably an officer's button, presumably imported from England as indicated by the spelling of "colour." Dismounted Mexican officers wore gold-plated buttons; mounted officers' buttons were silver plated.[35]

TYPE 4 (FIG. 5.17f)

One example: this is a two-piece button made of cast brass. The disc was shaped and thinned by being turned on a lathe, which gives it a "spun" back. The shank is missing, and the face is plain. Judging by the disc diameter, this is a coat button. A stamped backmark, "Standard Co.," is in English Gothic lettering. The English backmark reveals that Type 4 is an import.

TYPE 5 (FIG. 5.17g)

One example: this is a two-piece button made of cast brass. The button is domed, the shank well soldered and probably footed. A cast or etched design on the face consists of two sunflowers with stems and leaves and rouletting around the face. There is no backmark. Type 5 is a nonmilitary button of a style popular in Europe from approximately 1830 to the 1860s. Although meant for civilian use, such buttons have occasionally been found in Texas at Mexican and American military sites of the U.S.–Mexican War era as well as at Civil War sites. Type 5 was a relatively expensive button and, therefore, more likely to have been worn by an officer. Officers in both armies were given some latitude in the wearing of civilian clothing.

TYPE 6 (FIG. 5.17h)

One example: this is a three-piece button. A brass front and back are crimped together, the edge then rolled to make a solid bond. Although the shank is missing, the back shows an iron stain at the solder point, indicating that the shank was made of iron. "Standard Imperial," in Gothic lettering, is stamped onto the back, suggesting that this is an English button. Type 6 is probably an officer's coat button.

TYPE 7 (FIG. 5.17i)

One example: this is a one-piece, four-holed button made of cast-white metal, almost certainly made in the United States. Type 7 buttons were commonly used on fatigue clothing and occasionally by infantrymen as a substitute for the regulation brass jacket buttons. American troops used them on trousers from around the War of 1812 to the end of the Civil War.[36] This example was found on the battlefield, in the general area where we believe the American 4th Infantry was located toward the end of the battle.

Uniform Brass and Accoutrements

Possibly the most intriguing artifacts in the category of uniform brass and accoutrements are the Mexican regimental badges, since these items reveal the general locations of members of the regiments along the Mexican battle line. Map 11 shows the locations of Mexican regimental badges within SA 4. Their close proximity on the battlefield indicates that elements of the Mexican 6th and 10th Line Regiments—and possibly the 1st Line Regiment as well—stood and died within this sample unit. In addition, two cartridge-box belt plates signifying the Mexican 4th Line Regiment (and the 4th Line Regiment belt buckle described above) were found within SA 2 (map 9), located about five hundred feet to the southwest of SA 4. Apparently, Mexican soldiers from different regiments became intermingled, which reveals the tactical instability of the Mexican battle line. This instability prob-

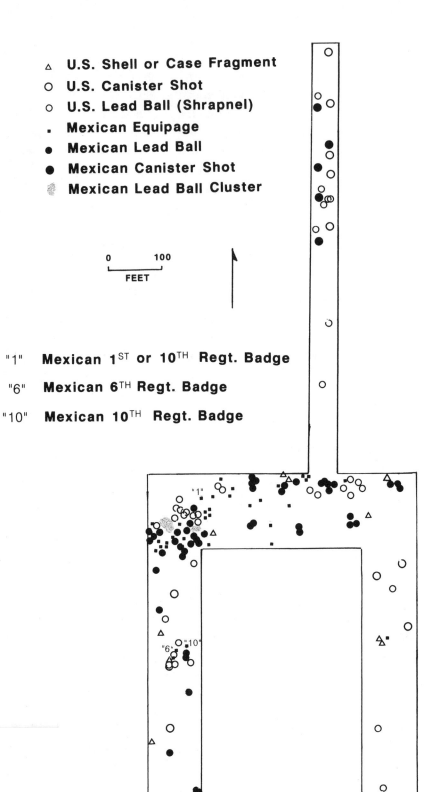

Legend

△ **U.S. Shell or Case Fragment**

○ **U.S. Canister Shot**

○ **U.S. Lead Ball (Shrapnel)**

. **Mexican Equipage**

● **Mexican Lead Ball**

● **Mexican Canister Shot**

⬤ **Mexican Lead Ball Cluster**

0 — 100

FEET

map 11. Search Area 4, artifact distribution. Produced by Charles M. Haecker

"1" **Mexican 1ST or 10TH Regt. Badge**

"6" **Mexican 6TH Regt. Badge**

"10" **Mexican 10TH Regt. Badge**

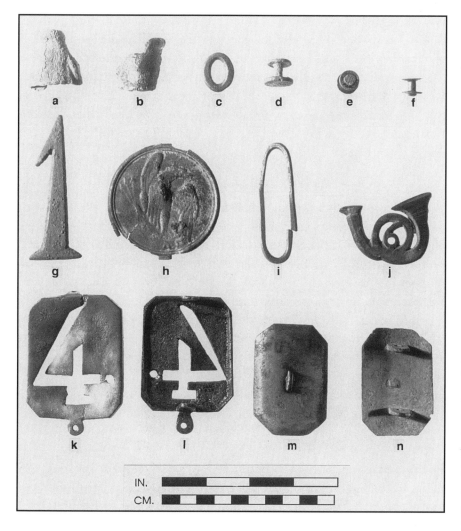

fig. 5.18. Uniform brass and parts of accoutrements. a, b: Canteen spouts; c: the zero portion of a Mexican Tenth Line regimental emblem; d: Mexican harness belt stud; e, f: U.S. rivets-and-burrs; g: the numeral one, either an emblem of the Mexican First Line Regiment or an emblem portion that signifies the Mexican Tenth Line Regiment; h: U.S. cartridge-box belt plate; i: Mexican belt suspension loop; j: Mexican Sixth Line regimental emblem; k, l: Mexican Fourth Regiment cartridge-box belt plates, obverse and reverse, respectively; m, n: Mexican cartridge-box belt plates (generic), obverse and reverse, respectively. Courtesy National Park Service

ably resulted from Mexican soldiers crowding closer together in an almost instinctive act of self-preservation. Crowding grows stronger as the distance from the enemy narrows, and crowding along a battle line increases exposure to enemy fire. Good leadership on the battle line will keep soldiers properly spaced. If leadership deteriorates or is poor at the outset, however, crowding escalates as the enemy is faced. Men press together for protection as extreme fear develops.[37] It should not be surprising that crowding took place, given that these soldiers stood still for hours while enduring a galling artillery attack.

CANTEEN SPOUT (FIG. 5.18a–b)

Two examples: both spouts are made of cast white metal. One came from the Mexican battle line, the other from where we believe Duncan's battery was positioned toward the end of the battle. This variety of spout was used on a tin or wooden canteen of the flat barrel type. Both spouts are similar in metal alloy, dimension, and shape, suggesting that they came from the same manufacturer. The disparity in provenience of the two spouts is notable, meaning that both the American and Mexican armies used this type of canteen. Mexican soldiers commonly used bottle gourds, a container eventually preferred by many American soldiers as well since it kept the water cooler than their metal-issue canteens.[38]

REGIMENTAL EMBLEM (FIG. 5.18c)

One example: this is a cast-and-filed brass zero. The reverse face is flat with two projecting prongs, each prong having a small hole to support a now-absent pin that attached the zero to cloth or leather. The emblem was found on the Mexican battle line. This artifact was presumably paired with the number one to form a "10," signifying the Mexican 10th Line Regiment. Regimental numbers were sometimes embroidered onto the high-neck collars of Mexican uniforms;[39] therefore, this artifact was probably attached to a Mexican leather shako or cloth forage cap.

HARNESS BELT STUD (FIG. 5.18d)

One example: a cast-and-filed brass object, used to secure and hold in place two overlapping harness belts. It was found on the Mexican battle line.

RIVET-AND-BURR (FIG. 5.18e–f)

Four examples: made of cast copper, with no makers' mark. All four were found in the vicinity of the American battle line. This type of rivet-and-burr is commonly found at American nineteenth-century military sites.[40] It was used to reinforce such accoutrements as knapsacks and cartridge boxes. Leather harness rivets are larger than these artifacts.

REGIMENTAL EMBLEM (FIG. 5.18g)

One example: this is a brass numeral one. It is either a regimental badge that signified the Mexican 1st Line Regiment or the "1" portion of a 10th Regiment badge. There are two fastening prongs on the reverse side, with one prong slightly longer and bent. This item may have been on a horseman's *shabraque*, a saddlecloth of French influence. The asymmetrical lengths of the fastening prongs would have allowed for attachment of decorative cords through the underside of the emblem.

CARTRIDGE-BOX BELT PLATE, AMERICAN (FIG. 5.18h)

One example: this is a thin-stamped brass plate; the back is lead-filled with an iron attachment wire embedded. The stamped design is the American eagle holding three arrows and an olive branch. This artifact was found in the vicinity where we believe Captain Duncan's battery stood toward the end of the battle. From about 1845 to 1872, this type of brass plate decorated the leather shoulder belt of the infantryman's cartridge box. As used on the cartridge-box belt, the plate had a fastener fashioned from iron wire. When used on sergeants' shoulder sword belts consisting of two branches, however, the plate was used to join the branches. For this purpose, it was fitted with three "arrowhead" or "puppy paw" hooks. The presence of a linear streak of rust on the back of this artifact indicates the iron wire that fastened the belt plate to the cartridge-box belt. Since artillerymen were not equipped with cartridge boxes, this object was probably lost by an infantryman. The only U.S. infantry unit on this side of the battlefield was the 8th Infantry, which supported Duncan's battery toward the end of the battle.

BELT SUSPENSION LOOP (FIG. 5.18i)

One example: drawn copper or brass wire that is square in cross section, the ends not soldered or welded. Its dimensions and shape approximate the Type 6 buckle, except the latter is round in cross section and the ends welded. This artifact may have been attached to a belt or knapsack. It was found along the Mexican battle line.

REGIMENTAL BADGE (FIG. 5.18j)

One example: an emblem of a horn, made of cast-and-filed brass, the number six inside the horn loop. There are two fastening prongs on the reverse side. This is a badge of the Mexican 6th Line Regiment. A nineteenth–century Mexican illustration of the horn emblem, but without a regiment number, shows it pinned onto a Mexican barracks cap made of cloth.[41] A similar horn emblem but displaying the regimental number seven was found in the excavated Mexican mass grave at Resaca de la Palma.

CARTRIDGE-BOX BELT PLATES, MEXICAN (FIG. 5.18k–l)

Two examples: flat, rectangular plates made of cast-and-filed brass. There is a pair of holed attachment prongs on the back side and one holed prong centered at the base. On the face of the plate is the number four in open-cut, European style. To the right of the "4" is a small open circle, the European symbol representing the number suffix th. No longer attached to the prong is the chain that once secured the musket vent-pricker and pan brush. These latter two items had to be readily accessible for in-field maintenance of the musket (see fig. 2.8, the 4th Line Regiment illustration). Although similar in overall design, the two 4th Regiment items differ somewhat in overall dimension, weight, prong shape, and design of the number four. This implies that each object either was made from a unique casting or came from different manufacturers. These three belt plates were discovered on the Mexican battle line.

Three examples: convex, rectangular brass plates that are cast and filed. There is a pair of attachment prongs on the back side and one holed prong centered on the front side. The three belt plates were found on the Mexican battle line. We believe these plates had the same function as those described in fig. 5.18*k* and 5.18*l* above (see fig. 2.7, the *cazador* illustration). The paired prongs on the back side were used to fasten the belt plate to the shoulder belt. The single-holed prong on the front side secured the chain that held the infantryman's musket vent-pricker and pan brush.

Personal Possessions (Fig. 5.19)

LEAD BALL PORTIONS

fig. 5.19. Personal possessions. a: One-quarter of a .62-caliber lead ball; b: one-eighth of a lead ball; c: Mexican one-quarter real *coin; d: religious medallion; e: fragment of a brass pot; f: fragment of a pendant (?). Courtesy National Park Service*

Two examples: (1) one-quarter of a cut-lead ball, the length revealing it was once a .62-caliber Baker rifle ball (fig. 5.19*a*), found just north of Arista Hill, near the Mexican battle line; and (2) one-eighth of a cut-lead ball, having three flat sides and one curved side (fig. 5.19*b*). The original caliber cannot be identified. This object was found on the Mexican battle line. Because of their modified nature, these artifacts are identified as personal possessions

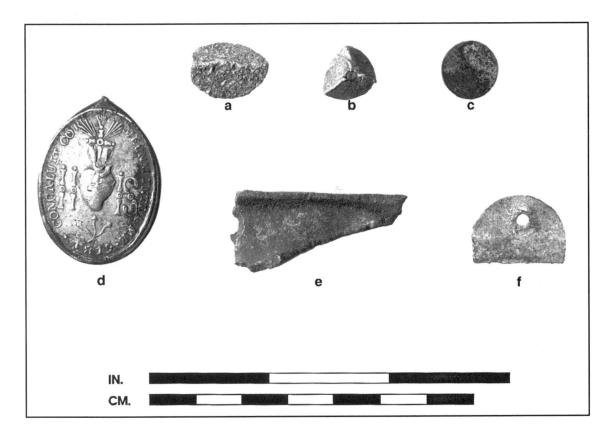

instead of lead ball ordnance. Soldiers of the American Revolution and the Civil War fabricated a wide variety of nonmilitary objects from lead projectiles, such as chess pieces, whistles, and toy cups. Civil War encampments in the Brownsville area have also yielded many halved and quartered lead balls. These latter objects may have been used as gaming counters and gambling chips.

ONE-QUARTER *REAL* COIN (FIG. 5.19c)

One example: this is a silver coin. The obverse side shows the head of Liberty facing left. To the right of the head are the letters *LR*, the initials of Luciano Rovira, an engraver at the Mexico mint. There is no mint mark, which means the coin was minted at San Luis Potosí: initials of this mint were not placed on one-quarter *reales*. The reverse side bears the fraction one-fourth, surrounded by "República de México" and the date 1843. Coins of this denomination were first minted in 1842 as a response to a lack of small change and as a replacement for the virtually worthless copper one-sixteenth and one-eighth *reales* issued by the federal and state governments. The minting of one-quarter *real* coins was suspended after 1863 following the changeover to the decimal system. By 1839, the Mexican private's monthly pay amounted to 15 pesos; a sergeant received 26 pesos, and a general 500. From this wage were deducted his monthly costs for laundry, barber, shoes, cigars, and so forth. A *real* was one-eighth of a peso, and a peso equaled one ounce of silver, or about one U.S. dollar of that period. A one-quarter *real* coin in 1846 was worth around one-thirtieth of a peso, or three cents American.[42]

RELIGIOUS MEDALLION (FIG. 5.19d)

One example: this is an ovoid silver medal minus its suspension loop. The medal was found between battle lines or possibly just in front of the American line. The obverse inscription, aligned around the border of the medal, reads *Concaluit cor meum intra me*, or "Aflame my heart within me." There is the central iconography of the Sacred Heart with a crown of thorns, three nails, and IHS; the date of 1819 is at the distal end. The reverse inscription is *Apprended de mi que soy manso y humilde de corazon:* "Learn from me that I am gentle and humble of heart." Given its inscription in Spanish and its battlefield provenience, this artifact was conceivably lost by a Mexican lancer engaged in the failed attack on the American eighteen-pounders and Foot Artillery Battalion.

METAL POT FRAGMENT (FIG. 5.19e)

One example: this is a rim fragment of a brass pot, which was made by casting and hammering. It was found between battle lines, or perhaps just in front of the American line. This object may be battle related; if so, it was part of a soldier's mess kit. Its battlefield provenience suggests that this object was deposited during the failed Mexican lancer attack on the American eighteen-pounders and Foot Artillery Battalion.

PENDANT (?) (FIG. 5.19f)

One example: this is a flat piece of brass with a punched hole at one end, presumably to accommodate a string or chain. The edges indicate that it was cut off from another piece of brass. The object was found on the Mexican battle line.

FRAGMENTS OF BOTTLE BASES (FIG. 5.20a–b)

Two examples: both bottle bases are of dark-green glass. The bases have high basal kick-ups, a characteristic of wine and champagne bottles. Neither kick-up has pontile marks, which is suggestive of a post-1840 manufacture date. One base diameter corresponds to French wine bottles found on the paddlewheel *Bertrand*, sunk in 1865; these wine bottles held 25.5 ounces. The base diameter of the other bottle approximates champagne bottles of the mid-nineteenth century that held 29 ounces.[43]

WINE-BOTTLE SEAL (FIG. 5.20c)

One example: this is a fragment of a wine-bottle shoulder with a glass seal gather impressed onto it. The seal gather is impressed with "St. Seurin Medoc" and a cluster of grapes. The dark-green bottle fragment was found on the Mexican battle line. Medoc is a region in the Bordeaux district of France

fig. 5.20. Personal possessions, wine-bottle fragments. a, b: Wine-bottle bases; c: wine-bottle seal. Courtesy National Park Service

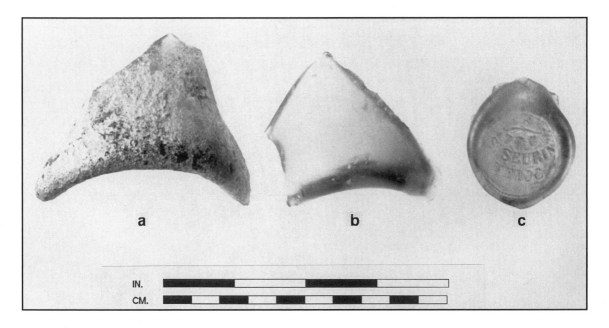

On the Prairie of Palo Alto

famous for producing red wine. Saint Seurin, its full name Saint-Seurin-de-Cadourne, is one of the smaller wine-producing communes or townships within the Haut Médoc, a subdistrict noted for finer wines. In the Classification of 1855, a wine-grading system introduced that year, wines produced from Saint Seurin were graded *Crus Bourgeois* and *Crus Artisans*, indicating wines of third and fourth levels of excellence, respectively. These commanded correspondingly lower premium prices compared to other wines from their subdistrict.[44] At Palo Alto, a bottle of imported wine would probably have been purchased by someone who could best afford such a high-status luxury—an officer. Presumably this individual was in the Mexican army, as suggested by the location of the artifact on the Mexican battle line.

Farriery and Horse Tack

HORSESHOES (FIG. 5.21a–b)

Fragments of three different horseshoes were recovered from the battlefield. Two fragments came from the general vicinity where we believe Captain Duncan's battery was stationed: the width, thickness, shape, and nail-hole spacing of these objects are typical of American mass-produced horseshoes

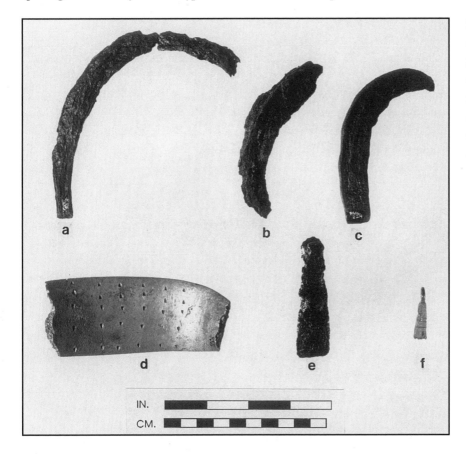

fig. 5.21. Farriery and horse tack. a, b: Horseshoe fragments; c: ox shoe half; d: Mexican stirrup (?) fragment; e: U.S. spur sideplate; f. Mexican coscojo. Courtesy National Park Service

used during the early to mid-nineteenth century. In contrast, Mexican horse-shoes of this period were wider and more reminiscent of horseshoe styles typical of the eighteenth century.[45] The third horseshoe fragment was found between the battle lines but is too decayed to attempt identification of national origin.

OX SHOE (FIG. 5.21c)

One example: an ox hoof is split; therefore, one shoe is needed for each side of the hoof. This artifact is a left-side shoe. It was found just south of Palo Alto Pond, near the wagon road. The object may be battle-related since oxen were used to pull the eighteen-pounder battery as well as American supply wagons.

STIRRUP FRAGMENTS (?) (ONE FRAGMENT SHOWN, FIG. 5.21d)

One example: two fragments of cast, filed, hammered, and punched brass. The fragments fit together to form what seems to have been a C-shaped object. The interior of the "C" has a series of triangular depressions made by using a punch. We believe this is part of a Mexican stirrup, the depressions added to provide better traction for the boot. The artifact was discovered on the Mexican battle line.

SPUR SIDEPLATE (FIG. 5.21e)

One example: this is a fragment of an iron or steel strap. It has two round-head rivets projecting out from one side. The artifact, identified as part of an American Army spur sideplate, was found where Captain Duncan's battery was likely stationed toward the end of the battle. One of the studs is for the upper strap, the other for the heel strap.

COSCOJO (FIGS. 5.21–23)

One example: this is a flat strip of filed and hammered brass or copper. There is a loop at one end and, at the opposite end, two filed notches that make a stylized hand. It was found on the Mexican battle line. *Coscojos* were arranged in a series on Mexican bridles and bits and were both decorative and pleasant to hear when traveling. *Coscojos* came in a variety of forms. One of the more common types, the *fica,* is represented by this artifact: a clasped hand with the thumb projecting between the first and second fingers. This was a common Old World symbol for warding off the Evil Eye[46] and is often found on Mexican bridles and stirrups.

Hardware (Fig. 5.24)

Forty-two cast-iron, wrought-iron, and steel hardware items were found on the battlefield. Six of these have been identified as agricultural in function,

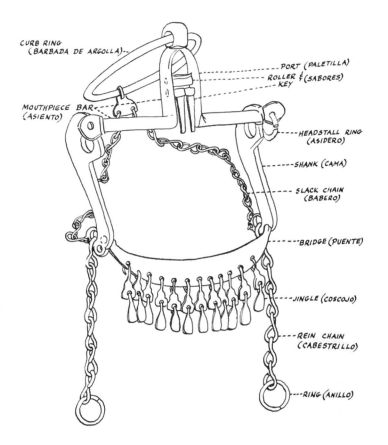

CURB RING
(BARBADA DE ARGOLLA)

PORT (PALETILLA)
ROLLER & (SABORES)
KEY

MOUTHPIECE BAR
(ASIENTO)

HEADSTALL RING
(ASIDERO)

SHANK (CAMA)

SLACK CHAIN
(BABERO)

BRIDGE (PUENTE)

JINGLE (COSCOJO)

REIN CHAIN
(CABESTRILLO)

RING (ANILLO)

fig. 5.22. Mexican bridle. Note the placement of the coscojos. Illustration by Frank Turley, in Simmons and Turley, Southwestern Colonial Ironwork: The Spanish Blacksmithing Tradition from Texas to California. *Courtesy Museum of New Mexico Press, Santa Fe*

fig. 5.23. Coscojo. Courtesy National Park Service

IN.

CM.

fig. 5.24. Hardware.
a: *Machine harvester tooth;*
b: *machinery fragment;*
c, d: *rings;* e: *wagon-support bracket;* f: *cold shut;* g: *hinge;* h: *linch- or drift pin;* i-k: *bolts;* l: *washer. Courtesy National Park Service*

thus postdating the battle. Most of the remaining thirty-six hardware items were discovered along the projected route of the old wagon road, as well as adjacent to Palo Alto Pond and the area where we believe American regiments once stood. Some of these include a cast-iron washer, cast-iron rings (two), cast-iron or steel bolts (three), a cast-iron wagon-support bracket, a brass hinge, and a portion of a steel rod that is tentatively identified as either a linchpin or drift pin. A drift pin is a tool used for ramming or driving down a heavy object or for enlarging or shaping holes. They would have been useful tools for an army smithy, although such a tool is not specifically listed in inventory stores for an army blacksmith's limber chest. A linchpin is used at the end of an axletree to prevent the wheel of a vehicle from

On the Prairie of Palo Alto

sliding off. Linchpins were used on wagons, caissons, and gun carriages, with spares stored in the limber chest of an artillery battery's wagon forge.[47]

Two hardware artifacts derive from the immediate vicinity of where Captain Duncan's battery was believed to have been positioned toward the end of the battle. These include a cast-iron or steel ring, similar in size and shape to those used to secure a gun carriage chain; and a cast-iron seat bracket, of a style used on nineteenth-century rolling stock. A cold shut, a piece of round stock used to repair a broken chain, was found to the immediate east of Palo Alto Pond, near where we believe the American wagon train was parked. The only piece of hardware that was recovered from the Mexican battle line was a brass bolt, the shaft unthreaded and its base sheared off.

Human Bone

Three human bone fragments were found on the surface. These remains were collected for further analysis. After examination, the bones were returned to the original surface locations. The widely dispersed proveniences of these remains suggest that they did not derive from a mass burial but instead were body parts not collected after the battle. Specimens 1 and 2 were found within SA 1, either between the battle lines or just in front of the American line; Specimen 3 was discovered within the extreme eastern end of the battlefield, possibly associated with the Mexican right flank attack toward the end of the battle.

Specimen 1: Distal end of a right human tibia, soil stained and weathered. It is fractured and splintered from unknown causes, possibly at the time of deposition. The overall diminutive dimensions of this bone suggest an adolescent or young adult of small stature.

Specimen 2: Proximal end of a left human femur, soil stained and weathered. There is a sharp break in the shaft, possibly at the time of deposition. The overall diminutive dimensions of the bone imply an adolescent or young adult of small stature.

Specimen 3: Right human talus. It is whole, soil stained, and weathered. The dimensions of the bone suggest an adult, stature unknown.

6

Conclusion

As noted in chapter 1, the primary goal of our investigations of the Palo Alto battlefield was to acquire enough archaeological and documentary data to determine the major battle line positions of the two opposing armies. Achieving this goal required the resolution of four mutually supportive research interests. These interests, and how they were resolved, are stated below.

(1) Identify and synthesize the documentary evidence of the battle, thus providing a basis of comparison with the archaeological data derived from the battlefield.

The battle of Palo Alto generated extensive documentary evidence that included both Mexican and American communiqués, battle maps, letters, and other materials. Critical analysis of the written evidence indicates that there is general agreement as to what occurred. However, as we also noted, a number of these documents are contradictory on several accounts. Of special note are discrepancies between Mexican and American battle maps. There was a need, then, to classify certain key documents as to their likelihood of reliability and to proffer explanations as to how and why these discrepancies might have occurred. This research approach proved useful since the reliable documents could then be used to direct where fieldwork should be conducted. It also lessened the possibility of comparing archaeological data with more or less imprecise historical data. We then used both written and schematic battle accounts derived from reliable sources for the interpretation of specific artifact patterns.

Of course, in a perfect world, one would experience a consistent correlation between presumed "good" documentary data and the archaeological pattern. This desired outcome was not realized for several historically documented battle events. Yet negative information—the absence of artifact patterning where it was hypothesized that such patterning should be found—

does not necessarily throw the historical accounts into question. This is because relic collecting and ground disturbances have resulted in a compromised archaeological record, and randomly placed survey units may simply have missed such evidence. Further fieldwork is required within these and other sectors of the battlefield, guided as always by data from documentary research.

(2) Compare specific topographic features described on the day of battle with similar features found at present-day Palo Alto to determine if there are correlations. If correlations exist, they can then be used as physical points of reference for determining locations of recorded battle events.

Comparisons of eyewitness descriptions of specific topographic features with those found on the battlefield today provided several correlations, actual physical links with the recorded past. These natural and cultural features were then used to select promising areas for archaeological study. For example, local tradition identified Area A as Palo Alto Pond. Unfortunately, vegetation removal, land leveling, and pond drainage in this part of the battlefield apparently destroyed any artifact patterning that may have once existed. There is no evidence of the earthworks that protected the American wagon train following the battle. A few artifacts, however, were located adjacent to the now-drained pond: an ox shoe, rivets typically found on American military equipment of the period, and an American officer's sword buckle. These relics lend some admittedly scanty support to our belief that Area A was the location of the original American battle line and wagon train.

We believe that Area B correlates with the resaca that figured prominently during the first phase of battle, when Mexican forces twice attempted to outflank the Americans here. This is because both Area B and the historically documented resaca occupy the same sector of the battlefield, they exhibit the same meandering configuration, and there are no other logical candidates for this resaca. Unfortunately, the thick vegetation cover west of Area B prevents conducting an archaeological survey to determine the tactical specifics of this battle event.

Analysis of an aerial photograph of the battlefield hints of a linear, manmade feature that we have termed Area C. This may be a vestige of the old Matamoros wagon road. Close inspection of the photograph reveals that Area C is forked, perhaps correlating with the fork in the road noted on period battle maps. Also, disturbance vegetation dominates within this feature, a vegetative patterning one would expect within a long-abandoned wagon road. However, our survey of Area C indicates that it is devoid of battle-related artifacts. Does this mean that little or no combat took place along this remaining road segment? Or is the circa 1846 roadbed actually located somewhere else? Future archaeological investigations of Palo Alto will need to address these questions.

Area D is our choice for the marshy obstacle that existed between the opposing battle lines. This feature is apparent on the aerial photograph and is further delineated in part by a distribution of battle-related artifacts along its southeastern periphery. Also, a botanical survey of the battlefield reveals that Area D extends along a northeast-southwest axis, which roughly corresponds with the axis of the final position of the Mexican battle line.

Local lore names one particular low rise that we have termed Area E as Arista Hill. This is the high ground where General Arista supposedly viewed the battle. Also, Berlandier's battle map revealed that this topographic feature was the terminus of the Mexican right, or eastern, flank. If these two features are one and the same, then archaeological evidence of the Mexican battle line should exist west of Area E. The resultant survey of this area did, in fact, locate a dramatic linear patterning of artifacts, which we interpret as a segment of the final position of the Mexican battle line. We can now identify the present-day low rise as the same *motita* that reportedly anchored the Mexican right flank. Because of its juxtaposition with Arista Hill, it follows that the present-day dirt road—Area G—must be the same one used by the Mexican army when it entered the Palo Alto prairie and formed its line of battle.

The *lomas tendidas*, or "low hills" labeled on Berlandier's maps, are not readily apparent on the battlefield today. We believe that at the time of the battle, they appeared as a low, wooded levee that extended in a southeasterly direction from Arista Hill. Post-1846 erosion, such as flooding caused by hurricanes, probably obliterated this feature and the vegetation that once covered it. In fact, heavy rains during the 1992 survey did delineate for a day the meager remnants of the old levee, which we have labeled Area F. Mexican accoutrements intermixed with American ordnance were found to the north and northwest of Area F. Such findings are appropriate within this sector of the battlefield. It was reported that the routed Mexican right flank, under severe artillery attack, retreated behind the *lomas tendidas* for protection. Unfortunately, the survey along the southern side of Area F did not produce evidence of either American artillery ordnance or Mexican-related artifacts.

We believe Areas A, B, and D–G share a commonality with the historic past; there is still some nagging doubt regarding whether Area C is the old wagon road. It is now possible to correlate period battle maps, notwithstanding all their maddening vagaries and contradictions, with the topography of Palo Alto as we see it today. Using these correlations, one can identify the same strip of land where the final Mexican battle line once stood, using as a guide the juxtapositions of present-day Arista Hill, the marshy area, and the resaca, along with each of their associated artifact patternings. We can also use the juxtapositions of Palo Alto Pond, the marshy area, and the resaca to interpolate where the final American battle line was positioned, even though few American-related artifacts were found within this sector of the battlefield.

(3) Assess the postbattle history of Palo Alto as it relates to topographic and artifact patterning modifications.

Damage to the archaeological record has definitely occurred at Palo Alto. Objects such as Mexican lances, swords, and shakos were prized as souvenirs by the victors and were removed from the battlefield almost as soon as the smoke of battle had cleared. Other easily visible objects, such as reusable solid iron shot, personal gear, and repairable equipage, would also have been gathered up by the American army. No doubt additional items were collected as souvenirs during the succeeding years. Vegetation regrowth eventually obscured the battle-damaged, thus visible, surfaces of the battlefield.

This initial period of artifact removal would not have destroyed the overall patterning of battle refuse since soil deposition over time hid from view many artifacts. Unfortunately, in recent years, relic collecting as a sport and a source of income has compromised or virtually destroyed the artifact patterning within several key areas of the battlefield. This damage appears to be confined to places with sparse vegetation and where artifacts are periodically exposed by plowing. Metal detectors are usually used by these collectors, so the problem of artifact loss is exacerbated. Battle interpretation may also be compromised by those collectors who have selectively taken only certain types of relics (for example, accoutrements made of brass). Such selective collecting pressures would leave behind a skewed artifact patterning consisting of mostly "rejected" items, such as nondescript fragments of iron shot. Fortunately, an impenetrable covering of tall cordgrass protects several sectors of the battlefield. These are archaeological preserves where artifact patternings might still exist.

Not all postbattle effects have been deleterious. Specifically, the dense growth of mixed mesquite-cordgrass vegetation west of Resaca de Palo Alto presently protects this portion of the battlefield. A recent biological survey reveals that this vegetation cover is at least forty years old. It is likely, therefore, that archaeological evidence of Mexican flank attacks and American countermeasures still exist here. Also, a dense covering of cordgrass protects the suspected locations of the Mexican wagon park and field hospital.

(4) Analyze the artifact types and their patterning on the battlefield to provide corroboration or refutation of reputed battle events.

There are some who believe that eyewitness accounts of a historic event are sufficient to tell the story of what happened and that associated archaeological findings are tantamount to expounding upon the obvious. Yet the correlations of archaeological data with historical accounts can provide the means for assessing the accuracy of these eyewitnesses. If the interpretations of the archaeological record indicate a positive correlation with a documented battle event, then the archaeological explanations are strengthened. There are also a number of instances where the historical record of the battle is vague or even silent on certain specific troop movements. In these situations, the archaeological data can help to clarify the record.

However, we also uncovered some instances wherein these data challenge the documentary evidence—this is when archaeological investigations become even more interesting. The artifacts recovered from Palo Alto have generally supported the testimony of the battle participants. Spatial analysis identified the following battlefield circumstances.

(1) There does appear to be a clustering of Mexican cannonballs where documentary evidence places Captain Duncan's battery. This clustering also confirms the accounts describing Mexican efforts to destroy American artillery by concentrated artillery attacks. Several American-related artifacts were also found within this general concentration of Mexican shot.

(2) Concentrations of Mexican canister shot occur to the northwest and west of the marshy area that separated the two opposing armies. We believe this shot supports the documented incident wherein Mexican artillery fired canister rounds at American dragoons when the latter attempted to cross the western half of the marsh.

(3) The effective range for American light artillery when using canister was no greater than four hundred yards. When using this type of round, therefore, they focused their aim on the closest Mexican units. This tactic is evidenced by significant accumulations of American light artillery canister shot just within and to the north of Area D, or less than four hundred yards from where we believe Duncan's battery had been stationed. In contrast, quantities of American eighteen-pounder shell and spherical case shrapnel lie deep within the Mexican battle line and south of Area D, well beyond the effective range of American light artillery.

(4) American spherical case shrapnel dramatically delineates a five-hundred-foot-long segment of the final Mexican battle line position. This segment extends along an almost north-south axis, which corroborates several American battle maps depicting the final Mexican battle line along this same axis. This patterning is especially significant because Mexican maps show their initial battle line position along an east-west axis. These documents portray the final deployment of the Mexican line as an aggressive northwestward advance that pivoted on the wagon road. However, for a Mexican north-south axis to exist, it would mean the Mexican left flank had, in fact, abandoned its defensive position on the road.

A north-south axis also points to a Mexican loss of tactical initiative. During the final phase of battle, the Americans advanced down the road to where the Mexican left flank once stood, then formed an east-facing battle line that closely paralleled the road. Significantly, the road extended along an almost north-south axis. In a concurrent development, the left flank of the Mexican army had retreated away from the road and toward the east or southeast. This retreat probably impinged upon the Mexican center line regiments. Their battle line would have become dangerously compacted, thereby offering an even better target for American artillery. Troop compaction also would have hindered the Mexican army's ability to use aggressive, battle-winning tactics. The Mexican center was forced to parallel its battle line with that of the enemy's, thereby forming a similar north-south battle line axis. Although compacted and its morale probably shaken, the Mexican center was still a cohesive fighting unit. This is indicated by the linear patterning of artifacts described above, a clear sign that tactical disintegration had not yet taken place.

Interestingly, there is one bit of Mexican documentary evidence that also challenges the Mexican battle maps. General Ampudia, in defending his actions at Palo Alto, stated that the soldiers under his command could not effectively return fire during the final phase of the battle because the setting sun shone directly into their eyes.[1] This meant that the Mexican army would have been facing a westerly direction and were aligned along a more or less north-south axis. The principal author visited Palo Alto during the late afternoon of May 8, 1993, the 147th anniversary to the hour of the final phase of the battle. He positioned himself on the previously discovered segment of the Mexican battle line, then faced the same northwesterly direction as the Mexican soldiers would have. He noted that visibility of the horizon was not hindered by the setting sun since the sun was to the left of his line of sight. Instead, the angled sunlight reflected off the open expanse of cordgrass in front of him, creating a partially blinding effect. In fact, the reflection was so great that most of the photographs taken of this phenomenon turned out overexposed. During the battle this light also would have reflected off the copious uniform brass worn by the Mexicans, making them even better targets for the east-facing American artillery.

(5) The greatest concentration of artifacts centers around the marsh of Area D, which we believe was the focus of the battlefield. A previous interpretation[2] places the battlefield nucleus approximately one-third mile to the east of Area D, with a corresponding extension of both battle lines much farther to the east than in our version. The patterning of Mexican-related artifacts to the immediate south of Area D is especially significant. We have stated that a linear patterning of artifacts indicates tactical stability, and we have offered an example of this type of patterning on the Mexican battle line. We have also related an example of Mexican tactical instability, which perhaps even signified a total collapse of army cohesion. In the previous chapter we noted the presence of insignias representing the Mexican 4th, 6th, and 10th Regiments (and possibly the 1st Regiment as well). All of these insignias were found within a three-acre area. The mingling of individuals from different regiments within such a small area points to crowding. As was noted by Fox in his study of the Little Bighorn fight, soldiers

under fire almost instinctively tend to draw closer together. This urge grows stronger as the distance from the enemy narrows, or as the deadly effects of incoming enemy fire increase. If not checked by good leadership, crowding will quickly escalate into extreme fear.[3] This probably happened at Palo Alto when the routed Mexican right flank rushed headlong into the crowded Mexican line regiments. At this point, the cohesive fabric of the entire Mexican army was destroyed.

(6) The broad prairie that extends northward from Arista Hill contains a widespread deposition of both American and Mexican ordnance and equipage. According to one relic collector, there also once existed a concentration of Mexican-related artifacts about one-third mile to the east of Area D. Our survey of this sector did not result in relocating these items. The deposition here of Mexican artifacts may have occurred during the retreat of the Mexican army from the battlefield or when the dead were collected for burial after the battle. It might also have been the location of the Mexican postbattle encampment. Unfortunately, since relic collectors have compromised this particular artifact patterning, we will probably never know what happened here.

(7) Mexican accoutrements recovered elsewhere from the battlefield include metal fittings from British India Pattern muskets and Paget carbines. These findings corroborate the documentary evidence establishing Mexico's heavy reliance on imported military arms and equipage, specifically from Great Britain. The archaeological record also hints of Mexico's industrial capabilities during this turbulent period of its history. Such objects as buttons for the enlisted men's uniforms, cartridge-box belt plates, belt buckles, regimental insignias, and canister shot were produced in large quantities within Mexico. We found, however, that measurements, weights, and shapes of comparable items (for example, canister shot) were never exactly the same. We believe this lack of standardization reflects the absence of a Modern Era industrial base in mid-nineteenth-century Mexico. Its entrepreneurial class of artisan metalworkers may have operated independently of one another, thereby producing military goods that varied in quality and appearance. Any attempt to standardize these "cottage industries" would have been hampered by Mexico's primitive transportation and communication network, compared to what existed in the United States and in European countries during this period.

In contrast is the military hardware manufactured in the United States. Simple but appropriate examples are the ubiquitous American-made lead balls, which were often found intermingled among the military products of Mexican artisans. Most of the American balls found at Palo Alto were made using the pressed, or "swage," method. Using this mass-production method, one factory worker could produce as many as forty thousand lead balls in one day, each ball having virtually the same weight and diameter as any other. Palo Alto, then, can also be viewed as the sanguinary judgment of the relative merits of two radically different manufacturing traditions. One warring nation upheld the ancient traditions of the artisan class; the other was an active participant in the Industrial Revolution.

This most recent archaeological study of Palo Alto resulted in the survey of approximately 17 percent of the estimated twelve hundred acres of the core battle area. In general, we were successful in meeting our stated goals. Yet there were some shortfalls as well. Discovery of the initial Mexican battle line should have been evidenced by a strong artifact patterning roughly along an east-west axis. In fact, no such patterning emerged through this survey. Possible definition of this battle line may only be obtained once surveys are allowed on the property south of the 1992 and 1993 project areas. Little archaeological evidence exists for the American battle lines. We attribute this latter negative finding largely to the fact that the American army experienced relatively little loss of men and equipment. Extensive land modifications within this sector of the battlefield also probably destroyed what artifact patterning may have once existed.

Evidence of flanking within the extreme western portion of the battlefield was also not found. Probably such evidence does exist but is presently inaccessible because of the dense mesquite forest that covers it. Significantly, a local informant declared that several Mexican Light Infantry belt buckles were recovered by a relic collector who favored working along the southern margins of this forest. Our survey of this particular area failed to produce any artifacts, possibly because the reputed collector was thorough. Although anecdotal, this information underscores the ongoing problem of battlefield depredation.

One desired outcome of this study was the identification of a pattern of use of smoothbore weaponry in the pre–Civil War era. It was theorized that linear-and-column tactics typical of this type of warfare would be recognized at Palo Alto as a linear and columnar deposition of artifacts. We did find a linear deposition; however, we also realize that such depositions might not always appear on Euro-American battlefields dating between circa A.D. 1650 and 1850. Each battle has its own unique set of parameters. This means that researchers of pre–Civil War battlefields should not depend on one or two axiomatic artifact patternings since each battle will probably posit a number of exceptions to the rule. Terrain, vegetative cover or lack thereof, weather, chosen tactics, competency of the commanders, morale of the soldiers, the degree of relic collecting—these and many other factors ultimately decide what type(s) of artifact patterning one will find. Also, the deployment of various combat units over the same terrain during the course of the battle might result in the intermingling of different patterns. Thus, the more complex the battle, the more difficult the task for researchers to identify and isolate specific troop deployments. Perhaps it is the case that some of the more subtle patternings characteristic of smoothbore warfare are best identified only on such battlefields as Palo Alto. The tactics employed here were fairly simple in concept and execution; the total number of combatants, auxiliary forces, and camp followers probably did not exceed eight thousand; and all of the major events of the battle took place within a two-square-mile area. The truly mammoth struggles of the smoothbore period—for example, Waterloo—would present a wholly different set of fascinating challenges for the battlefield archaeologist.

The battle itself was the single largest and most significant historical aspect of Palo Alto. We realize, however, there are other cultural resources not directly related to this battle. Future researchers might consider focusing on the identification of Worth's Camp, the American army encampment of March 24–27, 1846, located somewhere east of Palo Alto Pond. Worth's Camp may or may not be the same location of the Mexican army that bivouacked at Palo Alto on May 3–5, 1846. Neither do we know where the Mexican army positioned its field hospital and baggage train or where it encamped the night following the battle. Also, Palo Alto was an encampment site for American volunteers and regular soldiers both during and after the war. We know the approximate location of Palo Alto House, but we do not know the extent or complexity of the nascent frontier community that was abandoned during the 1850s. These, and other, research topics will be considered as the new park develops.

Although this study has set a number of research goals, one goal it definitely does not serve is the final and incontrovertible explanation as to what happened on the prairie of Palo Alto during the afternoon hours of May 8, 1846. There is ample room for additional research, which could lead to refinement—even radical reconstruction—of the hypothetical reconstructions given here. The present work provides a framework for further research. It is a starting point, not a conclusion.

Notes

Chapter 1. Introduction

1. K. Jack Bauer, *The Mexican War, 1846–1848*, p. 327.
2. John Keegan, *The Face of Battle*.
3. S. L. A. Marshall, *Men Against Fire*, pp. 123–28.
4. Keegan, *Battle*, p. 33.
5. Douglas D. Scott, conversation with Charles M. Haecker, October, 1995.
6. Richard A. Fox, Jr., and Douglas D. Scott, "The Post–Civil War Battle Pattern," *Historical Archaeology* 25, no. 2 (1991): 92–103; Douglas D. Scott, *A Sharp Little Affair*, p. 122.
7. Douglas D. Scott, Richard A. Fox, Jr., Melissa A. Connor, and Dick Harmon, *Archaeological Perspectives on the Battle of the Little Bighorn*.
8. Scott et al., *Archaeological Perspectives*; Raymond Wood, "Forward," in Richard A. Fox., Jr., *Archaeology, History, and Custer's Last Battle: The Little Bighorn Reexamined*, p. iii; Fox, *Custer's Last Battle*, p. 10.

Chapter 2. Historical Overview

1. Robert H. Ferrell, *American Diplomacy: A History*, pp. 188–90.
2. Llerena B. Friend, *Sam Houston: The Great Designer*, pp. 71–72; Ferrell, *American Diplomacy*, pp. 191–92; Richard Griswold del Castillo, *The Treaty of Guadalupe Hidalgo: A Legacy of Conflict*, p. 11. See also David M. Pletcher, *The Diplomacy of Annexation: Texas, Oregon, and the Mexican War*, pp. 113–29, for a detailed account of the Texas question.
3. Russell F. Weigley, *History of the United States Army*, pp. 104–10; John K. Mahon, *The War of 1812*, pp. 48–52. See Richard H. Kohn, *Eagle and Sword: The Federalists and the Creation of the Military Establishment*, for an excellent study of the impact of the Federalists. For a comprehensive study of the New Orleans campaign, see Robin Reilly, *The British at the Gates: The New Orleans Campaign in the War of 1812*.
4. William B. Skelton, "Professionalization in the U.S. Army Officer Corps during the Age of Jackson," in David C. Skaggs and Robert S. Browning III, eds., *In the Defense of the Republic: Readings in American Military History*, pp. 84–85, 89–90; James L. Morrison, *The Best School in the World: West Point in the Pre–Civil War Years, 1833–1866*, pp. 23–26.

5. Weigley, *History*, p. III.

6. *Niles National Register*, Sept. 21, 1839.

7. F. N. Sampanaro, "The Political Role of the Army in Mexico, 1821–1848," pp. 28–29, 32, 42; Michael P. Costeloe, *The Central Republic in Mexico, 1835–1846*, p. 2.

8. Ruth R. Olivera and Lilian Crete, *Life in Mexico under Santa Anna, 1822–1855*, pp. 167–70; Donald F. Stevens, *The Origins of Instability in Early Republican Mexico*, p. 11.

9. Jean Louis Berlandier, "Berlandier's Notes on Texas," pp. 517–18.

10. K. Jack Bauer, *Zachary Taylor: Soldier, Planter, Statesman of the Old Southwest*, pp. 1–28; Holman Hamilton, *Zachary Taylor, Soldier of the Republic*, pp. 21–58; Francis Paul Prucha, *The Sword of the Republic: The United States Army on the Frontier, 1783–1846*, p. 293; John K. Mahon, *The Second Seminole War*, pp. 226–29.

11. K. Jack Bauer, "The Battles on the Rio Grande: Palo Alto and Resaca de la Palma, 8–9 May 1846," in Charles E. Heller and William A. Stofft, eds., *America's First Battles, 1776–1965*, p. 57; Capt. William S. Henry, *Campaign Sketches of the War with Mexico*, pp. 14–52.

12. Bauer, "Battles," p. 60; James A. Huston, *The Sinews of War: Army Logistics, 1775–1953*, pp. 129–31; Philip R. Katcher, *The Mexican-American War, 1846–1848*, p. 9.

13. Norman A. Graebner, *Empire on the Pacific: A Study in American Continental Expansion*, pp. 117–21; Pletcher, *The Diplomacy of Annexation*, p. 289.

14. K. Jack Bauer, *The Mexican War, 1846–1848*, pp. 22–26.

15. Lt. M. Scarritt to Col. J. G. Totten, May 12, 1846; Henry, *Campaign*, pp. 61–62; Sgt. Maj. Charles Masland to Matthew H. Masland, April 15, 1846.

16. Robert Ryal Miller, *Shamrock and Sword: The Saint Patrick's Battalion in the U.S.-Mexican War*, p. 47; Zachary Taylor, "Mexican War Correspondence," pp. 302–303; Bauer, *Mexican War*, pp. 40–42.

17. Joseph M. Nance, *After San Jacinto: The Texas-Mexican Frontier, 1836–1841*, pp. 428–29; Robert M. Carreño, ed., *Jefes del ejército mexicano en 1847*, pp. 44–49; *Diccionario Porrúa de historia, biografía, y geografía de México*, p. III; Gene M. Brack, *Mexico Views Manifest Destiny, 1821–1846*, pp. 152–64.

18. Maj. Gen. George C. Meade, *The Life and Letters of George G. Meade, Major-General United States Army*, pp. 52–53; Gen. Cadmus M. Wilcox, *History of the Mexican War*, pp. 42–43.

19. William A. de Palo, *The Mexican National Army, 1822–1852*, p. 247.

20. Joseph P. Sanchez, "General Mariano Arista at the Battle of Palo Alto, Texas, 1846: Military Realist or Failure?" *Journal of the West* 24, no. 2 (April, 1985): 10; Bauer, *Mexican War*, pp. 46–48; Taylor, "Correspondence," pp. 96–97.

21. John S. Jenkins, *History of the War between the United States and Mexico*, pp. 48–49; José María Roa Bárcena, *Recuerdos de la invasión norteamericana, 1846–1848, por un joven de entonces*, p. 62; Sanchez, "Arista," p. 12.

22. Jenkins, *History*, p. 99; Justin H. Smith, *The War with Mexico*, pp. 162–68.

23. *Niles National Register*, June 13, 1846, p. 223; Taylor, "Correspondence," p. 24.

24. Roa Bárcena, *Recuerdos*, p. 64; Sanchez, "Arista," p. 13.

25. *Niles National Register*, June 20, 1846, p. 254; Taylor, "Correspondence," pp. 292–94.

26. George Gordon Meade to Margaret Meade, May 7, 1846; Taylor, "Correspondence," pp. 294–95; Hamilton, *Zachary Taylor*, pp. 177–81; Sanchez, "Arista," p. 12.

27. Sanchez, "Arista," p. 13.

28. John C. Rayburn, Virginia K. Rayburn, and Ethel N. Fry, eds., *Century of Conflict, 1821–1913: Incidents in the Lives of William Neale and William A. Neale, Early Settlers in Texas*, p. 40.

29. Taylor, "Correspondence," p. 177; Bauer, "Battles," p. 69; Bauer, *Mexican War*, p. 53.

30. Wilcox, *History*, p. 53; T. B. Thorpe, *Our Army on the Rio Grande*, p. 74.

31. Nathan C. Brooks, *A Complete History of the Mexican War: Its Causes, Conduct, and Consequences*, p. 127; Henry, *Campaign*, p. 57; James Longstreet, *From Manassas to Appomattox: Memoirs of the Civil War in America*, p. 25; Ezra J. Warner, *Generals in Gray: Lives of the Confederate Commanders*, p. 306; Taylor, "Correspondence," p. 2.

32. Jean Louis Berlandier, "Journal of Jean Louis Berlandier during 1846–1847," entry dated March 23, 1847.

33. Letter from Major W. W. S. Bliss to Major General Gaines, May 9, 1846, p. 1, states that the Mexican army had 5,800 soldiers; letter from Major General George A. McCall to "My Dear M—," n.p., states, "I estimate the Mexican army [at Palo Alto] to be near seven thousand." *Compana contra*, numero 1 (n.p.), which is a table, indicates that the Mexican army at Palo Alto consisted of "40 Gefes" (principal officers), "285 Oficiales" (minor officers), and "3461 tropa" (troops), for a total of 3786 soldiers.

34. Ramón Alcaraz et al., *Apuntes para la historia de la guerra entre México y los Estados Unidos. The Other Side: Or, Notes for the History of the War between Mexico and the United States*, Albert C. Ramsey, ed. and trans., pp. 46–47; *Compaña contra de los americanos, mayo de 1846*; c.f. Meade, *Life and Letters*, p. 83; *Niles National Register*, May 30, 1846, p. 196; Bauer, "Battles," pp. 69–70; Roa Bárcena, *Recuerdos*, p. 79; Joseph P. Sanchez, "The Defeat of the Army of the North in South Texas: An Examination of Mexican Military Operations in the First Battles of the Mexican War," p. 19; José López Uraga, *Sumaria mandada formar a pedimento del sr. coronel del 4. regimento de infantería de linea D. José López Uraga en la que se comprueba a conducta militar que observo en las acciones de guerra dadas a la tropas de las Estados-Unidos los días 8 y 9 mayo en los puntos de Palo Alto y Resaca de Guerrero*, pp. 13–14; Taylor, "Correspondence," p. 2; *New York Herald*, May 28, 1846, p. 2; Smith, *War*, p. 166; Jean Louis Berlandier, *Itinerario: Campaña de Palo Alto y Resaca de Guererro*, p. 166; Sanchez, "Arista," p. 16.

35. Bauer, "Battles," p. 71; Ulysses S. Grant, *Personal Memoirs of Ulysses S. Grant*, p. 92; Bvt. Col. J. S. McIntosh, letter report to Office of Adjutant General, Dec. 3, 1846.

36. C. M. Reeves, *Five Years an American Soldier*, p. 444.

37. Bauer, *Mexican War*, p. 55; Edward J. Nichols, *Zach Taylor's Little Army*, p. 76; Samuel R. Curtis, diary entry dated July 11, 1846; Brian Robertson, *Wild Horse Desert*, p. 58; Franklin H. Churchill, *Sketch of the Life of Bvt. Brig. Gen. Sylvester Churchill, Inspector General U.S. Army*, p. 71.

38. Smith, *War*, pp. 166–67; Bauer, "Battles," p. 70; Col. D. E. Twiggs, field report to 29th Congress, p. 19.

39. Scarritt to Totten, p. 3; McIntosh, letter report, p. 3; Capt. Ephraim K. Smith, *To Mexico with Scott: Letters of Captain E. Kirby Smith to His Wife*, p. 49; Taylor, "Correspondence," pp. 2–3.

40. George A. McCall, letter to unknown, n.d.

41. Alcaraz et al., *Apuntes para la historia*, p. 47; Lt. John J. Peck, *The Sign of the Eagle: A View of Mexico 1830–1855, Based on the Letters of Lieutenant John James Peck, with Lithographs of Mexico*, p. 23; Taylor, "Correspondence," pp. 2–3.

42. *The Congressional Globe*, appendix, p. 677.

43. Maj. Gen. George A. McCall, *Letters from the Frontier*, p. 453; Berlandier, *Itinerario*; Capt. James Duncan, letter report to Lieut. Col. W. G. Belknap, May 12, 1846; Grant, *Memoirs*, p. 60.

44. McIntosh, letter report, p. 3; Taylor, "Correspondence," p. 3.

45. Twiggs, field report, p. 2; Bauer, "Battles," p. 71; Alcaraz et al., *Apuntes para la historia*, p. 48.

46. Duncan, letter report.

47. Gen. Pedro de Ampudia, *Manifesto dando cuenta del conducto;* Sanchez, "Defeat," p. 20; Bauer, *Mexican War,* p. 55; John Porter Hatch to Eliza, May 19, 1846.

48. Bauer, *Mexican War,* pp. 55–57; Robert S. Henry, *The Story of the Mexican War,* p. 61; Lloyd Lewis, *Captain Sam Grant,* p. 146; Joseph P. Sanchez, "The Defeat of the Army of the North in South Texas: An Examination of Mexican Military Operations in the First Battles of the Mexican War," p. 21.

49. Meade, *Life and Letters,* p. 82; Brooks, *History,* p. 36; *Compaña.*

50. Capt. William H. Parker, *Recollections of a Naval Officer, 1841–1865,* pp. 51–52.

51. Bauer, "Battles," p. 73.

52. Surgeon Madison Mills, Diary of Surgeon Madison Mills, p. 14; *Niles National Register,* August 8, 1846.

53. *Niles National Register,* May 30, 1846.

54. Scarritt to Totten, p. 7.

55. Henry, *Campaign,* p. 93.

56. Lt. Col. W. G. Belknap, field report to Capt. W. W. S. Bliss, May 15, 1846.

57. John Frost, *History of the Mexican War,* pp. 669–70.

58. Mills, *Diary,* p. 15.

59. Thorpe, *Our Army,* p. 147; Rev. John Portmess, speech given at the commemoration of a monument dedicating the battle of Palo Alto.

60. A. A. Champion, "Historical Notes concerning the Battle of Palo Alto and Subsequent Events Which Took Place on the Battle Site."

61. *American Flag,* July 14, 1847.

62. Jake Ivey, "Reconnaissance Report on the Palo Alto Battlefield," January 21, 1992; Champion, "Notes"; Walter Plitt III, pers. comm., 1992.

63. Caleb Coker, ed., *The News from Brownsville: Helen Chapman's Letters from the Texas Military Frontier, 1848–1852,* pp. 92–93.

64. Portmess, speech; *Brownsville Herald,* May 9, 1893.

65. Gen. James Parker, "Report to War Dept., Adj. Gen. Office, Subject: Placing of Suitable Tablets to Mark Battlefield of Palo Alto," March 25, 1914.

66. Frank C. Pierce, *A Brief History of the Rio Grande Valley,* pp. 30–31, 105.

67. Champion, "Notes"; National Park Service, "Study of Palo Alto National Historic Site, Texas," p. 19.

68. Marrian Harr, pers. comm., 1992; Dr. Vidal Longoria, pers. comm., 1992; Clell L. Bond, "Palo Alto Battlefield: A Magnetometer and Metal Detector Survey," *Cultural Resources Laboratory Report* 4, p. 43.

69. Harry J. Shafer, "An Archaeological Reconnaissance of the Brownsville Relocation Study Area," *Texas A&M University Anthropology Laboratory Report* 1, p. 5.

70. Edward P. Baxter and Kay L. Killen, "A Study of the Palo Alto Battleground, Cameron County, Texas," *Texas A&M University Anthropology Report* 33, p. 26.

71. Bond, "Palo Alto," p. 4.

72. National Park Service, "Study," pp. 14–18; Walter E. Plitt III, "Palo Alto Battlefield National Park: A Metal Detector Survey"; Sanchez, "Arista."

Chapter 3. Weapons, Accoutrements, and the Soldier

1. Steven Ross, *From Flintlock to Rifle: Infantry Tactics, 1740–1866,* pp. 161–64.

2. Grady McWhiney and Perry D. Jamieson, *Attack and Die: Civil War Tactics and the Southern Heritage,* p. 29.

3. A. Nieto, A. S. Brown, and J. Hefter, *El soldado mexicano: Organización, vestuario, equipo. The Mexican Soldier: Organization, Dress, Equipment,* p. 53; José María Tornel,

Carta del general José María Tornel a sus amigos, sobre un artículo inserto en el Cosmopolita del día 17 de agosto del presente año, documento 3.

4. Anthony D. Darling, *Red Coat and Brown Bess*, p. 50; Philip J. Haythornthwaite, *Weapons and Equipment of the Napoleonic Wars*, pp. 31–32; Nieto et al., *El soldado mexicano*, p. 3; D. W. Bailey, *British Military Longarms, 1715–1815*, p. 17.

5. Garry James, "The Historic Baker Rifle," *Guns & Ammo* (November, 1983): 52; Nieto et al., *El soldado mexicano*, p. 54; Haythornthwaite, *Weapons*, p. 24; William A. Meuse, *The Weapons of the Battle of New Orleans*, pp. 10–12.

6. Haythornthwaite, *Weapons*, p. 25; Samuel P. Nesmith, "Analysis of Military Related Artifacts, La Villita Earthworks (41 BX 677), San Antonio, Texas: A Preliminary Report of Investigations of Mexican Siege Works at the Battle of the Alamo," *Archaeological Survey Report* 159: 67; James, "The Historic Baker Rifle," pp. 52–56; Tornel, *Carta*.

7. Haythornthwaite, *Weapons*, p. 23.

8. M. L. Brown, *Firearms in Colonial America, 1492–1792*, p. 172; Tornel, *Carta*.

9. Norman J. Bateman, *The Battle of Resaca de la Palma: An Electronic Metal Detector Survey*, pp. 32–33; Haythornthwaite, *Weapons*, p. 51.

10. U.S. War Dept., "Annual Report for 1846," p. 147; U.S. War Dept., "Annual Report for 1848," p. 343; Ulysses S. Grant, *Personal Memoirs of Ulysses S. Grant*, p. 46; James M. McCaffrey, *Army of Manifest Destiny: The American Soldier in the Mexican War 1846–1848*, p. 41.

11. David F. Butler, *United States Firearms: The First Century, 1776–1875*, pp. 34–35, 37.

12. Berkeley R. Lewis, *Small Arms and Ammunition in the United States Service*, pp. 34–35.

13. N. Bosworth, *A Treatise On the Rifle, Musket, Pistol, and Fowling-Piece*, pp. 80–81, in Lewis A. Garavaglia and Charles G. Worman, *Firearms of the American West, 1803–1865*, p. 113.

14. Garavaglia and Worman, *Firearms*, p. 113; statement from the Washington Arsenal, in U.S. Records of the Office of the Chief of Ordnance for 1846.

15. Bosworth, *Treatise*, pp. 100–102.

16. *Spirit of the Times*, Sept. 10, 1842, p. 2; Garavaglia and Worman, *Firearms*, pp. 113–14.

17. Steven Allie, pers. comm., 1993.

18. Butler, *United States Firearms*, p. 139.

19. Arcadi Gluckman, *Identifying Old U.S. Muskets, Rifles and Carbines*, pp. 137, 175.

20. Samuel E. Chamberlain, *My Confession: The Recollections of a Rogue*, p. 58.

21. Garavaglia and Worman, *Firearms*, p. 76; Joseph M. Nance, *After San Jacinto: The Texas-Mexican Frontier, 1836–1841*, p. 92.

22. J. C. Duval, *Early Times in Texas*, pp. 41–42.

23. Butler, *United States Firearms*, pp. 82–83; Kevin Young, pers. comm., 1993.

24. Garavaglia and Worman, *Firearms*, pp. 58–59.

25. Butler, *United States Firearms*, p. 201; Henry W. Barton, *Texas Volunteers in the Mexican War*, pp. 11–12; Michael J. Koury, *Arms for Texas: A Study of the Weapons of the Republic of Texas*, p. 43; Edward J. Nichols, *Zach Taylor's Little Army*, p. 59.

26. Butler, *United States Firearms*, pp. 141–46.

27. Nieto et al., *El soldado mexicano*, p. 33; *Washington Globe*, October 15, 1845, p. 1, col. 3; Gen. Cadmus M. Wilcox, *History of the Mexican War*, p. 51; Lt. Col. Louis C. Duncan, "A Medical History of General Zachary Taylor's Army of Occupation in Texas and Mexico, 1845–1847," *The Military Surgeon, Journal of the Association of Military Surgeons of the United States*, vol. 48 (1921): 95.

28. Haythornthwaite, *Weapons*, p. 26; Meuse, *Battle of New Orleans*, p. 13; Stephen J. Allie, *All He Could Carry: U.S. Army Infantry Equipment, 1839–1910*, p. 4.

29. T. F. Rodenbough, *From Everglade to Cañon with the Second Dragoons (Second United States Cavalry)*, p. 84; Haythornthwaite, *Weapons*, p. 52.

30. Nesmith, "Analysis," p. 68.

31. Ron G. Hickox, *U.S. Military Edged Weapons of the Second Seminole War, 1835–1842*, p. 6; Col. John R. Elting, *Military Uniforms in America, vol. 2: Years of Growth, 1796–1851*, p. 124; Sidney B. Brinckerhoff, "Metal Uniform Insignia of the U.S. Army in the Southwest, 1846–1902," pp. 2–4.

32. Hickox, *Edged Weapons*, p. 15.

33. U.S. Board of Artillery, *Instruction for Field Artillery, Horse and Foot, Compiled by a Board of Artillery Officers*, pp. 181–85; Capt. Robert Anderson, *Instruction for Field Artillery, Horse and Foot, Translated from the French, and Arranged for the Service of the United States*.

34. Maj. Gen. B. P. Hughes, *Firepower: Weapons Effectiveness on the Battlefield, 1630–1850*, p. 32; John E. Weems, *To Conquer a Peace: The War between the United States and Mexico*, p. 134.

35. Hughes, *Firepower*, p. 32; Capt. James Duncan, letter report to Col. W. G. Belknap, May 12, 1846.

36. Haythornthwaite, *Weapons*, p. 59.

37. Capt. Alfred Mordecai, *Ordnance Manual for the Use of Officers of the United States Army*.

38. Harold L. Peterson, *Round Shot and Rammers*, p. 107.

39. Hughes, *Firepower*, p. 33; L. Van Loan Naisawald, *Grape and Canister: The Story of the Field Artillery of the Army of the Potomac, 1861–1865*, pp. 537–38.

40. Maj. Gen. B. P. Hughes, *British Smooth-bore Artillery: The Muzzle Loading Artillery of the Eighteenth and Nineteenth Centuries*, p. 56; Lt. John Gibbon, *The Artillerist's Manual*, appendix, p. 35; John D. Bartleson, *A Field Guide for Civil War Explosive Ordnance, 1861–1865*, p. 5; Naisawald, *Grape and Canister*, p. 539.

41. Hughes, *Firepower*, p. 38; Gibbon, *Manual*, p. 387; Hughes, *British Smoothbore Artillery*, p. 56.

42. Gibbon, *Manual*, pp. 277–78.

43. Peterson, *Round Shot*, p. 107.

44. Grant, *Memoirs*, p. 44; Donald E. Houston, "The Role of Artillery in the Mexican War," *Journal of the West* 11 (April, 1972): 273–84.

45. Lester R. Dillon, Jr., *American Artillery in the Mexican War, 1846–1847*, p. 12.

46. Capt. Alfred Mordecai, *Artillery for the United States Land Service*, vol. 1, pp. 4–6; Dillon, *American Artillery*, pp. 12, 19; Peterson, *Round Shot*, p. 91; Elting, *Military Uniforms*, p. 122.

47. Peterson, *Round Shot*, pp. 88–90.

48. Waddy Thompson, Esq., *Recollections of Mexico*, p. 173; Luis de Agar, *Diccionario ilustrado de los pertechos de guerra y demas efertos pertenecientes al material de artillería*; Manuel Balbontín, *La invasión Americana, 1846 a 1848, apuntes del subteniente de artillería*; Hubert H. Bancroft, *History of Mexico, vol. 5, 1824–1861*, p. 173; Justin H. Smith, *The War with Mexico*, vol. 1, p. 156; Nieto et al., *El soldado mexicano*, p. 53; Sidney B. Brinckerhoff and Pierce A. Chamberlain, *Spanish Military Weapons in Colonial America, 1700–1821*, pp. 116–17; Jean Louis Berlandier, *Itinerario: Campaña de Palo Alto y Resaca de Guerrero*, p. 176.

49. George C. Furber, *The Twelve Months Volunteer; or, Journal of a Private in the Tennessee Regiment of Cavalry in the Campaign in Mexico, 1846–47*, pp. 199–200.

50. U.S. War Department, *General Regulations for the Army of the United States, 1841*; Elting, *Military Uniforms*, pp. 120–26; Brinkerhoff, "Metal Uniform Insignia," pp. 2–4; J. Duncan Campbell and Edgar M. Howell, *American Military Insignia*.

51. Allie, *All He Could Carry*, p. 5; R. T. Huntington, "Dragoon Accouterments and Equip-

ment, 1834–1849: An Identification Guide," *Plains Anthropologist* 12 (1967): 345–55.

52. Edward M. Coffman, *The Old Army: A Portrait of the American Army in Peacetime, 1784–1898*, pp. 139–41.

53. McCaffrey, *Army*, pp. 29–31.

54. Philip R. Katcher, *The Mexican-American War, 1846–1848*, p. 4; Thomas R. Irey, "Soldiering, Suffering, and Dying in the Mexican War," *Journal of the West* 11 (1972): 296; Chamberlain, *My Confession*, p. 226; Robert Ryal Miller, *Shamrock and Sword: The Saint Patrick's Battalion in the U.S.-Mexican War*, p. 102; Lloyd Lewis, *Captain Sam Grant*, pp. 187–88; George W. Smith and Charles Judah, eds., *Chronicles of the Gringos: The U.S. Army in the Mexican War, 1846–1848*, pp. 272, 289–90. See also George Ballentine, *Autobiography of an English Soldier in the United States Army*, for various eyewitness accounts detailing how U.S. enlisted men were treated by their officers and by civilians during the Mexican-American War.

55. Duncan, "Medical History," pp. 78, 87; U.S. War Dept., Office of the Surgeon General, *Army Medical Bulletin* 50: 49.

56. Capt. N. S. Jarvis, "An Army Surgeon's Notes of Frontier Service, Mexican War," *Journal of the Military Service* 40 (1907): 435–52.

57. U.S. War Dept., *Army Medical Bulletin*, p. 64.

58. Lewis, *Grant*, p. 133; Meade, *Life and Letters*, vol. 1, p. 45.

59. Nieto et al., *El soldado mexicano*, p. 53.

60. Ibid., p. 50; Katcher, *War*, pp. 26–27.

61. Katcher, *War*, p. 23.

62. Nieto et al., *El soldado mexicano*, p. 60.

63. Elizabeth Salas, *Soldaderas in the Mexican Military: Myth and History*, pp. 11, 29, 32–35, 121; Eric Ratliff, "Human Skeletal Remains from the Battle of Resaca de la Palma," in Charles M. Haecker, *A Thunder of Cannon: Archaeology of the Mexican–American War Battlefield of Palo Alto*, app. B, pp. 195–97.

64. Kevin R. Young, "Finding A Face: El Soldado Mexicano, 1835–1848," in Charles M. Haecker, *A Thunder of Cannon: Archaeology of the Mexican–American War Battlefield of Palo Alto*, app. C, p. 211.

65. Nieto et al., *El soldado mexicano*, pp. 76–77.

66. Katcher, *War*, p. 20.

67. T. Hooker, "Uniforms of the Mexican Army, 1837–1847, Part 1," *Tradition: The Journal of the International Society of Military Collectors* 65 (1976): 27–43; Nieto et al., *El soldado mexicano*, pp. 61–63. See also *Instrucción para la infantería ligera del ejército méxicano, mandada observar por el supremo gobierno*, for various detailed descriptions regarding Mexican military uniforms and accoutrements of the period.

68. Thompson, *Recollections*, p. 173; George W. Hockley to Albert Sydney Johnston, March 28, 1839; Smith, *Mexico*, p. 10; Young, "Finding a Face," p. 212.

69. Darling, *Red Coat and Brown Bess*, pp. 9–10; Maj. Gen. Winfield Scott, *Infantry Tactics; or, Rules for the Exercise and Manoevres of the United States Infantry*, vol. 1, *Schools of the Soldier and the Company*; *Instrucción para la infantería ligera del ejército mexicano*.

70. Edward Hagerman, *The American Civil War and the Origins of Modern Warfare, Ideas, Organization, and Field Command*, p. 6; Ross, *Tactics*, p. 153; Nieto et al., *El soldado mexicano*, p. 50; Antoine Henri de Jomini, *Summary of the Art of War*, trans. O. F. Winship and E. E. McLean; Denis Hart Mahan, *An Elementary Treatise on Advanced-Guard, Out-Post, and Detachment of Service of Troops, and the Manner of Posting and Handling Them in the Presence of an Enemy*.

71. George Deas, "Reminiscences of the Campaign of the Rio Grande," *Historical Magazine*, February, p. 103.

72. Lynn Montrose, *War through the Ages*, p. 336.

73. Col. John R. Elting, *Swords around a Throne: Napoleon's Grande Armeé*, p. 481; John Keegan, *The Face of Battle*, p. 141.

74. McWhiney and Jamieson, *Tactics*, p. 34; Darling, *Red Coat and Brown Bess*, p. 11.

75. Richard A. Preston, *Men at Arms: A History of Warfare and Its Interrelationships with Western Society*, pp. 192–93.

76. Philip J. Haythornthwaite, *Wellington's Military Machine*, p. 91.

77. Philip Lord, Jr., *War over Walloonscoick: Land Use and Settlement Pattern on the Bennington Battlefield—1777*, p. 39.

78. Grant, *Memoirs*, p. 95; Luther Giddings, *Sketches of the Campaign in Northern Mexico in Eighteen Hundred Forty-Six and Seven*, p. 181.

Chapter 4. Topographic and Documentary Analyses

1. Ulysses S. Grant, *Personal Memoirs of Ulysses S. Grant*, p. 94.

2. Zachary Taylor, "Official Reports from General Taylor," p. 2; Lt. Jeremiah Scarritt to Col. J. G. Totten, May 12, 1846.

3. Scarritt to Totten.

4. Ibid.

5. Ibid.

6. Jean Louis Berlandier, *Itinerario: Campaña de Palo Alto y Resaca de Guerrero*, p. 12.

7. Ibid., p. 161.

8. *Campaña contra los americanos, mayo de 1846*, pp. 10–11; Josef de Orga, *Prontuario en que se han reunido las obligaciones del soldado, cabo y sargento*, p. 128; A. Nieto, A. S. Brown, and J. Hefter, *El soldado mexicano: Organización, vestuario, equipo. The Mexican Soldier: Organization, Dress, Equipment*, p. 51.

9. Cf. Berlandier, *Itinerario*, pp. 59–61; Capt. William S. Henry, *Campaign Sketches of the War with Mexico*, p. 92.

10. John Keegan and R. Holmes, *Soldiers*, p. 263.

11. Justin H. Smith, "Official Military Reports," *American Historical Review* 21 (1915): 96–97.

12. Cf. Henry, *Campaign Sketches*, p. 92; J. W. Stewart, map showing troop movements at the battle of Palo Alto.

13. Alcaraz et al., *Apuntes para la historia de la guerra entre México y los Estados Unidos. The Other Side: Or, Notes for the History of the War between Mexico and the United States*, p. 186; Stewart, Palo Alto battle map.

14. Nathan C. Brooks, *A Complete History of the Mexican War: Its Causes, Conduct, and Consequences*, p. 126; Gen. Cadmus M. Wilcox, *History of the Mexican War*, p. 53; Stewart, Palo Alto battle map.

15. Henry, *Campaign Sketches*, p. v; *Life and Public Services of Gen. Z. Taylor*.

16. Scarritt to Totten.

17. Ibid.

18. Ibid.

Chapter 5. The Physical Evidence of the Battle

1. William L. Calver and Reginald P. Bolton, "Consider the Revolutionary War Bullet," *The New York Historical Society Quarterly Bulletin* 11 (1928): 120; David F. Butler, *United States Firearms: The First Century, 1776–1875*, p. 18.

2. Berkeley R. Lewis, *Small Arms and Ammunition in the United States Service*, pp. 108, 111, 115.

3. Ibid., pp. 167–68.

4. U.S. War Dept., "Annual Report for 1846," p. 147; Maj. Gen. Winfield Scott, *Infantry Tactics; or, Rules for the Exercise and Manoevres of the United States Infantry, vol. 1, Schools of the Soldier and the Company.*

5. Berkeley R. Lewis, "Small Arms and Ammunition in the United States Service, 1776–1865," *Smithsonian Miscellaneous Collections* 29: 175–76, 185.

6. Lt. John Gibbon, *The Artillerist's Manual*, appendix, p. 35.

7. A. Nieto, A. S. Brown, and J. Hefter, *El soldado mexicano: Organización, vestuario, equipo. The Mexican Soldier: Organization, Dress, Equipment*, p. 53.

8. Anthony D. Darling, *Red Coat and Brown Bess*, p. 51; Nieto et al., *El soldado mexicano*, p. 53; Lawrence E. Babits and Richard Manesto, "An Investigation of Minié Ball Manufacture to Determine Effects of Prolonged Firing," p 3.

9. Lewis, *Small Arms*, p. 32.

10. Joseph P. Sanchez, "General Mariano Arista at the Battle of Palo Alto, Texas, 1846: Military Realist or Failure?" *Journal of the West* 24, no. 2 (April, 1985): 16. Six officers under Arista were interrogated by General Francisco Pardo, *fiscal militar*, before a formal board of inquiry in June, 1846, regarding Arista's actions at Palo Alto. This quote was from General Ampudia during the inquiry. The various statements made by these officers are in *Fallo definitivo del supremo tribunal de la guerra, al examinar la conducta militar del exmo. sr. general d. Mariano Arista en las acciones de guerra que sostuvo al principio de la invasión americana*, Biblioteca Nacional de México.

11. Philip J. Haythornthwaite, *Weapons and Equipment of the Napoleonic Wars*, p. 60.

12. Calver and Bolton, "Bullet," p. 76.

13. Lewis, *Small Arms*, pp. 115–16.

14. Gibbon, *Manual*, p. 27.

15. Ibid.

16. Maj. Gen. George G. Meade, *The Life and Letters of George G. Meade, Major-General United States Army*, vol. 1, p. 79; Lester R. Dillon, Jr., *American Artillery in the Mexican War, 1846–1847*, p. 12; Lt. Jeremiah Scarritt to Col. J. G. Totten, May 12, 1846; Wilcox, *History*, p. 60.

17. Ulysses S. Grant, *Personal Memoirs of Ulysses S. Grant*, p. 94; Dillon, *American Artillery*, p. 12.

18. Bvt. Col. J. S. McIntosh, letter report to Office of Adjutant General, Dec. 3, 1846.

19. Gibbon, *Manual*, appendix, p. 29.

20. Zachary Taylor, "Official Reports from General Taylor," pp. 21–22.

21. Harold L. Peterson, *Round Shot and Rammers*, p. 107.

22. George C. Furber, *The Twelve Months Volunteer; or, Journal of a Private in the Tennessee Regiment of Cavalry in the Campaign in Mexico, 1846–47*, p. 199.

23. Capt. C. A. May to Lt. John McDonald, Adj. Second Dragoons, letter report, May 10, 1846, in Taylor, "Official Reports from General Taylor," pp. 21–22.

24. McIntosh, letter report, Dec. 3, 1846.

25. Gibbon, *Manual*, appendix, p. 27.

26. Peterson, *Round Shot*, p. 41.

27. Seymour de Lotbiniere, "English Gunflint Making in the Seventeenth and Eighteenth Centuries," *Colonial Frontier Guns*, pp. vii–viii; Nancy Kenmotsu, "Gunflints: A Study," *Historical Archaeology* 24, no. 2 (1990): 100.

28. Robert H. McNulty, "A Study of Bayonets in the Department of Archaeology, Colonial Williamsburg, with Notes on Bayonet Identification," in *Colonial Williamsburg Occasional Papers in Archaeology, vol. 1: Five Artifact Studies*, p. 66, fig. 6, no. 12.

29. Arthur Woodward, "Spanish Trade Goods," in Charles C. Di Peso, ed., *The Sobaipuri Indians of the Upper San Pedro River Valley, Southeastern Arizona*, p. 203; Eric A. Ratliff, "Human Skeleton Remains from the Battle of Resaca de la Palma," in Charles M. Haecker, *A Thunder of Cannon: Archaeology of the Mexican–American War Battlefield of Palo Alto*, app. B, p. 201; George C. Neumann and Frank J. Kravic, *Collector's Illustrated Encyclopedia of the American Revolution*, p. 59, fig. 48.

30. Marc Simmons and Frank Turley, *Southwestern Colonial Ironwork: The Spanish Blacksmithing Tradition from Texas to California*, p. 114, fig. 4.

31. Lee Hanson and Dick Ping Hsu, *Casemates and Cannonballs: Archaeological Investigations at Fort Stanwix, Rome, New York*, p. 93, fig. 51r.

32. Ibid., fig. 51l.

33. Samuel P. Nesmith, "Analysis of Military Related Artifacts, La Villita Earthworks (41 BX 677), San Antonio, Texas: A Preliminary Report of Investigations of Mexican Siege Works at the Battle of the Alamo," *Archaeological Survey Report* 159: 93; Samuel P. Nesmith, "Military Artifacts," *Archaeological Survey Report* 205: 61–62; Stanley J. Olsen, "Dating Early Plain Buttons by Their Form," *American Antiquity* 28, no. 4 (1963): 552. See also Carl J. Clausen, "The Fort Pierce Collection," pp. 1–43, for illustrations of a variety of U.S. Army equipage used during the 1840s.

34. Stanley South, "Analysis of the Buttons from Brunswick Town and Fort Fisher," *Florida Anthropologist* 17, no. 2 (1964): 116, 118; Olsen, "Buttons," p. 552.

35. Nieto et al., *El soldado mexicano*, p. 51.

36. David F. Johnson, *Uniform Buttons: American Armed Forces, 1784–1948*, vol. 1, pp. 51–52; J. Duncan Campbell, "Military Buttons, Long-lost Heralds of Fort Mackinac's Past," *Mackinac History, Leaflet* 7, fig. 17.

37. Anne A. Fox, *Archaeological Investigations in Alamo Plaza, San Antonio, Bexar County, Texas, 1988 and 1989*, p. 33.

38. Col. John R. Elting, *Military Uniforms in America*, vol. 2: *Years of Growth, 1796–1851*, p. 122.

39. Nieto et al., *El soldado mexicano*, plates 1, 4, 5, 9, 12, 13.

40. Cf. Robert M. Herskovitz, "Fort Bowie Material Culture," *Anthropological Papers of the University of Arizona* 31: 64; W. Dean Wood and Karen G. Wood, *Soldiers and Citizens: Civil War Actions around Latimer's Farm, Cobb County, Georgia*, p. 74.

41. Nieto et al., *El soldado mexicano*, plate 8e.

42. T. V. Buttrey and Clyde Hubbard, *A Guide Book of Mexican Coins, 1822 to Date*, pp. 54–55; Nieto et al., *El soldado mexicano*, p. 62.

43. G. Kendrick, *The Antique Bottle Collector*, p. 20; Ronald R. Switzer, *The Bertrand Bottles: A Study of Nineteenth-Century Glass and Ceramic Containers*, pp. 27–29, 91, 92.

44. André L. Simon, *The Noble Grapes and the Great Wines of France*, pp. 15–27.

45. Ivor Noël Hume, *A Guide to Artifacts of Colonial America*, p. 238; Association for Preservation Technology, *Illustrated Catalogue of American Hardware of the Russell Erwin Manufacturing Company*, p. 250; Woodward, "Spanish Trade Goods," p. 194; Edward Chappell, "A Study of Horseshoes in the Department of Archaeology, Colonial Williamsburg," in Noël Hume, ed., *Colonial Williamsburg Occasional Papers in Archaeology*, vol. 1: *Five Artifact Studies*, p. 107.

46. Simmons and Turley, *Southwestern Colonial Ironwork*, pp. 101, 103, 115.

47. Gibbon, *Manual*, appendix, pp. 17, 21.

Chapter 6. Conclusion

1. Gen. Pedro de Ampudia, *Manifesto dando cuenta del conducto*, in Joseph P. Sanchez, "General Mariano Arista at the Battle of Palo Alto, Texas, 1846: Military Realist or Failure?" *Journal of the West* 24, no. 2 (April, 1985): 18.

2. National Park Service, "Study of Palo Alto Battlefield National Historic Site, Texas," p. 39.

3. Richard A. Fox, Jr., *Archaeology, History, and Custer's Last Battle: The Little Bighorn Reexamined*, pp. 7–10.

Glossary

AIDE-DE-CAMP. Junior staff officer attached to a general.

ARM (of service). Cavalry, infantry, artillery, or other branch.

BALDRIC. A shoulder belt, worn diagonally from shoulder to hip.

BALL. Musket ball.

BALLISTICS. Science of projectiles in motion.

BATTALION. A military unit of two or more companies but smaller than a regiment.

BATTALION COMPANY. The "center" company of an infantry battalion.

BATTERY. Originally a gun emplacement. By the mid-nineteenth century, this term referred to a company-size artillery unit equipped for mobile warfare with a variable number of guns—usually four to eight, depending on standardized method of artillery organization of a nationality or availability and expediency. *See* FIELD BATTERY.

BLOUSE. Smock-type garment.

BOMB. Mortar shell; loosely applied to all explosive projectiles.

BORE. Interior of a firearm and cannon barrel.

BREASTPLATE. Small badge worn on the shoulder belt.

BREECH. Rear or closed end of a firearm and cannon barrel.

BREECHLOADER. A firearm that receives its load at the breech.

BREVET. A commission to an officer that confers higher rank without higher pay.

BRIGADE. Military unit larger than a regiment and smaller than a division.

BRIQUET. An infantry sword; a type of HANGER.

BROWN BESS. Nickname applied to long Land Pattern British muskets and later patterns, including the India Pattern musket.

BULLION. Gold or silver LACE.

BUTT. Rearward portion of the stock of a firearm.

BUTT CAP. A metal cap used to cover and protect the butt of a pistol.

BUTT PLATE. A reinforcing plate used to cover and protect the butt of a shoulder arm.

CAISSON. Ammunition wagon accompanying mobile artillery.

CALIBER. Diameter of the bore of a cannon and firearm. For a firearm, caliber is usually expressed in hundredths of an inch. For a cannon, this is expressed either as the weight of the solid shot or the inches of diameter of the bore.

CANISTER. A tin projectile containing small shot.

CANNON. All tube artillery: includes guns, howitzers, and mortars.

CAP. A small metal device containing a percussion-ignited compound designed to ignite the main charge of a firearm.

CARBINE. A shortened form of musket or rifle used by mounted troops.

CARRIAGE. Wheeled mount for a cannon.

CARTRIDGE.

(1) For firearms, the paper tube containing the lead ball and gunpowder; the paper was used as wadding once its contents were poured into the musket or rifle barrel.

(2) For a cannon, the bag or case containing the propelling charge.

CASE or SPHERICAL CASE. A hollow round similar to a SHELL in that it has a bursting gunpowder charge. The cavity of a case round, however, is packed with lead balls held in a mass of melted sulfur or resin and includes a fuse to cause it to burst at the correct point on the trajectory.

CAZADOR. Spanish term; same as light infantry; elite troops specifically employed as skirmishers and sharpshooters, ususally armed with rifles.

CHARGE. The propellant and round in a firearm and cannon.

COATEE. A short military coat, cut to the waist in front, with short tails that just covered the buttocks.

COCKADE. A rosette of national colors worn on hats and helmets.

COLOR SERGEANT. A top-ranked, noncommissioned officer.

COLUMN FORMATION. Several adjacent files of infantrymen. A column on the march had a frontage of up to eight men and an immense length. When a column attacked, its frontage was usually greater in length than in depth. The purpose of an attack column was to deliver a decisive impact at the point where the head of the column struck the enemy LINE FORMATION.

COMMISSARY.

(1) A supply officer.

(2) A military supply depot or dump.

COMPANY. Military unit smaller than a battalion.

CONE. A small tube of a percussion firearm on which is placed the PERCUSSION CAP.

CORPS. A tactical unit consisting of several divisions.

CUIRASS. Breastplate.

CYLINDER. The part of a multifiring firearm holding a number of cartridges presenting the loads in succession for firing by revolution about an axis.

DIRECT FIRE. Fire against a visible target.

DIVISION. Military unit larger than a brigade.

DRAGOON. Mounted infantryman and forerunner of American cavalryman. The latter meaning was in use by the Civil War.

DUCK. A fine, bleached linen canvas, used for summer wear.

ELEVATION. Angle formed between the axis of the cannon bore and the horizontal.

ELEVATION SCREW. A hand screw under the cannon breech for adjusting elevation.

ENFILADE. Fire from a flank, raking the entire length of a formation.

ENSIGN. Infantry second lieutenant; a brevet rank in the U.S. military at the time of the U.S.-Mexican War.

EPAULET (or EPAULETTE). An ornamental shoulder piece. During the period of the U.S.-Mexican War, its shape, size, and color were used to indicate the wearer's grade and branch of service.

ESCOPETA. A short musket with a bell-mouthed or sawed-off barrel, used by Mexican mounted irregulars; also called a "scuppet" by U.S. soldiers.

EXFOLIATION. As the term is used in this text, it is the condition of metal artifacts whose original surfaces have scaled or flaked off due to oxidation and absorption of water with attendant ground salts.

FACINGS. Lapels, cuffs, and collars of a uniform coat that were covered or "faced" with a different color than the coat. The colors used often indicated the regiment or service branch of its wearer.

FIELD BATTERY.
(1) A company of artillery equipped with guns, horses, and vehicles to serve as field artillery.
(2) A specific term used to emphasize the difference between such a unit and a conventional, less mobile BATTERY.

FIELD OFFICER (or FIELD GRADE OFFICER). A major, lieutenant colonel, or colonel.

FIXED AMMUNITION. Propellant and projectile complete as a single unit; artillery projectile with a wooden SABOT affixed.

FLINT. A variety of hard quartz stone, possessing fracture properties for a sharp edge that produced sparks when the edge was struck against steel.

FLINTLOCK. A firearm equipped with a gunlock in which the impact of a piece of flint against steel created sparks that set off the priming.

FOOT ARTILLERY. An artillery unit in which only the officers, senior noncommissioned officers (NCOs), trumpeters, and drivers were mounted. The other enlisted men marched on foot.

FORAGE CAP. A light, soft leather or cloth cap worn with the undress uniform; same as a barracks cap.

FOREARM. The part of the stock in front of the trigger guard extending under the barrel toward the muzzle.

FRIZZEN. The upright, pivoted part of the flintlock mechanism that, when struck by the flint, produced sparks. Also termed "battery."

FROG. A short sheath attached to a belt, designed to hold a scabbard.

FULL DRESS UNIFORM. The showy uniform worn for parades and other military ceremonies.

FURNITURE. Metal fittings on a musket or rifle.

FUSE (alternate nineteenth-century spelling, FUZE). Device to detonate a shell or other weapon.

FUSIL. Light musket.

GAUGE. The diameter of the bore of the firearm expressed in the number of spherical balls of corresponding size to the pound. For example, sixteen gauge indicates a diameter that would take a round ball weighing sixteen such balls to equal a pound.

GRAPESHOT (GRAPE). A type of artillery ammunition consisting of metal balls (the number and diameter depending on the caliber of the gun) placed in a canvas bag and tied to form a rough cylinder that fitted the gun's bore. The metal balls used in canister rounds were also informally called grapeshot, although they were of smaller caliber and greater number. By the early nineteenth century, true grapeshot was reserved for use by Navy and coastal artillery since it was found that CANISTER was more effective for field artillery.

GREATCOAT. An overcoat. During this period, it was usually long and had an attached shoulder cape.

GUN. Long-barreled cannon with a characteristic high muzzle velocity and flat trajectory.

HANDSPIKE. A short wooden pole for moving the trail of a carriage either left or right.

HANGER. A short, heavy cutting sword with a curved blade; generally an infantry weapon.

HAVERSACK. For infantrymen, a haversack was a canvas or heavy linen bag used in the field for carrying rations. Soldiers usually carried the bag over the right shoulder so that it rode the left hip and thus did not interfere with the cartridge box. For artillerymen, a haversack was a leather bag used to transport the powder cartridge from the LIMBER to the field cannon.

HORSE ARTILLERY. An artillery unit in which all men had personal mounts. It could, therefore, move rapidly enough to keep up with cavalry.

HOUSINGS. Horse trappings.

HOWITZER. Short-barreled cannon with a characteristic high angle of fire.

INDIRECT FIRE. Fire against a target not visible from the cannon.

JACKET. A term synonymous with waistcoat or vest; also a short coat with sleeves.

KERSEY. A coarse woolen cloth, usually ribbed.

KNAPSACK. An infantryman's pack. In the Mexican Army, it was made of cowhide with the hair left on the outside; in the U.S. Army, the knapsack was made of heavy canvas, varnished to make it waterproof.

LACE. Flat braid used for trimming lapels, cuffs, and other portions of the uniform.

LANCER. Light cavalryman armed with a lance.

LIGHT ARTILLERY. During this period, a very loose term applied to either foot or horse artillery; field artillery as compared to fortress or siege artillery.

LIGHT INFANTRY. Troops selected for agility, marksmanship, courage, and reliability; used for advance guard operations, raids, and skirmishing. In some cases, they were issued lighter weapons and equipment.

LIMBER. Two-wheeled, horse-drawn vehicle for pulling gun carriages or caissons.

LINE. A term describing ordinary infantry, cavalry, and other soldiers; meaning "infantry of the line of battle."

LINE (or LINE FORMATION). One or more files of infantrymen in close proximity. Firing within this formation was conducted by

(1) a massed volley of the entire formation;

(2) one file firing while the other file(s) were reloading and then firing in turn; or

(3) company or platoon subdivision, so that musketry fire would be issuing from some part of the line at all times (a "rolling volley").

LINE OF SIGHT. Straight line from the muzzle of a piece to the target or point of impact.

LINSTOCK. An artilleryman's implement: a staff three feet long with a forked iron head to hold a slow match; used to fire a cannon.

LOCK. The mechanism of a firearm. The function was to ignite the explosive.

LONGARM. A classification name for the longer type of firearms, such as muskets, rifles, and carbines.

MAGAZINE. Storage space for munitions; a supplementary container for musket or rifle ammunition carried on the individual soldier.

MINIÉ BULLET. An elongated bullet with a cup-shaped hollow in the base that, when expanded by the action of the gases, causes the bullet to take the rifling. It was named after C. E. Minié, captain of infantry (French Army) to whom the invention of the system is credited. The Minié was adopted by the U.S. Army in 1855.

MORTAR. Very short-barreled cannon with a low muzzle velocity and a very high trajectory.

MUSKET. A smoothbore barrel shoulder arm.

MUSKETOON. A shortened musket, commonly used by artillerymen and some mounted units.

MUZZLE. The end of the barrel from which the bullet leaves the arm.

PAN. The receptacle for holding the priming charge for a flintlock.

PARK. Artillery reserve.

PATCH. A leather or cloth wrapper, usually greased, used around the bullet of rifled muzzleloading arms to facilitate loading.

PERCUSSION CAP. A small metal, cup-shaped device charged with fulminate or other percussion-ignited compound and placed on the cone of a percussion arm. When struck by the hammer, the explosive compound was ignited by the blow, and the flash was transmitted through the hollow cone to the main charge in the barrel.

PERCUSSION WEAPON. A firearm with a gunlock that fired by striking a PER-
CUSSION CAP. It replaced the flintlock during this period.

PICKET (derived from the French *piquet*). Infantry or light cavalry outpost.

PIECE. A firearm, including any cannon.

PIPING. A narrow fold of cloth usually colored to contrast with the surrounding
cloth material. It was often used as a decoration on nineteenth-century uniforms.

PLASTRON. Colored chest-panel on a jacket.

POINT-BLANK. Coincident point of the TRAJECTORY and LINE OF SIGHT.

PORTFIRE. A tube, usually of thin metal, containing a quick-burning PRO-
PELLANT, such as alcohol mixed with gunpowder. It gradually replaced the
LINSTOCK during the late eighteenth and early nineteenth centuries.

PRESIDIALES. Mexican soldiers who guarded Mexico's northern frontier and
conducted their operations from a string of small forts, or presidios, situated
along the frontier.

PRICKER. Wire needle used for clearing musket touch hole.

PROJECTILE. Portion of a ROUND intended for delivery to the target; cannonball, musket ball.

PROPELLANT. Explosive charge; gunpowder in a ROUND of ammunition.

QUOIN. A wedge-shaped device used to elevate or depress the cannon tube. By
the late eighteenth century, a number of countries (for example, England and
France) had replaced the quoin with the elevation screw.

RAMMER. A wooden staff with a head to force the powder charge and projectile
into the cannon barrel.

RAMROD. A wooden or metal rod used for ramming down the charge of muzzleloading arms.

REGIMENT. Military unit larger than a battalion and smaller than a brigade.

REGULAR ARMY. The permanent Army of a country, maintained both in peacetime and war; the "Standing Army."

RIFLE. A shoulder-fired longarm with a rifled small-caliber barrel.

RIFLE MUSKET. A term used by the Ordnance Department in the mid-nineteenth
century to designate the new musket-size rifled arms and long, slim rifle-caliber
barrels.

RIFLING. Grooves cut in the sides of the bore or the process of cutting such grooves.

ROUND. One complete load of ammunition for one piece.

SABER (or SABRE).
(1) A curved cavalry sword.
(2) A cavalryman; for example, "a regiment of 800 sabers."

SABOT. Wooden block on artillery FIXED AMMUNITION.

SAPPER. Originally one who dug narrow siege trenches; later the generic term for
engineers. *See* ZAPADOR.

SCALES. A type of shoulder knot made of brass scales. During this period, it was
worn only by mounted troops.

SHABRAQUE (alternate spelling SHABRAK). A cloth cover fitting over the saddle and saddle blanket; ornamental horse furniture. In the United States mounted service, it was used mostly for full-dress ceremonies, but the Mexican mounted soldiers used them in the field.

SEMIFIXED AMMUNITION. One complete round with adjustable components, such as a powder charge.

SEPARATE LOADING AMMUNITION. Powder cartridge and projectile independent of each other.

SHAKO. A cylindrical military cap made of felt and leather. It originated in Austria and was adopted by England, France, Spain, the United States, Mexico, and other nations as standard infantry headgear by the early nineteenth century.

SHELL. Hollow PROJECTILE containing powder and fused to detonate.

SHOT. Spherical PROJECTILE.

SIEGE TRAIN. Heavy artillery, for besieging fortresses and fortified towns, accompanying an invading army. It normally marched with the baggage train.

SMOOTHBORE. A firearm whose bore is not rifled.

SPADROON. Light, straight-bladed sword.

SPATTERDASHES. Long leggings worn on eighteenth- and nineteenth-century uniforms, used to protect trouser legs from mud, snow, and moisture.

SPONGE. A woolen bag covering a wooden cylinder; for fieldpieces the sponge was attached to the opposite end of the same staff as the RAMMER. The sponge soaked in water extinguished sparks left after discharge and also helped remove black powder residue.

SQUARE FORMATION. A defensive formation executed by infantry when about to be attacked by cavalry. Squares were formed from COLUMN or LINE FORMATIONS. With a ten-company battalion in line, three companies would stand fast, the remainder falling back at right angles and the flanks turning at right angles again to close the rear of the square (or more commonly an oblong formation). The square was almost always hollow, with officers, musicians, colors, and baggage in the center.

STANDARDS. The flags of a cavalry regiment.

STEEL. *See* FRIZZEN.

STOCK.

(1) The wooden part of a firearm.

(2) A wide, stiff neck covering.

SWIVEL. A mechanism permitting motion on a part of an arm so that it remains a part of the piece; for example, a "swivel ramrod" was a ramrod attached to the arm yet capable of the movement required for loading.

THUMBSTALL. A buckskin cover for the thumb to protect it from heat while stopping the cannon vent during loading.

TRAIL. That part of a CANNON CARRIAGE resting on the ground.

TRAIN. Troops responsible for driving transport, artillery, and other cargo.

TRAJECTORY. Path of a PROJECTILE in flight.

TRIGGER GUARD. The frame placed about the trigger to minimize the possibility of accidental discharge by unintentional pressure on the trigger.

TRIGGER PLATE. The metal part of the firearm through which the trigger projects.

TUBE. The cannon, synonymous with barrel.

UNDRESS UNIFORM. A uniform worn for normal military duties; less showy but more comfortable than FULL DRESS.

UNLIMBER. Unhitch from LIMBER and prepare to fire.

VALISE. A leather case carried behind the cantle on the saddle to hold a horseman's cloak and other articles.

VENT. A small hole, tube, or channel used to convey the flash of the ignited priming from the exterior of the BREECH to the main CHARGE in the chamber.

VOLTIGEUR. A French term for a light infantryman, introduced during the Napoleonic wars. The name was borrowed for the Tenth Infantry Regiment with one horse for each two men, permitting double-mounting for rapid movement. Early plans to give it a special organization, uniform, and equipment fell through. Eventually, this regiment actually differed from other regular U.S. infantry regiments only in its name.

WAD. The paper, felt, or other material used to retain the CHARGE in the barrel of a firearm and cannon (or in a cartridge).

WORM. A twisted, corkscrew-shaped metal device used on the end of a ramrod in withdrawing the CHARGE in muzzleloading arms.

ZAPADOR. The Spanish word for SAPPER. *Zapadores* were elite troops in the Mexican Army.

Bibliography
with Selected Annotations

Manuscript Collections

Beaman, Jenks. Papers. The Houghton Library. Harvard University.

Bee, Hamilton P. Papers. The University of Texas Library.

Belknap, William G. Papers. Princeton University Library.

Brooks, Sumner. Papers. The Beineke Library. Yale University.

Buchanan, Robert Christie. Papers. Maryland Historical Society.

Chapman Family Papers. United States Military Academy at West Point, Special Collections.

Cochrane, Richard. Papers. The University of Texas Library.

Craig, Henry Knox. Papers. The Carnegie Library.

Crimmins, Martin. Papers. The University of Texas Library.

Deas, George. Papers. Mississippi Department of Archives and History.

Duncan, James. Papers. United States Military Academy at West Point, Special Collections.

Dyer, Alexander B. Papers. Library of Congress.

French, Samuel Gibbs. Papers. Mississippi Department of Archives and History.

Hatch, John Porter. Papers. Library of Congress.

Hays, Alexander. Papers. Historical Society of Western Pennsylvania.

Hazlitt, Robert. Papers. United States Military Academy at West Point, Special Collections.

Henshaw, John C. Papers. Brown University.

Hitchcock, Ethan Allen. Papers. Library of Congress.

Hunter, Nathaniel Wyche. Papers. The University of Georgia Library.

Jesup, Thomas Sidney. Papers. Library of Congress.

Judah, Henry Moses. Papers. Library of Congress.

Kendall, George W. Papers. The University of Texas at Arlington.

McCall, George A. Papers. United States Military Academy at West Point, Special Collections.

McLaws, Lafayette. Papers. Southern Historical Collection. The University of North Carolina.

Mansfield, Joseph F. Papers. United States Military Academy at West Point, Special Collections.

Meade, George Gordon. Papers. Historical Society of Pennsylvania.

Mexican Military Manuscripts, 1842–46. United States Military Academy at West Point, Special Collections.

Mills, Madison. Papers. The Filson Club.

Myers, Abraham. Journal. Historical Society of Pennsylvania.

National Archives. Office of the Adjutant General. Papers captured with General Arista's baggage. Record Group 54.

Papers captured with General Arista's baggage. New York Historical Society.

Peck, John James. Papers. United States Military Academy at West Point, Special Collections.

Pemberton, John C. Correspondence in Pemberton Family Papers. Historical Society of Pennsylvania.

Reynolds, John Fulton. Papers. The Franklin and Marshall College Library, Lancaster, Pennsylvania.

Smith, Edmund Kirby. Papers. Southern Historical Collection. The University of North Carolina.

Smith, Sidney K. Correspondence in the Seth Shetterly Collection. The Bentley Library. University of Michigan.

Taylor, George William. Papers. The Clements Library. University of Michigan.

Taylor, Zachary. Papers. Library of Congress.

Mexican Sources

Archivo General de la Nación (AGN)

Hemeroteca del AGN:

> *Amigo del pueblo*
>
> *Boletín de noticias*
>
> *Católico*
>
> *Diario del gobierno*
>
> *Diario del gobierno de la república mexicana*
>
> *Don Simplicio*
>
> *Indicador de la federación mejicana*
>
> *Memorial histórico*
>
> *El monitor constitucional*
>
> *El monitor republicano*
>
> *La voz del pueblo*

Hemeroteca del Museo Nacional de Antropología:

> *Aurora*
>
> *El memorial histórico*
>
> *La reforma*
>
> *El republicano*

Hemeroteca de la Universidad Nacional Autónoma de México:

> *Alcance al boletín republicano de Jalisco.* 11 Agosto, 1846, no. 5, Tomo I.
>
> *La columna de la libertad.* Periódico oficial del estado de Querétaro. 1846.
>
> *Diario del gobierno.* 15 Agosto, 1846, no. 9, Tomo I.
>
> *Diario oficial del gobierno de México*
>
> *Diario oficial del gobierno mexicano*
>
> *Don Simplicio*
>
> *El pasatiempo.* 10–24 Mayo, 1846, nos. 15–17, Tomo I.
>
> *El Sonorense.* Periódico oficial del gobierno de Sonora. 21 Agosto, 1846, no. 5, Tomo I.

Hemeroteca Miguel Lerdo de Tejada, perteneciente a la secretaria de hacienda y crédito público (SHCP), en el Centro Histórico

Registro Oficial del Gobierno del Departamento de Durango

Books and Articles

Agar, Luis de. *Diccionario ilustrado de los pertechos de guerra y demas efertos pertenecientes al material de artillería*. Madrid: D. Joaquín de Aramburu, 1866. Definitions and detailed descriptions of Spanish military items, with sketches; theorizes what the Mexican Army may have had in its arsenals and supply depots in 1846–48.

Alcaraz, Ramón, et al. *Apuntes para la historia de la guerra entre México y los Estados Unidos. The Other Side: Or, Notes for the History of the War between Mexico and the United States*. Translated and edited in the United States by Albert C. Ramsey. New York: John Wiley, 1850. First published in Mexico City, this work was a joint effort by Alcaraz and a dozen other Mexican war veterans who recorded their accounts of the war. Excellent descriptions of military actions from the Mexican viewpoint, although some of the information is highly questionable. For example, Alcaraz states that both armies at Palo Alto numbered around three thousand, denying virtually all other historical accounts that a Mexican army of superior force lost to an American force about half its size. Numerous maps and battle plans.

Allie, Stephen J. *All He Could Carry: U.S. Army Infantry Equipment, 1839–1910*. Fort Leavenworth, Kans.: Frontier Army Museum Pub., 1991. A good, basic description of what the U.S. foot soldier wore and carried.

American Flag. Article regarding Palo Alto House dated July 14, 1847. Newspaper published by U.S. occupation forces in Matamoros, Mexico.

Ampudia, General Pedro de. *Manifesto dando cuenta del conducto*. Mexico City, 1846.

Anderson, Captain Robert. *Instruction for Field Artillery, Horse and Foot, Translated from the French, and Arranged for the Service of the United States*. Philadelphia: Robert P. Desilver, 1845.

Association for Preservation Technology. *Illustrated Catalogue of American Hardware of the Russell Erwin Manufacturing Company*. Ottawa: facsimile edition, Association for Preservation Technology, 1980. Initially printed by Russell and Erwin Manufacturing Co., New Britain, Conn., 1865.

Babits, Lawrence E., and Richard Manesto. "An Investigation of Minié Ball Manufacture to Determine Effects of Prolonged Firing." Paper presented at the Society for Historical Archaeology Conference on Historical and Underwater Archaeology, Vancouver, B.C. (Canada), January 5–9, 1994.

Bailey, D. W. *British Military Longarms, 1715–1815*. Harrisburg, Pa.: Stackpole Books, 1971. A classic, referenced by all other sources dealing with eighteenth-century small arms; detailed photos of the famous "Brown Bess," with closeups of musket furniture.

Balbontín, Manuel. *La invasión Americana, 1846 a 1848, apuntes del subteniente de artillería*. Mexico City, 1883. Contains interesting accounts regarding the Mexican military, specifically the quality of Mexican artillery used at Palo Alto.

Ballentine, George. *Autobiography of an English Soldier in the United States Army*. New York: Stringer and Townsend, 1853. Ballentine was in Scott's command. Contains observations that seem accurate, although the author did not display the revulsion for camp life and military discipline expressed by most soldiers.

Bancroft, Hubert Howe. *History of Mexico, vol. 5, 1824–1861*. San Francisco: A. L. Bancroft and Co., 1885. A thorough history of the U.S.-Mexican War. Bancroft's interpretations on the causes of the war are unusually pro-Mexican.

Barbour, Philip, and Martha Barbour. *Journals of the Late Brevet Major Philip Norbourne Barbour and His Wife Martha Isabella Hopkins Barbour, Written during the War with Mexico—1846*. New York: Rhoda van Bibber Tanner Doubleday, ed., G. P. Putnam's Sons, 1936. A lively, personal account about such fellow officers as General Taylor. It also provides insights into values and mores of the officer class in mid-nineteenth-century United States and covers the period from March 28 to September 20, 1846, when Barbour was killed at Monterrey, Mexico.

Bartleson, John D. *A Field Guide for Civil War Explosive Ordnance, 1861–1865*. Washington, D.C.: Government Printing Office, 1973.

Barton, Henry W. *Texas Volunteers in the Mexican War*. Waco: Texian Press, 1970. As one might expect, it glosses over the brutal aspects of guerrilla warfare as conducted by the Texans; provides detailed information regarding recruitment, dress, and attitudes of the Texan volunteer.

Bateman, Norman J. *The Battle of Resaca de la Palma: An Electronic Metal Detector Survey*. Brownsville, Tex.: Norman J. Bateman, 1982. On file, National Park Service, Southwest Regional Office, Santa Fe.

Bauer, K. Jack. *The Mexican War, 1846–1848*. New York: Macmillan, 1974. A thorough, scholarly account that is also readable; emphasizes strategy and tactics of both nations' Armies.

———. *Zachary Taylor: Soldier, Planter, Statesman of the Old Southwest*. Baton Rouge: Louisiana State University Press, 1985.

———. "The Battles on the Rio Grande: Palo Alto and Resaca de la Palma, 8–9 May 1846." In *America's First Battles, 1776–1965*. Charles E. Heller and William A. Stofft, eds. Lawrence: University Press of Kansas, 1986, pp. 57–80. Goes into even greater detail than his 1974 book on the tactics used at Palo Alto; a must for anyone conducting research on this battle.

Baxter, Edward P., and Kay L. Killen. "A Study of the Palo Alto Battleground, Cameron County, Texas." College Station: *Texas A&M University Anthropology Laboratory Report* 33, 1976.

Belknap, Lieutenant Colonel W. G. Field report addressed to Captain W. W. S. Bliss, Assistant Adjutant General, Army of Occupation, on the actions of the First Brigade at the battle of Palo Alto, letter dated May 15, 1846. Washington, D.C.: report published in 29th Cong., 1st sess., House Executive Document 209, pp. 23–26. Reports from General Taylor.

Berlandier, Jean Louis. "Itinerario: Campaña de Palo Alto y Resaca de Guerrero." Yale University: Western America Collection, MS S-310, 1846. MS translation by Frank Mares.

———. "Journal of Jean Louis Berlandier during 1846–1847, Including the Time When He Was Driven from Matamoros by the Americans." Thomas Phillips Collection, MS 15512 (Berlandier), Library of Congress, Washington, D.C. Copy on file at the Arnulfo L. Oliveira Library, University of Texas at Brownsville.

———. "Berlandier's Notes on Texas." MS copy on file at the Texas Historical Commission, Austin.

Bond, Clell L. "Palo Alto Battlefield: A Magnetometer and Metal Detector Survey." College Station: *Cultural Resources Laboratory Report* 4, Texas A&M University, 1979.

Bosworth, ———. *A Treatise on the Rifle, Musket, Pistol, and Fowling-Piece*. Huntington, W.Va., 1846.

Brack, Gene M. *Mexico Views Manifest Destiny, 1821–1846*. Albuquerque: University of New Mexico Press, 1973.

Bray, M., and K. J. Irwin. *Observations on Amphibians and Reptiles in the Lower Rio Grande Valley, Texas*. Alamo, Tex.: U.S. Fish and Wildlife Service, 1991.

Brinckerhoff, Sidney B. "Metal Uniform Insignia of the U.S. Army in the Southwest, 1846–1902," *Arizona Pioneers' Historical Society Museum Monograph* 3, 1965. A good reference, with sketches of insignias.

Brinckerhoff, Sidney B., and Pierce A. Chamberlain. *Spanish Military Weapons in Colonial America, 1700–1821*. Harrisburg, Pa.: Stackpole Books, 1972. Discusses the arms of the Mexican soldier, especially those weapons that would have been antiquated but still useful during the U.S.-Mexican War.

Brooks, Nathan C. *A Complete History of the Mexican War: Its Causes, Conduct, and Consequences*. Chicago: Rio Grande Press, 1965. First published in 1849. A well-balanced evaluation of the causes of the war, but there is no mention of slavery, expansionism, or California. It states that Polk provoked the war by ordering Taylor to the Rio Grande.

Brown, M. L. *Firearms in Colonial America, 1492–1792*. Washington, D.C.: Smithsonian Institution Press, 1980.

Brownsville Herald. "Commemoration of Palo Alto Battlefield," p. 1, May 9, 1893.

Butler, David F. *United States Firearms: The First Century, 1776–1875*. New York: Winchester Press, 1971. Detailed descriptions of gun parts with copious photos.

Buttrey, T. V., and Clyde Hubbard. *Guide Book of Mexican Coins, 1822 to Date*. Iola, Wisc.: Krause Pub., 1992.

Calver, William L., and Reginald P. Bolton. "Consider the Revolutionary War Bullet." *New York Historical Society Quarterly Bulletin* 11 (1928): 55–120.

Campbell, J. Duncan. "Military Buttons, Long-lost Heralds of Fort Mackinac's Past." Mackinac Island, Mich.: *Mackinac History, Leaflet* 7, 1965. A significant study on this category of artifacts; it gives history and development of the military button, although application to the U.S.-Mexican War is limited.

Campbell, J. Duncan, and Edgar M. Howell. *American Military Insignia*. Washington, D.C.: Smithsonian Institution, 1963. An important archaeological reference.

Carlson, Gayle F. "Archaeological Investigations at Fort Atkinson (25WN9), Washington County, Nebraska, 1956–1971." Lincoln: *Nebraska State Historical Society Publications in Anthropology* 8, 1979.

Carreño, Albert M., ed. *Jefes del ejército mexicano en 1847*. Mexico City: Secretaria de Fomento, 1914.

Chamberlain, Samuel E. *My Confession: The Recollections of a Rogue*. New York: Harper, 1956. This dramatic, first-hand account and its color sketches did not come to light until 1955 when, amid some controversy regarding its authenticity, it was abridged in *Life* magazine. Little doubt of its validity remains today. It is especially valuable for views on soldier and camp life.

Champion, A. A. "Historical Notes concerning the Battle of Palo Alto and Subsequent Events Which Took Place on the Battle Site." Unpublished MS on file, National Park Service, Southwest Regional Office, Santa Fe.

Chappell, Edward. "A Study of Horseshoes in the Department of Archaeology, Colonial Williamsburg." *Colonial Williamsburg Occasional Papers in Archaeology, vol. 1: Five Artifact Studies*, pp. 100–16. Edited by Ivor Noël Hume. Williamsburg, Va.: Colonial Williamsburg Foundation, 1973.

Chipman, Donald E. *Spanish Texas, 1519–1821*. Austin: University of Texas Press, 1992.

Churchill, Franklin H. *Sketch of the Life of Bvt. Brig. Gen. Sylvester Churchill, Inspector General U.S. Army*. New York: Willis McDonald and Co., 1888. He was the father of Lieutenant William Churchill, the officer in charge of the eighteen-pounders at Palo Alto. The father briefly mentions the actions of his son during that battle.

Clausen, Carl J. "The Fort Pierce Collection." *Bureau of Historic Sites and Properties Bulletin* 1. Tallahassee: Florida Department of State, 1970, pp. 1–43. A good reference on U.S.

military and civilian buttons used during the Seminole War (1835–42), with applications to U.S.-Mexican War buttons.

Coffman, Edward M. *The Old Army: A Portrait of the American Army in Peacetime, 1784–1898*. New York: Oxford University Press, 1986. Organization of the Army during various periods of its history; insights into the differing, evolving attitudes and values of the U.S. officer caste and enlisted man over time.

Coggins, Jack. *Arms and Equipment of the Civil War*. New York: Doubleday, 1962.

Coker, Caleb, ed. *The News from Brownsville: Helen Chapman's Letters from the Texas Military Frontier, 1848–1852*. Austin: Texas State Historical Assoc., University of Texas, 1992. An army officer's wife's impressions of early Brownsville and vicinity. Helen Chapman visited the battlefields of Resaca de la Palma and Palo Alto and described battlefield appearances two years after the combat took place.

Compaña contra los Americanos, mayo de 1846. Mexico D.F.: Biblioteca Nacional de México, 1846.

Congressional Globe. An equivalent to the *Congressional Record*. Appendix, 29th Cong., 1st sess., 1847.

Costeloe, Michael P. *The Central Republic in Mexico, 1835–1846*. New York: Cambridge University Press, 1993.

Crimmins, Martin L. "First Stages of the Mexican War, Initial Operations of the Army in 1846." *Army Ordnance* 15 (1939): 222–25.

Curtis, Samuel R. Diary entry of Samuel R. Curtis, Third Ohio Volunteer Regiment, July 11, 1846. A copy of the diary, with entries dating to 1846–47, is on file with Dr. Joseph E. Chance, University of Texas–Pan American, Edinburg.

Darling, Anthony D. *Red Coat and Brown Bess*. Alexandria Bay, N.Y.: Museum Restoration Service, Historical Arms series 12, 1981. Not as detailed as Bailey's book on the Brown Bess, but still a good reference; gives interesting information about the eighteenth-century British soldier and linear tactics.

Deas, George. "Reminiscences of the Campaign of the Rio Grande." *Historical Magazine*, January, p. 20; February, p. 103 (1870).

Diccionario Porrúa de historia, biografía, y geografía de México. Editorial Porrúa, México, 1964.

Dillon, Lester R., Jr. *American Artillery in the Mexican War, 1846–1847*. Austin: Presidial Press, 1975. The only book in print to date on this critical branch of the U.S. Army during the U.S.-Mexican War.

Downey, Fairfax. "The Flying Batteries." *Army* (November, 1956): 66–72.

———. *Sound of the Guns: The Story of American Artillery from the Ancient and Honorable Company to the Atom Cannon and Guided Missile*. New York: David McKay Co., 1956.

———. "The Flying Batteries." *Army* (January, 1957): 60–64.

Dufour, Charles R. *The Mexican War: A Compact History, 1846–1848*. New York: Hawthorn Books, 1968. A popular treatment with emphasis on campaigns.

Duncan, Captain James. Letter report to Lieutenant Colonel W. G. Belknap, commander, First Brigade, describing the battles of Palo Alto and Resaca de la Palma, dated May 12, 1846. In "The Artillery in the Mexican War, Reports of Capt. James Duncan, Second U.S. Artillery." *Journal of the U.S. Artillery* 29 (1908): 313–16.

Duncan, Lieutenant Colonel Louis C. "A Medical History of General Zachary Taylor's Army of Occupation in Texas and Mexico, 1845–1847." *The Military Surgeon, Journal of the Association of Military Surgeons of the United States*. Edited by James Robb Church. Vol. 48 (1921): 76–104.

Du Picq, A. *Battle Studies*. Harrisburg, Pa.: Military Service Pub., 1946.

Duval, J. C. *Early Times in Texas*. Austin, 1892.

Dyer, Gwynne. *War*. New York: Crown Pub., 1985.

Eaton, Jack D. *Excavations at the Alamo Shrine (Mission San Antonio de Valero)*. San Antonio: Center for Archaeological Research, Special Report 10, University of Texas, 1980.

Eisenhower, John S. D. *So Far from God: The U.S. War with Mexico, 1846–1848*. New York: Anchor Books-Doubleday, 1989. A popular, readable account but has little primary documentation on the battle of Palo Alto.

Elting, Colonel John R., ed. *Military Uniforms in America, vol. 2: Years of Growth, 1796–1851*. San Rafael, Calif.: Presidio Press, 1977. Color drawings, each associated with texts that detail uniform specifics.

———. *Swords around a Throne: Napoleon's Grand Armeé*. New York: The Free Press (a division of Macmillan), 1988.

Falk, Stanley L. "Artillery for the Land Service: The Development of a System." *Military Affairs* 28, no. 3 (fall, 1964): 97–110.

Fallo definitivo del supremo tribunal de la guerra, al examinar la conducta militar del exmo. sr. general Mariano Arista. Mexico City: Torres, 1850. Investigation of Arista for his loss of Palo Alto and Resaca de la Palma.

Farley, James J. *Making Arms in the Machine Age: Philadelphia's Frankford Arsenal, 1816–1870*. University Park, Pa.: Pennsylvania State University Press, 1994.

Farmer, Mike. "National Resource Survey of Palo Alto National Battlefield." MS on file, National Park Service, Denver, 1992.

Ferrell, Robert H. *American Diplomacy: A History*. New York: W. W. Norton, 1975.

Fox, Anne A. Archaeological Investigations in Alamo Plaza, San Antonio, Bexar County, Texas, 1988 and 1989. *Center for Archaeological Research Report 205*. San Antonio: University of Texas, 1992.

Fox, Richard A., Jr. *Archaeology, History, and Custer's Last Battle: The Little Big Horn Reexamined*. Norman: University of Oklahoma Press, 1993.

Fox, Richard A., Jr., and Douglas D. Scott. "The Post–Civil War Battle Pattern." *Historical Archaeology* 25, no. 2 (1991): 92–103.

Friend, Llerena B. *Sam Houston: The Great Designer*. Austin: University of Texas Press, 1954.

Frost, John. *The Mexican War and Its Warriors*. New Haven: Mansfield Pub., 1849.

———. *History of the Mexican War*. New Haven: Mansfield Pub., 1859.

Furber, George C. *The Twelve Months Volunteer; or, Journal of a Private in the Tennessee Regiment of Cavalry in the Campaign in Mexico, 1846–47*. Cincinnati: J. A. & U. P. James, 1848. The author was a veteran of Scott's campaign. This is considered one of the best contemporary works. It emphasizes four topics: camp life, physical description of the country, manners and customs of Mexicans as Furber saw them, and military operations. In Furber's mind, the Mexicans caused the war.

Garavaglia, Louis A., and Charles G. Worman. *Firearms of the American West, 1803–1865*. Albuquerque: University of New Mexico Press, 1984.

Gibbon, Lieutenant John. *The Artillerist's Manual*. New York: D. Van Norstrand, 1860. Although printed fourteen years after Palo Alto, its specification tables are still relevant regarding the U.S.-Mexican War.

Giddings, Luther. *Sketches of the Campaign in Northern Mexico in Eighteen Hundred Forty-six and Seven*. New York: George P. Putnam, 1853.

Gluckman, Arcadi. *Identifying Old U.S. Muskets, Rifles, and Carbines*. New York: Bonanza Books, 1965.

Graebner, Norman A. *Empire on the Pacific: A Study in American Continental Expansion*. New York: Ronald Press Co., 1959.

Grant, Ulysses S. *Personal Memoirs of Ulysses S. Grant*. New York: Charles L. Webster Co.,

1885. Some interesting, wry observations concerning events leading up to the U.S.-Mexican War as well as anecdotes about Palo Alto and Resaca de la Palma. Grant believed this was a most shameful war on the part of an aggressive United States.

———. *The Papers of Ulysses S. Grant*. Edited by John Y. Simon. Vol. 1, 1837–61. Carbondale, Ill.: University of Southern Illinois Press, 1967.

Griswold del Castillo, Richard. *The Treaty of Guadalupe Hidalgo: A Legacy of Conflict*. Norman: University of Oklahoma Press, 1990.

Haecker, Charles M. *A Thunder of Cannon: Archaeology of the Mexican-American War Battlefield of Palo Alto*. Professional Papers 52. Santa Fe: National Park Service, Southwest Regional Office, Divisions of Anthropology and History, 1994.

Hagerman, Edward. *The American Civil War and the Origins of Modern Warfare, Ideas, Organization, and Field Command*. Bloomington: Indiana University Press, 1988.

Hamilton, Holman. *Zachary Taylor, Soldier of the Republic*. Indianapolis: Bobbs-Merrill, 1941.

Hanson, Lee, and Dick Ping Hsu. Casemates and Cannonballs: Archaeological Investigations at Fort Stanwix, Rome, New York. *Publications in Archaeology* 14. Washington, D.C.: National Park Service, 1975.

Haythornthwaite, Philip J. *Weapons and Equipment of the Napoleonic Wars*. Dorset, England: Blandford Press, 1979. Detailed information on arms and tactics that speaks to how U.S.–Mexican War battles were conducted by both sides.

———. *Wellington's Military Machine*. Tunbridge Wells, Kent, England: Spellmont Ltd., 1989.

Henry, Robert S. *The Story of the Mexican War*. New York: Bobbs-Merrill Co., 1950. Although well researched and readable, it is now out of date because of the many studies following its publication.

Henry, Captain William S. *Campaign Sketches of the War with Mexico*. New York: Arno Press, 1973. Originally printed in 1847. A diary of Taylor's operations; interesting descriptions of everyday camp life as well as battles and skirmishes. Henry was breveted major for his actions at Monterrey.

Herskovitz, Robert M. "Fort Bowie Material Culture." *Anthropological Papers of the University of Arizona* 31. Tucson: University of Arizona Press, 1978.

Hickox, Ron G. *U.S. Military Edged Weapons of the Second Seminole War, 1835–1842*. Published by Ron G. Hickox, Gainesville, Fla., 1984. Detailed line drawings of swords; some treatment of U.S. equipage used during the U.S.-Mexican War.

Hicks, Major James E. *Notes on United States Ordnance, vol. 1: Small Arms, 1776–1946*. Published by James E. Hicks, Mount Vernon, N.Y., 1940. With excellent line drawings by André Jandot, this is one of the clearest and most useful general coverages of U.S. regulation firearms.

Hockley, George W. Letter to Albert Sidney Johnston dated March 28, 1839. Austin: Texas State Archives, Army Papers.

Hooker, T. "Uniforms of the Mexican Army, 1837–1847, Part 1." *Tradition: The Journal of the International Society of Military Collectors* 65 (1976): 27–43.

———. "Uniforms of the Mexican Army, 1837–1847, Part 2." *Tradition: The Journal of the International Society of Military Collectors* 66 (1976): 5–19.

Houston, Donald E. "The Role of Artillery in the Mexican War." *Journal of the West* 11 (April, 1972): 273–84.

Hoyt, E. *Practical Instructions for Military Officers*. Westport, Conn: Greenwood Press, 1971. First published in 1811 by John Denio.

Hughes, Major General B. P. *British Smooth-bore Artillery: The Muzzle Loading Artillery of the Eighteenth and Nineteenth Centuries*. Harrisburg, Pa.: Stackpole Books, 1969. Detailed line drawings.

————. *Firepower: Weapons Effectiveness on the Battlefield, 1630–1850*. London: Arms and Armour Press, 1974.

Huntington, R. T. "Dragoon Accouterments and Equipment, 1834–1849: An Identification Guide." *Plains Anthropologist* 12 (1967): 345–55.

————. *Accouterments of the United States Infantry, Riflemen, and Dragoons, 1834–1849*. Alexandria Bay, N.Y.: Museum Restoration Service, 1987.

Huston, James A. *The Sinews of War: Army Logistics, 1775–1953*. Washington, D.C.: Office of the Chief of Military History, 1966.

Instrucción para la infantería ligera del ejército mexicano, mandada observar por el supremo gobierno. Ciudad de México: Imprenta de V. García Torres, 1846.

Irey, Thomas R. "Soldiering, Suffering, and Dying in the Mexican War." *Journal of the West* 11 (1972): 285–98.

Ivey, Jake. "Reconnaissance Report on the Palo Alto Battlefield." 1992. Report on file with the National Park Service, Southwest Regional Office, Division of History, Santa Fe.

James, Garry. "The Historic Baker Rifle." *Guns & Ammo* (November, 1983): 52–56.

Jarvis, Captain N. S. "An Army Surgeon's Notes of Frontier Service, Mexican War." *Journal of the Military Service* 40 (1907): 435–52.

Jenkins, John S. *History of the War between the United States and Mexico*. Philadelphia: J. E. Potter, 1848.

Johnson, David F. *Uniform Buttons: American Armed Forces, 1784–1948*. Watkins Glen, N.Y.: Century House, 1948.

Jomini, Antoine Henri de. *Summary of the Art of War*. Translated by O. F. Winship and E. E. McLean. New York, 1857.

Katcher, Philip R. *The Mexican-American War, 1846–1848*. London: Osprey Pub., 1976.

Keegan, John. *The Face of Battle*. New York: Viking Press, 1976.

Keegan, John, and R. Holmes. *Soldiers*. New York: Viking Penguin, 1986.

Kendrick, G. *The Antique Bottle Collector*. Sparks, Nev.: Western Printing and Pub. Co., 1967.

Kenmotsu, Nancy. "Gunflints: A Study." *Historical Archaeology* 24, no. 2 (1990): 92–124. A thorough, analytical approach; especially informative regarding gunflint edge wear.

Kohn, Richard H. *Eagle and Sword: The Federalists and the Creation of the Military Establishment*. New York: Free Press, 1975.

Koury, Michael J. *Arms for Texas: A Study of the Weapons of the Republic of Texas*. Fort Collins, Colo.: Old Army Press, 1973.

Larnard, Captain Charles H. Inventory of property captured from the Mexican Army, May 9, 1846. National Archives and Records Service, Record Group 94, records of the adjutant general's office (1780s–1917), letters received (main series), file T-160-AGO-1846, Washington, D.C.

Lewis, Berkeley R. *Small Arms and Ammunition in the United States Service*. Washington, D.C.: Smithsonian Institution, 1956.

————. "Small Arms and Ammunition in the United States Service, 1776–1865." *Smithsonian Miscellaneous Collections*, vol. 29. Washington, D.C.: Smithsonian Institution, 1960.

Lewis, Lloyd. *Captain Sam Grant*. New York: Little, Brown and Co., 1950. Personal insights into Grant as a young lieutenant during the Mexican War. It uses letters, documents, and extensive quotes and is enjoyable reading.

Life and Public Services of Gen. Z. Taylor. New York: H. Long and Brother, 1846.

Longstreet, James. *From Manassas to Appomattox: Memoirs of the Civil War in America*. Philadelphia, 1896.

Lord, Philip, Jr. "War over Walloonscoick: Land Use and Settlement Pattern on the

Bennington Battlefield—1777." *New York State Museum Bulletin* 473, 1989 (Albany).

Lotbiniere, Seymour de. "English Gunflint Making in the Seventeenth and Eighteenth Centuries." In *Colonial Frontier Guns*. Chadron, Nebr.: Fur Press, 1980, pp. 154–59.

McCaffrey, James M. *Army of Manifest Destiny: The American Soldier in the Mexican War, 1846–1848*. New York: New York University Press, 1992. Describes varied backgrounds, attitudes, and training of the American soldier during this period; also includes battlefield accounts.

McCall, Major General George A. *Letters from the Frontier*. Gainesville: University Press of Florida, 1974. Originally published in 1868. Contains a section on U.S.–Mexican War experiences.

McIntosh, Brevet Colonel J. S. Report submitted to the Office of Adjutant General on the military actions of the Fifth Infantry Regiment at Palo Alto and Resaca de la Palma, dated December 3, 1846. Copy on file at the National Park Service, Southwest Regional Office, Division of Anthropology, Santa Fe.

McNeil, William H. *The Pursuit of Power: Technology, Armed Force, and Society since A.D. 1000*. Chicago: University of Chicago Press, 1982.

McNulty, Robert H. "A Study of Bayonets in the Department of Archaeology, Colonial Williamsburg, with Notes on Bayonet Identification." In *Colonial Williamsburg Occasional Papers in Archaeology, vol. 1: Five Artifact Studies*. Williamsburg, Va.: Colonial Williamsburg Foundation, 1973, pp. 54–77.

McWhiney, Grady, and Perry D. Jamieson. *Attack and Die: Civil War Military Tactics and the Southern Heritage*. University: University of Alabama Press, 1982.

McWhiney, Grady, and Sue McWhiney. *To Mexico with Taylor and Scott, 1845–1847*. Waltham, Mass.: Blaisdell Pub., 1969.

Mahan, Dennis Hart. *An Elementary Treatise on Advanced-Guard, Out-Post, and Detachment Service of Troops, and the Manner of Posting and Handling Them in the Presence of an Enemy*. New York, 1847.

Mahon, John K. *The Second Seminole War*. Gainesville, Fla.: University of Florida Press, 1967.
———. *The War of 1812*. Gainesville, Fla.: University of Florida Press, 1972.

Marshall, S. L. A. *Men Against Fire*. Gloucester, Mass.: Peter Smith, ed., 1978.

Masland, Sergeant Major Charles. Published letter of Sergeant Major Charles Masland to Matthew H. Masland, describing the march of Taylor's command from Corpus Christi to Matamoros, March 8–28, 1846. Masland's letter is on file at the U.S. Army Military History Institute, Carlisle Barracks, Carlisle, Pa.

Meade, Major General George G. *The Life and Letters of George G. Meade, Major-General United States Army*. Vol. 1. New York: Charles Scribner's Sons, 1913. Meade was an officer under both Taylor and Scott; contains rather acerbic observations about Taylor's competency or lack thereof.

Mejía, Francisco. *Sumaria mandada formar a pedimento en los puntos del Palo Alto y resaca de guerrero*. Navarro, Mexico, 1846. A forty-page pamphlet, it is one of several "explanations" as to why the Mexicans lost the first two battles of the war.

Meuse, William A. *The Weapons of the Battle of New Orleans*. Edited by Charles L. Dufour and Leonard V. Huber. New Orleans: Louisiana Landmarks Society, New Orleans chapter, 1965. The Battle of New Orleans 150th Anniversary Committee of Louisiana. General information on weaponry, with some application to the U.S.-Mexican War.

Meyer, Michael C., and William L. Sherman. *The Course of Mexican History*. New York: Oxford University Press, 1983.

Miller, Robert Ryal. *Shamrock and Sword: The Saint Patrick's Battalion in the U.S.-Mexican War*. Norman: University of Oklahoma Press, 1989. This battalion, composed of American deserters, fought for Mexico.

Mills, Madison. Diary of surgeon Madison Mills, March 11, 1846–November 6, 1847. Copied by Mrs. Joseph Gray from the original diary and given to the Filson Club by Mrs. Gray (Louisville, Kentucky, September, 1933). Original MS on file, Filson Club, Jefferson, Kentucky.

Montrose, Lynn. *War through the Ages*. London, 1960.

Mordecai, Captain Alfred. *Ordnance Manual for the Use of Officers of the United States Army*. Washington, D.C., 1841.

———. *Artillery for the United States Land Service*. 2 vols. Washington, D.C.: J. and G. S. Gideon, 1849. The first volume of text and the second (folio) volume of plates represent the most detailed and exhaustive compilation of American artillery equipment in print to date.

Morrison, James L. *The Best School in the World: West Point in the Pre–Civil War Years, 1833–1866*. Kent, Ohio: Kent State University Press, 1986.

Naisawald, L. Van Loan. *Grape and Canister: The Story of the Field Artillery of the Army of the Potomac, 1861–1865*. New York: Oxford University Press, 1960.

Nance, Joseph M. *After San Jacinto: The Texas-Mexican Frontier, 1836–1841*. Austin, 1963.

National Park Service. "Study of Palo Alto Battlefield National Historic Site, Texas." MS on file, National Park Service, Santa Fe, 1979.

Nesmith, Samuel P. "Analysis of Military Related Artifacts, La Villita Earthworks (41 BX 677), San Antonio, Texas: A Preliminary Report of Investigations of Mexican Siege Works at the Battle of the Alamo." Edited by Joseph H. Labadie. In *Archaeological Survey Report* 159, pp. 62–94, 1986. San Antonio: University of Texas, Center for Archaeological Research.

———. "Military Artifacts" in "Archaeological Investigations in Alamo Plaza, San Antonio, Bexar County, Texas, 1988 and 1989." Edited by Anne A. Fox. In *Archaeological Survey Report* 205, pp. 56–62, 1992. San Antonio: University of Texas, Center for Archaeological Research.

Neumann, George C., and Frank J. Kravic. *Collector's Illustrated Encyclopedia of the American Revolution*. Harrisburg, Pa.: Stackpole Books, 1975.

New York Herald. "Battles along the Rio Grande." Newspaper article dated May 28, 1846, p. 2.

Nichols, Edward J. *Zach Taylor's Little Army*. Garden City, N.Y.: Doubleday, 1963. Appears well researched but lacks documentation; a readable narrative.

Nieto, A., A. S. Brown, and J. Hefter. *El soldado mexicano: organización, vestuario, equipo. The Mexican Soldier: Organization, Dress, Equipment*. Mexico City, 1958. A classic: specifically deals with the Mexican soldier of that period; includes color and line-drawing illustrations of Mexican uniforms and equipment. The author admits that the illustrations represent the ideal and not the real, vis-à-vis what the Mexican soldier of the period really wore and used in battle.

Niles National Register. September 21, 1839. Weekly newspaper published in Baltimore; good, relatively objective reporting.

———. "War News." May 30, 1846, p. 196.

———. "War News." June 6, 1846, pp. 215–17.

———. "War News." June 13, 1846, pp. 229–34.

———. "War News." June 20, 1846, pp. 249–55.

———. "War News." June 27, 1846, p. 264.

———. "War News." August 8, 1846.

Noël Hume, Ivor. *A Guide to Artifacts of Colonial America*. New York: Alfred A. Knopf, 1970.

———. *Historical Archaeology*. New York: Alfred Knopf, 1969.

Olivera, Ruth R., and Lilian Crete. *Life in Mexico under Santa Anna, 1822–1855*. Norman: University of Oklahoma Press, 1991.

Olsen, Stanley J. "Uniform Buttons As Aids in the Interpretation of Military Sites." *Curator* 5, no. 4 (1962): 346–52.

———. "Dating Early Plain Buttons by Their Form." *American Antiquity* 28, no. 4 (1963): 551–54.

Ordnance Board. Proceedings of March, 1846. Washington, D.C.: textual records of the Office of the Chief of Ordnance, Record Group 156, National Archives.

Orga, Josef de. *Prontuario en que se han reunido las obligaciones del soldado, cabo y sargento.* Valencia, 1808.

Palo, William A. de. *The Mexican National Army, 1822–1852.* College Station: Texas A&M University Press, 1997.

Parker, General James. "Report to War Dept., Adj. Gen. Office, Subject: Placing of Suitable Tablets to Mark Battlefield of Palo Alto." War Department document dated March 25, 1914. Washington, D.C.: National Archives, Record Group 94, Records of the Adjutant General's Office, 1780–1917.

Parker, Captain William H. *Recollections of a Naval Officer, 1841–1865.* New York: Charles Scribner's Sons, 1883.

Peck, Lieutenant John James. *The Sign of the Eagle: A View of Mexico 1830–1855, Based on the Letters of Lieutenant John James Peck, with Lithographs of Mexico.* San Diego: Copley, commissioned by James S. Copley, Union-Tribune Pub., 1970. Period illustrations of Mexico interspersed with texts giving American views of Mexican culture during the early to mid-nineteenth century.

Peterson, Harold L. *Round Shot and Rammers.* New York: Bonanza Books, 1969. A solid introduction to the history and evolution of artillery from the sixteenth century to the Civil War. Besides guns, there are sections on ammunition, loading and firing equipment, and gunners' instruments; an analysis of the role of artillery in each era; and copious drawings (no photos).

Pierce, Frank C. *A Brief History of the Rio Grande Valley* Menasha, Wisc.: George Banta Pub., 1917.

Pletcher, David M. *The Diplomacy of Annexation: Texas, Oregon, and the Mexican War.* Columbia: University of Missouri Press, 1973.

Plitt, Walter E. III. "Palo Alto Battlefield National Park: A Metal Detector Survey." MS on file, National Park Service, Santa Fe, 1992.

Portmess, Reverend John. Speech given at the commemoration of a monument dedicating the battle of Palo Alto, May 8, 1893. Copy on file, National Park Service, Santa Fe.

Preston, Richard A. *Men at Arms: A History of Warfare and Its Interrelationships With Western Society.* New York: Frederick A. Praeger, 1956.

Prucha, Francis Paul. *The Sword of the Republic: The United States Army on the Frontier, 1783–1846.* Bloomington, Ind.: Indiana University Press, 1973.

Rappole, J. H., and J. Klicka. "Status of Six Populations of Rio Grande Birds." MS on file, U.S. Fish and Wildlife Service, Caesar Kleberg Wildlife Research Institute, Kingsville, Tex., 1991.

Ratliff, Eric A. "Human Skeleton Remains from the Battle of Resaca de la Palma." In *A Thunder of Cannon: Archaeology of the Mexican–American War Battlefield of Palo Alto*, by Charles M. Haecker. Professional Papers 52. Santa Fe: National Park Service, Southwest Regional Office, Divisions of Anthropology and History, 1994. Appendix A, pp. 190–208.

Rayburn, John C., Virginia K. Rayburn, and Ethel N. Fry, eds. *Century of Conflict, 1821–1913: Incidents in the Lives of William Neale and William A. Neale, Early Settlers in Texas.* Waco: Texian Press, 1966.

Records of the Office of the Chief of Ordnance. Record Group 156, 1842. National Archives, Washington, D.C.

———. Statement from Fort Monroe Arsenal, Record Group 156, 1845. National Archives, Washington, D.C.

———. House Committee Report 86, 28th Cong., 2nd sess., serial no. 468, 1846. National Archives, Washington, D.C.

———. Senate Exec. Doc. no. 1, 34th Cong., 1st sess., serial no. 811, 1855. National Archives, Washington, D.C.

Reeves, C. M. *Five Years an American Soldier*. Cincinnati: H. Howe, 1860.

Reilly, Robert M. *United States Military Small Arms, 1816–1865: The Federal Firearms of the Civil War*. The Eagle Press, 1970.

Reilly, Robin. *The British at the Gates: The New Orleans Campaign in the War of 1812*. New York: George P. Putnam, 1974.

Ripley, R. S. *The War with Mexico*. 2 vols. New York: Burt Franklin, 1970. Originally published in 1849. The earliest major history of the war; detailed and accurate considering its early date; a good account of Palo Alto. The major causes of the war are mentioned objectively without discussion or interpretation, and Ripley does not attempt to affix blame on either nation. The author, a professional soldier and officer in Scott's command, was more interested in the military engagements but perceptively discusses the effects of both U.S. and Mexican domestic politics.

Rives, George Lockhart. *The United States and Mexico, 1821–1848*. 2 vols. New York: Charles Scribner's Sons, 1913. Most of volume 2 pertains to the U.S.-Mexican War. Considered by some historians to be an especially valuable account, it has useful and accurate battle maps.

Roa Bárcena, José María. *Recuerdos de la invasión norteamericana, 1846–1848, por un joven de entonces*. Mexico City: Editorial Porrúa, S.A., 1947 (3rd ed.). Considered the standard work from the Mexican viewpoint. Most of the book deals with military actions for which the author frequently praises the Mexican troops. He states that the war was caused by U.S. expansionism; some U.S. historians (for example, Justin Smith [1915: 96–98]) found the work "partisan" (presumably unlike American historians?) and thus unreliable.

Robertson, Brian. *Wild Horse Desert*. Edinburg, Tex.: New Santander, 1985.

Rodenbough, T. F. *From Everglade to Cañon with the Second Dragoons (Second United States Cavalry)*. New York: D. Van Nostrand, 1875. Romantic account, minimally useful.

Ross, Steven. *From Flintlock to Rifle: Infantry Tactics, 1740–1866*. London: Associated University Presses, 1980.

Salas, Elizabeth. *Soldaderas in the Mexican Military: Myth and History*. Austin: University of Texas Press, 1990.

Sampanaro, F. N. "The Political Role of the Army in Mexico, 1821–1848." Ph.D. diss., State University of New York at Stony Brook, 1974.

Sanchez, Joseph P. "The Defeat of the Army of the North in South Texas: An Examination of Mexican Military Operations in the First Battles of the Mexican War." MS on file, National Park Service, Santa Fe, 1980.

———. "General Mariano Arista at the Battle of Palo Alto, Texas, 1846: Military Realist or Failure?" *Journal of the West* 24, no. 2 (April, 1985): 8–22. A thorough account of General Arista's actions before, during, and after Palo Alto.

Scarritt, Lieutenant Jeremiah. Letter written May 12, 1846, to Colonel J. G. Totten, commander of topographical engineers, describing the battles of Palo Alto and Resaca de la Palma. National Archives, Record Group 77, records of the Office of the Chief of Engineers, letters received, 1838–66.

Scott, Douglas D. *A Sharp Little Affair*. Lincoln: J & L Reprint Co., *Reprints in Anthropology* 45, 1994.

Scott, Douglas D., Richard A. Fox, Jr., Melissa A. Connor, and Dick Harmon. *Archaeological Perspectives on the Battle of the Little Bighorn*. Norman: University of Oklahoma Press, 1989.

Scott, Major General Winfield. *Infantry Tactics; or, Rules for the Exercise and Manoevres of the United States Infantry, vol. 1, Schools of the Soldier and the Company*. Reprinted from the original 1840 copy by McCrain Pub., Dallas (n.d.).

Shafer, Harry J. "An Archaeological Reconnaissance of the Brownsville Relocation Study Area." *Texas A&M University Anthropology Laboratory Report 1*. College Station: Texas A&M University, 1974.

Simmons, Marc, and Frank Turley. *Southwestern Colonial Ironwork: The Spanish Blacksmithing Tradition from Texas to California*. Santa Fe: Museum of New Mexico Press, 1980.

Simon, André L. *The Noble Grapes and the Great Wines of France*. New York: McGraw-Hill Co., 1957.

Skelton, William B. "Professionalization in the U.S. Army Officer Corps during the Age of Jackson." *In the Defense of the Republic: Readings in American Military History*, edited by David C. Skaggs and Robert S. Browning III. Belmont, Calif: Wadsworth Pub., 1991, pp. 83–106.

Smith, Lieutenant Edmund Kirby. Letter written by Lieutenant Edmund Kirby Smith to his mother and father, dated May 13, 1846. Letter on file at Southern Historical Collection, University of North Carolina, Chapel Hill.

Smith, Captain Ephraim Kirby. *To Mexico with Scott: Letters of Captain E. Kirby Smith to His Wife*. Edited by Emma Jerome Blackwood. Cambridge, Mass.: Harvard University Press, 1917.

Smith, George W., and Charles Judah, eds. *Chronicles of the Gringos: The U.S. Army in the Mexican War, 1846–1848*. Albuquerque: University of New Mexico Press, 1968. A chronologically arranged collection of excerpts from first-hand accounts of U.S. participants in the war.

Smith, Justin H. "Official Military Reports." *American Historical Review* 21 (1915): 96–98. A brief essay on the trustworthiness of military reports for historical purposes.

———. *The War with Mexico*. 2 vols. Gloucester, Mass.: Macmillan, 1919. Detailed research with copious citations and extensive use of primary resources, including manuscripts from the Mexican archives. Smith's interpretation of the war reveals that he was obviously biased in favor of manifest destiny.

South, Stanley. "Analysis of the Buttons from Brunswick Town and Fort Fisher." *Florida Anthropologist* 17, no. 2 (1964): 113–33.

Spirit of the Times. Periodical, dated September 10, 1842.

Steffen, Randy. *The Horse Soldier, 1776–1943, vol. 1: The Revolution, the War of 1812, the Early Frontier, 1776–1850*. Norman: University of Oklahoma Press, 1977.

Stevens, Donald F. *The Origins of Instability in Early Republican Mexico*. Durham, N.C.: Duke University Press, 1991.

Stewart, J. W. Map showing the order of battle at Palo Alto. Map on file at Brownsville Historical Association, Brownsville, Texas, 1887.

Switzer, Ronald R. *The Bertrand Bottles: A Study of Nineteenth-Century Glass and Ceramic Containers*. Washington, D.C.: National Park Service, 1974.

Taylor, Zachary. "Mexican War Correspondence." 30th Cong., 1st sess., House Exec. Doc. 60, 1846.

———. "Official Reports from General Taylor." Doc. 209, 29th Cong., 1st sess., 1846, pp. 2–31.

Thompson, Waddy. *Recollections of Mexico*. New York: Wiley and Putnam, 1846.

Thorpe, T. B. *Our Army on the Rio Grande*. First published in 1846. Philadelphia: Carey and Hart, 1950.

Tornel, José María. *Carta del general José María Tornel a sus amigos, sobre un artículo inserto en el Cosmopolita del día 17 de agosto del presente año*. Mexico City: Ignacio Cumplido, 1839. Copy on file, National Park Service, Division of Anthropology, Santa Fe.

Tuchman, Barbara W. "Problems in Writing the Biography of General Stillwell." In *Practicing History: Selected Essays by Barbara W. Tuchman*. New York: Ballantine Books, 1982, pp. 65–75.

Twiggs, Colonel D. E. Field report by the right wing commander, Army of Occupation, on right wing actions of the U.S. Army during the battle of Palo Alto. In "Official Reports from General Taylor," House Exec. Doc. 209, 29th Cong., 1st sess., 1846, pp. 19–20.

Uraga, José López. *Sumaria mandada formar a pedimento del sr. coronel del 4. regimento de infantería de linea D. Jóse López Uraga en la que se comprueba a conducta militar que observo en las acciones de guerra dadas a la tropas de las Estados-Unidos los días 8 y 9 mayo en los puntos de Palo Alto y Resaca de Guerrero*. Navarro, Mexico: 1846. A thirty-four-page defense of the actions of Mexican officers at Palo Alto and Resaca de la Palma.

U.S. Board of Artillery. *Instruction for Field Artillery, Horse and Foot, Compiled by a Board of Artillery Officers*. Washington, D.C., 1845. This manual is largely based on what Captain Robert Anderson translated from the French and published in 1839. It provides specifics on the operation of light artillery pieces (six-pounder guns and twelve-pounder field howitzers).

U.S. Ordnance Dept. *The Ordnance Manual for the Use of the Officers of the United States Army*. Washington, D.C., 1841. In addition to ordnance information, it contains detailed descriptions of ancillary equipment, such as regulation saddlery and harnesses.

U.S. Records of the Office of the Chief of Ordnance for 1846, House Comm. Rept. 86, 28th Cong., 2nd sess., ser. no. 468.

U.S. War Department. *General Regulations for the Army of the United States*. Washington, D.C., 1841.

———. "Annual Report for 1846." *Annual Reports of the War Department, 1822–1907*. Washington, D.C.: National Archives Microfilm Pub. M997, rolls 7–9: 147.

———. "Annual Report for 1847." *Annual Reports of the War Department, 1822–1907*. Washington, D.C.: National Archives Microfilm Pub. M997, rolls 7–9: 684.

———. "Annual Report for 1848." *Annual Reports of the War Department, 1822–1907*. Washington, D.C.: National Archives Microfilm Pub. M997, rolls 7–9: 343.

———. Office of the Surgeon General. *Army Medical Bulletin* 50. October, 1939: 30–70.

Vázquez, Josefina Zoraida, and Lorenzo Meyer. *The United States and Mexico*. Chicago: University of Chicago Press, 1977.

Warner, Ezra J. *Generals in Gray: Lives of the Confederate Commanders*. Baton Rouge: Louisiana State University Press, 1993.

Washington Globe. October 15, 1845, p. 1, col. 3. Newspaper article regarding the respective qualities of Mexican and American troops.

Weems, John E. *To Conquer a Peace: The War between the United States and Mexico*. Garden City, N.Y.: Doubleday, 1974.

Weigley, Russel F. *History of the United States Army*. Bloomington, Ind.: Indiana University Press, 1984.

Wilcox, General Cadmus M. *History of the Mexican War*. Edited by Mary Rachel Wilcox. Washington, D.C.: Church News Pub., 1892. Largely concerned with military actions about which Wilcox, as an aide first to Zachary Taylor and then to Winfield Scott, was qualified to write.

Wood, W. Dean, and Karen G. Wood. *Soldiers and Citizens: Civil War Actions around Latimer*

Farm, Cobb County, Georgia. Athens, Ga.: Southeastern Archaeological Services, 1990.

Wood, W. Raymond. "Forward." In *Archaeology, History, and Custer's Last Battle*, by Richard A. Fox, Jr. Norman: University of Oklahoma Press, 1993, pp. xi–xiii.

Woodward, Arthur. "Spanish Trade Goods." In *The Sobaipuri Indians of the Upper San Pedro River Valley, Southeastern Arizona*. Edited by Charles C. Di Peso. Dragoon, Ariz.: Amerind Foundation, 1953, report 6. Contains line drawings and photos of Spanish colonial artifacts; has some relevance to mid-nineteenth-century Mexican material culture.

Young, Kevin R. "Finding A Face: El Soldado Mexicano, 1835–1848." In *A Thunder of Cannon: Archaeology of the Mexican–American War Battlefield of Palo Alto*, by Charles M. Haecker. Professional Papers 52. Santa Fe: National Park Service, Southwest Regional Office, Divisions of Anthropology and History, 1994.

Index

Note: Pages with illustrations are indicated by italics